Stepfamilies in Therapy

DON MARTIN
MAGGIE MARTIN
with the assistance of Pat Jeffers

Stepfamilies in Therapy

UNDERSTANDING SYSTEMS, ASSESSMENT, AND INTERVENTION

Jossey-Bass Publishers · San Francisco

For sales outside the United States, contact Maxwell Macmillan International Publishing Group, 866 Third Avenue, New York, New York 10022.

Manufactured in the United States of America.

 The paper used in this book is acid-free and meets the State of California requirements for recycled paper (50 percent recycled waste, including 10 percent postconsumer waste), which are the strictest guidelines for recycled paper currently in use in the United States.

Library of Congress Cataloging-in-Publication Data

Martin, Don, date.
    Stepfamilies in therapy : understanding systems, assessment, and intervention / Don Martin and Maggie Martin ; with the assistance of Pat Jeffers. — 1st ed.
        p.   cm. — (The Jossey-Bass social and behavioral science series)
    Includes bibliographical references and index.
    ISBN 1-55542-453-8
    1. Family psychotherapy.   2. Stepfamilies—Psychological aspects.
I. Martin, Maggie.   II. Jeffers, Pat, date.   III. Title.
IV. Series.
RC488.5.M369   1992
616.89′156—dc20   92-12519
                                                                        CIP

FIRST EDITION
HB Printing   10 9 8 7 6 5 4 3 2 1   *Code 9256*

THE JOSSEY-BASS
SOCIAL AND BEHAVIORAL
SCIENCE SERIES

To Paige, Sean, and Erin

—Don Martin and Maggie Martin

To Jack

—Pat Jeffers

Contents

Preface

This is a book about stepfamilies and the treatment of the problems they encounter. In a way, it is a guidebook for helping therapists navigate the many roads that must be traveled to assist the stepfamilies they counsel. Each family story is different, but we hope that we have provided some valuable clues for therapists to use in their daily work with stepfamilies. It may surprise some people, but the stepfamily is rapidly becoming the norm in American society. The numbers that support this statement are staggering. A 1989 Gallup poll in *USA Today* (August 15, p. 1) revealed that between 50 and 75 percent of all first marriages end in divorce, and these results substantiate earlier findings. At the same time, the number of remarriages has surged. Almost 80 percent of divorced or widowed single parents remarry within three to five years after the loss of a spouse. Among divorced people, nearly 83 percent of men and 76 percent of women remarry. These figures are increased by the growing number of never-married single parents who are now marrying.

Most divorced couples have children. Because parents remarry, about one of every six children in the United States has become part of a stepfamily, and one of every eight children under eighteen is a stepchild living with a biological parent or stepparent. It seems almost inconceivable, but one of every four children in the United States will live with a stepparent before reaching the age of sixteen.

Uniting individuals who previously belonged to other nuclear families carries the potential for complex family dynamics. New relationships must be formed, new territory must be defined, and new roles have to be assumed. Adding to the complexity is the new extended family, which includes not only current and former blood relatives but also relatives from all previous marriages. Healthy stability is the goal, but the path is often strewn with difficulties that make the intervention of a skilled therapist critical.

The traditional nuclear family structure now accounts for only a small percentage of modern American families. Nevertheless, many human service professionals (teachers, counselors, psychologists, and social workers) were raised in such families. Moreover, the traditional training of such professionals has not included emphasis on or understanding of stepfamilies. To compound the problem, there is a gap in the literature available to therapists who are trying to help stepfamilies.

Human service professionals may soon find that stepfamilies constitute the majority of their caseloads, yet many are unsure of how to proceed in counseling them. General systemic concepts are helpful, but traditional techniques may not always work, given the many intricacies related to intimacy issues in stepfamilies. Such issues may not exist in traditional families, or at least not to such an extent.

This book seeks to help professionals fill the gap between experience, training, and the existing literature, on the one hand, and these new clients, on the other. The book is structured around stepfamily issues, therapeutic assessment, and intervention.

Overview of the Contents

Basic considerations are presented in Part One. Chapter One concentrates on defining the stepfamily — what it is, how it differs from the traditional family, what its major issues are, how it is stereotyped in our society, and what its developmental stages are. Chapter Two concerns processes and patterns common in stepfamily therapy and discusses a paradigm for helping stepfamily members. A primary theme of the book is the need for therapists to serve as advocates for children in dysfunctional stepfamilies, and so Chapter Three examines the effects of marital disintegration on the formation of the new stepfamily unit.

Part Two concerns assessment and intervention, the twin tools of therapy. Chapter Four begins with a discussion of the initial contact and offers guidelines and suggestions. A detailed assessment instrument is included at the end of the chapter. Chapter Five considers basic strategies for therapists, which are explored in further detail in Chapters Six through Nine. Case studies reflecting typical interventions and methods are recommended in these chapters. Chapter Six examines the dynamics of the marital couple in detail, including specific issues related to remarriage and developing effective stepparenting philosophies. Chapter Seven discusses issues with ex-spouses with a particular focus on dysfunctional ex-spouse relationships that are troubled by significant discord. Helping the stepparent adjust to being a parent is the emphasis of Chapter Eight. Guidelines for creating healthy stepparent/stepchild interactions are examined through applicable case studies. Chapter Nine discusses the dilemmas of stepchildren as they attempt to cope within two family systems (biological and stepfamily). Major issues of treatment when the child is considered the focus of theory are explained, as well as intervention strategies.

Because our underlying assumption is that there is a model of healthy stepfamily functioning to be used for comparison, Chapter Ten investigates that model and reminds therapists of the special benefits attainable through work with stepfamily units, despite what are often tumultuous beginnings.

Acknowledgments

The issues covered in this book are well known to the three of us, personally and professionally. On our way to completing this project, our friends, colleagues, and students reached out to us when we needed their support and guidance. We are also very appreciative of comments and suggestions made by Byron

Medler of Denton, Texas, Jim Gumaer of Radford, Virginia, and an additional anonymous reviewer.

For more than a decade, two of us have been clinical supervisors for students in graduate counseling programs. We are thankful to our students and to the many individuals and families who willingly participated as clients in those programs. Special thanks go to the graduate student interns involved in the at-risk family project in the Pulaski County school system and to the Virginia State Department of Education, which provided the funding for that unique project.

Finally, we want to thank the many families who have allowed us access to their lives, their private domains, and their struggles. Their willingness to share their stories, coupled with their perseverance, helped sustain us through the final chapter of this book.

June 1992   Don Martin
                                               Maggie Martin
                                               Charleston, South Carolina

                                               Pat Jeffers
                                               Radford, Virginia

The Authors

Don Martin is coordinator of graduate programs in counselor education in the Department of Education at The Citadel, Charleston, South Carolina. He also has a private practice, specializing in marital and family therapy. He received his B.A. degree from Roanoke College in psychology, his M.S. degree from Radford University in counseling and guidance, and his Ph.D. degree from the University of North Texas in counseling.

Martin has been involved in teaching and training therapists for over a decade and has been director of several university counseling clinics. He coauthored *Families in Transition: Divorce, Remarriage, and the Stepfamily* (1985, with M. Martin) and *Step by Step: A Guide to Helping Stepfamilies* (1992, with M. Martin). He has also written numerous articles for research journals and popular magazines about family therapy, with a special emphasis on stepfamilies.

Maggie Martin is professor of counselor education in the Department of Counselor Education and Psychological Foundations at South Carolina State University, Orangeburg, South Carolina. She also has a private practice, specializing in marital and family therapy, in Charleston. She received her B.S. degree from Colorado State University in psychology, her M.Ed. degree from Colorado State University in counselor education, and her Ed.D. degree from the University of Tulsa in counseling psychology.

Much of her career has been devoted to the training and supervision of female and minority therapists. Her primary research emphasis is on understanding the role of women in families, particularly minority families. She coauthored *Families in Transition: Divorce, Remarriage, and the Stepfamily* (1985, with D. Martin) and *Step by Step: A Guide to Helping Stepfamilies* (1992, with D. Martin). She has also published numerous articles in research journals and popular magazines on therapeutic concepts and techniques in systems theory.

Pat Jeffers is a freelance writer living in Radford, Virginia. She received B.A. degrees from the College of William and Mary in cultural anthropology, and from Radford University in music. She also received her M.S. degree from Radford University in guidance and counseling. A former assistant director of continuing education at Radford University, she established the Adult Degree Program, for older students returning to college. With Don and Maggie Martin, she has coauthored several articles about family therapy and stepfamilies for popular magazines. She is a member of the International Women's Writing Guild.

Stepfamilies
in Therapy

PART ONE

Unique Structures, Systems, and Needs

In this section, we have compiled a broad range of theoretical and research information on the structure of stepfamilies and the major issues they face. We have also placed those findings in a general systems framework. Systems theory has features that set it apart from other approaches, and we adopt some of those in this section. Our primary goal, however, is to present an overview of the unique nature of the phenomenon called a *stepfamily:* the stepfamily system, its subsystems, and its issues. An understanding of this foundational material will make the clinical portions of this book more useful to the reader.

Part One defines the stepfamily, examines its issues, explores its developmental models, and investigates the stages of a stepfamily's integration.

Many stepfamilies enter treatment because of the maladaptive behavior of children. We have found that children's issues can usually be related to "residues" from the divorce process, as well as to the children's own inability to be integrated into the emerging stepfamily. Therefore, we also dissect the process of moving from divorce to stepfamily formation, particularly from a child's perspective, and we discuss ways of creating healthy environments for children. Too often, children do not have well-developed coping mechanisms, an ability to communicate their turmoil concretely, or adults who can try to understand and care for them; we strongly believe that therapists need to be acutely aware of the dilemmas of young people.

Work with stepfamilies can be a rewarding part of a therapist's career. Watching family members learn skills for better communication, process unresolved divorce issues, bond with one another (particularly stepparents with stepchildren), and ultimately become a functional, caring family is a heartwarming experience. Nevertheless, for a therapist untrained in working with stepfamilies, therapeutic contact with them can feel like being ringmaster for a disorganized circus. In correlation with its degree of dysfunction, a stepfamily can take every conceivable twist and turn. The methods that work with traditional families may not work with stepfamilies at all. Therefore, to help therapists understand the overall context of the stepfamily, we will begin by defining the modern stepfamily and describing the complex dilemmas that it encounters in its daily existence.

1

Understanding Stepfamilies

The stepfamily, which has been misrepresented by a variety of labels (Wald, 1981; Furstenberg & Spanier, 1984; Skeen, Covi, & Robinson, 1985), is a special unit, different from other varieties of family. By comparison with traditional families, it has unique structural characteristics. It is a unit typically associated with complications, chaos, hurt, loss, change, instability, and confusion: "While the word 'family' may denote hearth and home, pictures of Cinderella shivering by the ashes of the fire tend to accompany 'stepfamily'" (Visher & Visher, 1988, p. 3). Yet projections indicate that the stepfamily will be the norm by the year 2000 in the United States (Glick, 1984; Glick & Lin, 1986). Therefore, understanding this unit is no longer merely an option for therapists; it has become an essential task.

Definitions of the term *stepfamily* are numerous, but most refer to the stepfamily as a two-parent unit initiated by the legal remarriage of a divorced or widowed person (Coleman & Ganong, 1985). Visher and Visher (1988, p. 9) offer their definition: "a household in which there is an adult couple at least one of whom has a child from a previous relationship. . . . [These are] households in which the children may reside for periods of time varying from none to full time. Because of basic similarities, [stepfamilies] include couples who may not be legally married, but who do have a significant commitment to one another." We believe that the couple, legally married or not, is the focal point of the stepfamily, and marital commitment (or lack of it) will dramatically affect the development of the family unit.

3

The most common combination for stepfamilies is biological mother with stepfather (Glick, 1984; Skeen, Covi, & Robinson, 1985). This combination appears with such frequency because women are awarded custody of children in 85 to 90 percent of divorces (Furstenberg & Nord, 1985). Families with a biological mother and a stepfather tend to have less stress than other types of stepfamilies (Clingempeel, Brand, & Ievoli, 1984; Furstenberg & Spanier, 1984). Male children usually welcome the presence of a man in the household (Santrock, Warshak, & Elliott, 1982), and over time these boys may form deep, satisfying relationships with their stepfathers. When the stepfather has no children other than his stepchildren, the likelihood of this bonding increases (Furstenberg & Spanier, 1984).

Both of the other types of stepfamilies — those with a female stepparent, and those with children from both previous marriages — display more stress than stepfather families (Clingempeel, Brand, & Ievoli, 1984; Hetherington, 1987; Furstenberg & Nord, 1985; Santrock & Sitterle, 1985; White & Booth, 1985). White and Booth (1985) report, in addition to greater stress, the highest level of divorce among those stepfamilies with children from both previous marriages. Visher and Visher (1979, 1988) find that stepmother families are overrepresented in therapy and appear to be the most overtly stressful. The youngsters involved in these families may be biological children or adopted children from previous marriages. They may or may not live with the remarried couple on a regular basis, but there are still ongoing emotional and legal connections with noncustodial parents. The birth of a child into such stepfamilies often complicates the structure still more.

This potential for complexity in the family structure is a hallmark that differentiates stepfamilies from intact nuclear families. They are clearly not the same. Life in a stepfamily is radically different from life in a traditional family (Martin & Martin, 1985). A traditional family's connectedness results from biological and shared historical factors; a stepfamily must be formed. The legal ties that create a stepfamily are not translated immediately into family intimacy and a sense of belonging.

In each role and subsystem in a stepfamily — the couple, the ex-spouse, the stepparent or parent, the stepchildren or biological children, and the extended family — there are structural dissimilarities from traditional families. Loss is one primary difference, and it affects each role and subsystem in the stepfamily. Stepfamilies are born of grief and separation from the past. During the postdivorce/premarriage stage, many future stepfamilies do not adequately work through the loss and mourning of past relationships. Therapists should not see this as a failure, however. Most people in our culture have difficulty with death and loss. It is hard to grieve, and the loss involved with divorce is tremendous. Not only do people lose mates and sometimes parents, they also change emotional and financial lifestyles, ways of living, and perceptions of the world.

Beyond the fact that many families are prone to economic troubles after divorce, the emotional ramifications may be quite difficult. Because very few people know how to process these issues effectively, family members may try to work through these issues by themselves, leaving others in the family stranded and alone. For example, a parent overwhelmed by the loss of a mate through divorce may not spend the necessary time or energy to understand issues confronting the children. Whether a stepfamily has been together for one month or six years, we have found that a good number of issues can be traced to unresolved loss. Too often, stepfamilies avoid the sorrow of loss and change rather than talk about it (Martin & Martin, 1992). The consequences of admitting that a relationship has ended or drastically changed are difficult to bear, but to ignore this reality and its impact is to defeat the formation of a healthy stepfamily before it has had a chance to grow.

Stepfamily Issues

Stepfamilies do have the potential to become large and complex through multiple marriages and liaisons; but, regardless of size, the tendency toward instability is always present (Visher & Visher, 1982). There is great variety in the patterns of stepfamily households, and so such issues as boundary setting and role definition are not the same in all stepfamilies and may be very unclear. Furthermore, even when the confusing and stressful factors of forming a new family are handled with healthy dynamics, the happiness that the new stepfamily seeks may be elusive. According to Visher and Visher (1988, p. 15), "much of this may be caused by stepfamily ambiguity," inherent complexity, and lack of fit with cultural norms for the "ideal" family.

Various issues contribute to chaos and confusion in stepfamilies. For example, there is the marital relationship. The couple must establish stability and open communication. The possible intrusion of an ex-spouse must also be faced, so that boundaries can be drawn satisfactorily. Likewise, the stepparent/parent relationship must be solidified; here, the goals are to establish family rules and to form a parental coalition. Strength of the parental union is directly correlated with difficulty in integrating stepparents and biological parents into the stepfamily unit. Therapists working through these complex issues must help stepfamily members as they interact with various family subsystems and move toward healthy family development. The issues discussed in therapy include setting boundaries, defining roles, and learning good communication and parenting skills, as well as issues of money, time, space, and stereotyping (see Table 1).

The Couple Relationship

Despite the risks and difficulties, it appears that participants in second marriages have the same high hopes as those in first marriages (Furstenberg, 1987). In remarriage, however, each member of the couple may have high expectations of his or her partner. Each is seeking to avoid the problems of the first marriage (Coleman & Ganong, 1987; Visher & Visher, 1979). Wanting to step into a relationship, the partners also seek guarantees that such a move will be accepted and approved of. Without total commitment, the couple stays on the edge instead of truly uniting, never deciding who is to take the first step in the marital dance. Then, rather than dancing, the partners may stare at each other, become bored or disillusioned, and ultimately disengage.

Table 1. Stepfamily Issues and Solutions.

Issues	Solutions
Loss and change	Deal with loss and change
Marital relationship	Establish stability with open communication
Ex-spouse relationship	Define boundaries
Stepparent/parent relationship	Establish family rules and parental coalition
Subsystems	Keep communication open and define relationships
Family development	Be congruent within a healthy family life-style

This leads to the question of whether second marriages end in divorce more frequently than first marriages do. It is a proposition that has often been debated. Weed (1980) and Cherlin (1981) say that people who remarry do have a slightly higher divorce rate, by comparison with those in first marriages. The data indicate that remarried couples divorce at a rate of nearly 60 percent (Pasley & Ihinger-Tallman, 1987; Visher & Visher, 1988). Not enough is known about the complexities of stepfamily life to explain this differential; any of the stepfamily issues could be causes. One additional factor may also play a role: since the majority of remarried people have experienced divorce, they are more aware of the process — the benefits as well as the pain — and so they may be more likely to repeat the separation process or be less committed to the new relationship in its initial stages. These couples have been through it before and may wish to circumvent pain. As a result, they may be quicker to leave a troubled relationship. More research is needed in this area, but Weed's findings support the impression of an inherent potential for instability in stepfamilies.

The Ex-Spouse Relationship

The well-being of most children is affected when parents have a high level of conflict, whether the conflict exists in the remarried couple or is between ex-spouses. Such conflict usually entails fighting over past issues that have not been or never can be resolved. Such disagreement affects parenting styles. Contrary to popular belief, most divorced couples disengage after marriage. Rather than establishing "coparenting," they are more likely to engage in "parallel-parenting" (Furstenberg, 1987). This may mean that there is not much communication between the ex-spouses about their children; each parent attends to the children when they are within his or her own new family.

Parallel parenting has positive as well as negative aspects. If the marriage was dysfunctional when the couple divorced, the former spouses probably helped create an "identified patient" or "problem child" in the original family. Paradoxically, we have discovered that it is a "detrimental benefit" for one of the parents to keep the "identified patient" maintaining his or her maladaptive behavior: if the child refused to continue the behavior, then the parent would have to face his or her own dilemmas. For example, a child of a past marriage may be chemically dependent, and the child's chemical dependency obscures major problems of a remarried parent. Another example is the child who is angry and abusive with his or her divorced parent. The child may act in this manner because of loyalty issues.

Children who have experienced family conflict over long periods may unconsciously try to continue conflict in the new family. A typical scenario would involve a family in which the new stepparent is seen as an incoming savior, whose job is to initiate change. For the savior to succeed, the spouses need to be very supportive of each other, but there are often hidden agendas in stepfamilies. For example, the biological parent who seeks a savior may also act as a saboteur: if the stepparent succeeds in helping a child change, then that success can be interpreted to mean that the biological parent has been a failure in the past. This is a double bind. If the stepparent fails, the spouse may actually be relieved: "I am a failure, but at least I have company." The parent could also rationalize that the child is at fault, so that all can be forgiven. It is difficult to free children and parents from these conflictual roles, but it is possible when both parents in the remarried couple have made the commitment to a common system of parenting.

It is intriguing that stepmothers and biological mothers appear to have more conflict over children than stepfathers and biological fathers do. Most of the evidence (Clingempeel, Brand, & Ievoli, 1984; Furstenberg, 1987) indicates that children are more confused about stepmothers, and that both female parents seem quite competitive about the raising of the children. It is very obvious in our culture that mothers still have greater identification with children than fathers do. They are involved in more of the day-to-day parenting issues and dilemmas that concern children. We have discovered that even when both mothers agree on how the children should be raised, they still have trouble accepting or determining what is best for the child because of their own nurturance issues.

These issues are different for most men. Nearly 90 percent of noncustodial parents are men (Furstenberg, Nord, Peterson, & Zill, 1983). Even though many therapists espouse the idea of joint custody for children, this is usually not the decision rendered by judges. The majority of men do not pay child support on a regular basis (Pasley & Ihinger-Tallman, 1987; Glick, 1984). Men also appear to have trouble visiting their children. Approximately 16 percent manage to see their children as often as once a week (Furstenberg, Nord, Peterson, & Zill, 1983; Pasley & Ihinger-Tallman, 1987); the vast majority see their children much less than that, and a good number do not see them at all. Furstenberg and Nord (1985) discovered, in a random sample of divorced couples, that 75 percent of the children had no contact with their fathers.

The biological father's absence and lack of financial support can aggravate conflicts in a stepfamily, particularly if money was an issue in the previous marriage. It is helpful when stepparents commit themselves to the economic support of stepchildren, because this commitment indicates involvement in caring for the child, and the child realizes that part of the responsibility of a parent is providing financial support. Nevertheless, when a stepparent does support the stepchildren, a variety of conflicts may ensue. For example, children may see a stepfather's financial support as his way of caring for them, but they may also feel anger toward their biological father, who has "given up" on them and, in their opinion, is not supportive. Lack of support is difficult for a child to understand, and so the child may create an idealized picture of a parent. If the father visits only occasionally, the child may invent a mythical parent figure, in order to feel better. The child's reaction is quite natural but may push the stepfather away, and he may be confused because even though he sees the noninvolvement of the biological parent, he still experiences the child's lack of commitment to him. He may feel angry with the biological parent for not being involved. He may retreat because he feels rejected, or he may feel sad for the children and try to protect them. Such lack of involvement on the part of the children must be discussed, so that the family members involved can discontinue this hidden agenda.

Even when the biological father is involved, however, parenting of the children is rarely discussed between ex-spouses. Most decide their own courses of action. If both parents agree to this approach, come to terms, and accept each other, then there are usually few problems. This solution lets the family permit a child to learn how to function with a variety of parenting and family options. Children can move between families and maintain their integrity as long as they know the boundaries and limitations of each family unit, and these circumstances are not atypical for children. Every day, they experience different types of boundaries in school and among their peers, and they discover what behavior is appropriate to which environments.

One benefit for children who share two families is involvement with stepgrandparents, aunts, uncles, and numerous other relatives. There has not been much research to substantiate whether such relationships grow stronger over time, but it seems that the extended family has been helpful to children. It enables them to connect with other people while observing other types of families, marriages, and relationships and to learn from this experience. Stepgrandparents do appear to get involved with children and can contribute both emotional and financial support (Furstenberg, 1987).

The Stepparent-Parent Relationship

Maladaptive misbehavior is often exhibited because a child feels disloyal to one parent (whether a stepparent or a biological parent) and is attempting to please the other. The stepchild endeavors to solidify the relationship with the favored parent through maladaptive behavior. Therapists may find it difficult to direct these relationships to become more productive as a child moves between the biological parents and stepparents and attempts to please a variety of adults in the process.

Whatever type of behavior a child is exhibiting, the family must provide a foundation and the stability for the child to develop a healthy self-concept. Caring and involved parents determine the necessary climate for family development. This need for closeness and parent-child bonding in the stepfamily may provide the solution to many difficulties. Good parenting requires hard work and consistency, however. Unlike some other therapists, we believe it is the responsibility of the adults to determine the pace for developing relationships between stepparent and child. Children do not have a limited quantity of love, and we expect adults to overcome their own jealousies and insecurities in order to help the parent-child relationship grow stronger.

According to Pasley, Ihinger-Tallman, and Coleman (1984), there have been many conflicting ideas about levels of interpersonal relationships in stepfamilies. Most stepparents have difficulty with parenting roles and appear reluctant to administer discipline. They may think that their stepchildren will not accept them as parents, and both parties may be afraid to make a commitment to the relationship. As a result, adults often put limits on steprelationships, causing confusion and friction for the children (Visher & Visher, 1979). When a stepparent becomes an instant authority figure but puts limits on love, conflicts may result, particularly in families where there are adolescents, because adolescents in general do not agree with their parents; they are in the process of working out their dependence and independence issues. Authority figures are questioned and often disregarded if not disdained.

In our view, there can be no intimacy without conflict, but too much or too little is destructive. We have seen stepparents shy away from conflict because they fear intimacy, becoming too involved and escalating loyalty issues, or suffering further loss (Martin & Martin, 1985, 1992). For example,

Louis was a very outgoing, charismatic parent who formed an immediate close bond with his seven-year-old stepson, Andy. Because Andy's biological father was a long-distance trucker, his meetings with Andy were infrequent, and the relationship was tenuous. In a therapy session, Louis talked about his commitment to and love of Andy, along with his reluctance to "get in the way of Andy and his Dad." He saw Andy's excitement when his father called, and Louis was unsure of his place. In his frustration, Louis began to cry as he questioned his role with Andy: "Should I tell him I love him? What about my resentment for his father and what he's done? Where do I fit in Andy's life?"

Beyond their commitment issues, stepparents may also perceive a potential lack of support from their mates (the biological custodial parents) when they set rules and limits that are vital to the integration and well-being of the family. If the stepparent's input into the family's structure and discipline is negated, the family may quickly become chaotic. We believe that, without order, family intimacy is virtually impossible.

It is this feeling of being stranded that leaves the stepparent a friend or an outsider, rather than a committed and involved family member. This alienation may dissipate over time (Martin & Martin, 1985), but if the stepparent is not initially committed, it is much harder to achieve intimacy later on. Such relationships may be easier with younger children who will have more time at home with the stepparent. Nevertheless, if the stepparent is not committed to this child and chooses to stay free of conflict, then the same distancing scenario will develop.

Many stepparents, when children refuse to accept them, retreat rather than face these dilemmas. Therapists need to help adults understand that *relationships* develop over time, but appropriate, respectful *behavior* from all family members must be immediate. Children may be quite vocal and very open in their opinions. They may actively criticize a stepparent and try to unite the biological parents over issues. At the beginning stage of the stepfamily, it is important for the biological spouse to support the stepparent, because lack of confidence may exclude the stepparent from disciplinary and other caring situations.

Biological parents may experience the same types of problems with stepparents as their children do. They may see the stepparents as failing to assume responsibility in the family and acting uninvolved. Such lack of commitment is a means of protection from hurt and fear. Furstenberg (1987) says that children in stepfamilies tend to do less with stepparents and are less emotionally tied to them, but the involvement that comes from doing things together and sharing family responsibilities, chores, and events is what draw people closer. Intimacy grows, even though children may move in and out of the family on weekends and at other times. A stepfamily must develop a consistent plan for involving everyone in the family. Children in stepfamilies are no more doomed to maladjustment than are most other children in our society (Furstenberg, 1987). If the remarried couple is happy and united in parenting the children, then the children are more than likely to exhibit healthy characteristics.

The Stepchildren-Children Relationship

Children are another factor affecting stability in stepfamilies. In fact, the children must often make the greatest adjustments after a parent's remarriage. Previous authority figures and role models may be replaced, and ordinal positions may change. They may be separated from biological siblings or have to share space with new siblings. They may have to move, frequently from one parent to another, according to visitation rights. Another adjustment may be required if the new couple goes on to have a biological child. Where is home, and who is family?

In reacting to such adjustments, some children may not seem particularly agreeable to keeping the new couple together, and they may actively disrupt the family. Others have a more wary attitude: they want to be certain that the couple is functioning adequately before they participate and risk relationships. The adults had the opportunity to date and make their choices before the remarriage, but the children probably had very little voice in the decision.

The ways in which stepfamily members determine the amount of time they will spend with one another may also confuse and frustrate children. Of course, the remarried partners must find time for themselves; yet, as in any other family, the children demand a great deal of attention. If it is lacking, they will seek it through negative behavior. Because emotional bonding and boundaries around relationships take time to develop, it is important that stepfamily members make a clear commitment to spend time together. That may be a challenge when children shift geographically between family units — they may feel that they do not have enough parental time for the relationships they need in either unit — yet it is a task that stepfamilies must undertake. Messinger and Walker (1981) discuss the need for permeable boundaries, so that children who see both biological parents can move easily between households. The need for permeability remains even after the children are grown.

Children in a newly formed stepfamily may resent having to move to a new neighborhood, attend a new school, and find new friends. If they also have to share living space (such as a bedroom) with new stepsiblings, conflict may escalate. Older siblings may resent having their status or place in the family changed by the addition of new family members. Moreover, biological children typically believe that they have higher standing with their biological parents than any stepchildren do. This belief may contribute to conflict and confusion when stepchildren perceive disparity in the amount of time spent with their stepsiblings and biological parents.

In considering children and attention in stepfamilies, it is easy for parents to spend nearly all their available time answering the demands of their children and little time together as a couple. Children do provide plenty of conversation for marital couples, but the partners may soon find they have little else to share with each other if all their energies are focused in that one direction. In fact, such a one-dimensional focus probably contributes to marital discord (Messinger, 1984).

Children's problems may be educational, social, or psychological. Typical types of school problems for children in stepfamilies are decreased academic performance, missed classes, truancy, vandalism or violence, and general lack of attention in class. Unfortunately, parents often wait until these problems become crises before they seek counseling. This delay makes the process of intervention crisis-oriented and may hamper the chances of success. In therapy, children often reveal that their school problems hide deeper emotional issues, such as the resentment, anger, anxiety, alienation, or confusion associated with both divorce and stepfamily adjustment. If these underlying issues are not addressed and alleviated, a child may withdraw from the family and move toward a negatively oriented peer group, and such problems as chemical dependency, an unwanted pregnancy, and other maladaptive behaviors may result. Child and family service agencies report that many runaway children are stepchildren, as are a disproportionate number of children who are abused. Events that require the placement of stepchildren in foster homes occur all too frequently, and probation officers report working with this population far too often.

Stereotyping Stepfamilies

Our society has negative perceptions of stepfamilies. These families are seen as deficient by comparison to nuclear or traditional families. A new stepfamily is a group of individuals who need to work out their interactional patterns, some of which may be quite dysfunctional. Being seen in this position generates a type of self-fulfilling prophecy, whereby families become afraid to face the inherent dynamics of being a stepfamily and sometimes will not even admit to being stepfamilies. Stepfamilies often hide from the world (Visher & Visher, 1988). Members of a stepfamily may use the name of the full-time family in which they reside (whether it is their legal name or not), or they may deny to the people around them that there was a remarriage and that they belong to a stepfamily. Others confide only with a small group of people whom they believe open to understanding the nature of their unique problems (these people may also be stepfamily members). Stepfamilies are afraid, perhaps justifiably, that the world will view them negatively.

New stepfamily members often speak of culture shock (Visher & Visher, 1979, 1989). Self-consciousness about their own behavior and acute awareness of the behavior of others in the household may create an unfamiliar, even alien, environment. Seemingly trivial things can become important and must be respected by others (Martin & Martin, 1985; Visher & Visher, 1988).

Several research studies have found that school personnel, teachers, and administrators treat stepfamily members more negatively than they treat students from traditional families (Bryan, Ganong, Coleman, & Bryan, 1985). For example, in one study (Touliatos & Lindholm, 1980), the researchers showed videotapes of children and said sometimes that maladaptive children were from traditional families and sometimes that they were from stepfamilies. Almost invariably, the teachers or administrators would say that the stepfamily members were more maladaptive, and that those children were suffering because of a divorce.

Counselors and other therapists, prejudiced or lacking training and insight, may engage in the same type of stereotyping. Bennett (1981) found that when therapists who were either stepparents or had been stepchildren were asked if they thought there was special training needed for work with stepfamilies, the great majority of them said yes. Only 14 percent of nonstepfamily therapists said that they would need special training to work with these family units.

In addition to being subjected to negative stereotyping, many stepfamily members are uncomfortable with the variety of labels applied to them. These labels may not accurately describe family members and, again, are perceived as being viewed negatively. In our practice, we have seen stepfamily members who were unsure about what to call one another, because of conflicts or loyalty issues (Martin & Martin, 1985). They also felt uncomfortable calling each other by names that seemed negative.

Negative stereotypes can distort perceptions of how people treat one another (Furstenberg & Allison, 1985). They can constitute a kind of self-fulfilling prophecy that affects individual family members and the family unit as a whole. If members enter the family with negative expectations about a stepparent or about how a stepparent will treat a child, then these expectations may be lived out. Interpersonal relationships may be especially damaged because individuals may not be given the chance to be seen as they wish to be or truly are. It is difficult to develop understanding and intimacy while fighting negative stereotypes, within the stepfamily and in society (Ganong & Coleman, 1983).

Stress and the Family

Therapists know that stepfamilies are families under stress. Their members face the stressors common to other individuals in our culture, as well as a host of additional ones resulting from the effort to form a family. Visher and Visher (1978, 1988) have identified six sources of tension and stress for stepfamilies.

The first source cannot be overestimated: stepfamilies are families born of loss. Unfortunately, our society underestimates the time needed to recover from the effects of grieving over loss. Many think that the process takes only a year or two, but in fact the full cycle of grieving may take nearly five years. Therefore, remarriages often occur before the grief process is complete, and the unresolved loss contributes to disharmony in new stepfamilies (Wallerstein, 1985; Wallerstein & Kelly, 1980).

The second source of tension and stress is personal history. Stepfamily members do not have clean slates before becoming a stepfamily. They have life-style, communication, and behavior patterns. They have played various roles and fulfilled certain responsibilities. Couples, despite having enough in common to bring them to remarriage, are quite likely to clash over some decisions and have misunderstandings. This source of tension is particularly difficult for children, who did not choose the remarriage partner and may not understand this person's behavior, communications, and feelings.

Perhaps the greatest source of stress is the preexistence of subsystems in the stepfamily, particularly the biological parent-child subsystem (Visher & Visher, 1985). The continuity in the biological parent-child relationship severely challenges stepfamily formation. Wallerstein (1990) reports that the process of moving into parenthood stresses even intact traditional families.

The situation may be worse in stepfamilies, where the new spouses have little time to bond as a marital couple or to develop a philosophy of parenting before children arrive. Whereas babies in intact families grow up experiencing the parenting styles of both their father and their mother, in a stepfamily one adult's style is known and accepted, but the stepparent's is unfamiliar and may not be understood (Pasley & Ihinger-Tallman, 1982).

A fourth stressor is the existence of another biological parent. Whether that person is actively involved in the stepfamily or not, there is a history that influences the development of new relationships. Children are especially vulnerable to these influences, and loyalty conflicts often result.

The existence of another parent leads to a fifth stressor: children are frequently members of two households, and these households are often in conflict. What is particularly damaging to children is an inability of each household to resolve its own conflicts, not to mention conflict between the households. The children are caught between two contentious family units and must attempt to deal with different expectations, rules, inconsistencies, and hidden agendas in each one. It is an unenviable position.

The final stressor is the need to integrate the varying developmental stages of family members with divergent family life cycles. Developmental stages influence behavior and goals, and tension is produced when these are not congruent. Wallerstein and Kelly (1980) have found that divergent developmental stages spawn increased stress when stepchildren are adolescents or are approaching that age.

Of course, none of these sources of stress operates in isolation. Stepfamilies need to develop excellent coping skills, because they face many stressors from several different sources. To reduce the effects of these stressors and help families cope with them are primary goals of therapy.

Stages of Stepfamily Integration

All families pass through several developmental stages (Bray & Berger, 1990; Clingempeel & Segal, 1986). While stepfamilies as well as traditional families progress through such experiences as the birth of a first child, children's entering school, or the last child's departure, stepfamilies also have another series of stages superimposed on these. These involve such factors as custody arrangements, the birth of a new child to the remarried couple, the absence of one parent, and the age when children are incorporated into the family structure. Issues generated during the various stages may help family relationships develop positively or may create future crises to which family members will have to adjust. Therapists must remember that general lack of bonding may cause problems that would not be typical of traditional families, and routine developmental situations may escalate rapidly into crises (Bray & Berger, 1990).

A major but underlying obstacle for many stepfamilies seeking therapy is the lack of a shared family history. Members of these families have joint memories that go back only to the period of courtship. For children, memories of the original family, with its life-style and relationships, may be stronger than those connecting them to the new family unit (Visher & Visher, 1988). A frequent mistake in stepfamily formation is for adults to push bonding too quickly. Just as they may have high expectations of their new marital partners, they may also expect family togetherness instantly upon remarriage (Coleman & Ganong, 1987). Instead of the desired intimacy, however, these stepfamilies find increasing discomfort.

Postdeath/Postdivorce and Premarriage Stage

This is the critical stage when adults and children need to begin the healthy transition toward forming a new family. It is the stage at which loss and grief should be addressed. Functional, newly single adults and single-parent families may pass through the grief stages: denial, depression, anger, bargaining, and acceptance (Kübler-Ross, 1969). That adults learn to be truly single again is crucial (Shapiro, 1984). It is a time to move past the hurts and memories of previous relationships, but that does not mean running away from them. It means a positive move to the point where the individual can feel equally comfortable alone or in a new relationship. When individuals halt their progress at the denial stage, problems surface later, and it is unlikely that these adults will be able to develop other intimate relationships. Concurrently, children of divorce should have the opportunity to adapt to the new relationship with the noncustodial parent. Adaptation will help minimize loyalty issues surrounding a future stepparent. Overall, this stage is a time for healing and personal growth.

Unfortunately, many couples have unresolved emotional issues from their previous marriages. The remarried couple must overcome these issues if the stepfamily is to survive (Trotzer & Trotzer, 1986). When a new marriage begins before healing takes place, problems quickly become apparent. New partners who have not sought therapy or undertaken self-examination to resolve the issues of a previous marriage will probably find the same issues reappearing in the new marital relationship. In fact, individuals may marry the same types of people they divorced. The similarities may not be realized until the courtship ends and marriage begins.

As this stage proceeds, individuals move toward the formation of a stepfamily. This move presents a variety of dilemmas, particularly in the arena of parent-child bonding. In single-mother households, there may be greater potential for developing friendships with children, rather than effective parent-child relationships (Martin & Martin, 1992). Single mothers may also become overly protective or enmeshed with younger children and encourage older male children to become the "men" of the family. In single-father families, a reverse pattern seems to exist, whereby daughters frequently assume spouselike roles (Kalter, 1990). Engaged in such roles, daughters appear more responsible than is healthy for their age, while boys in single-father families may become less task-oriented and more irresponsible (Kelly, 1988).

Remarriage signifies to such children that they must give up these special roles, and this is not always a welcome change. Along with their inappropriate roles, these children have acquired power, privilege, and importance. Nevertheless, it is a change essential to the healthy formation of the stepfamily. At the same time, the biological parent and the future stepparent need to determine a process for family integration and a philosophy of parenting.

Adjustment to the stepfamily is easier for young children than for adolescents, particularly when custody arrangements are clearly defined. Roles among family members are more easily solidified when children are younger because, even though the stepparent needs to take more responsibility in the family, the expected roles are defined and structured. With adolescents, however, much of the struggle with parents involves assuming more responsibility and independence as they demonstrate their ability to handle new tasks. The normal struggles of adolescence are out of step with a new stepfamily's attempts to bond as a unit.

The length of time between marriages can also have an effect on stepfamily integration (Sager and others, 1983). If the period between marriages has been a long one, the family or individual adult may have mastered a number of developmental tasks (paradoxically, however, the individual or the family may have become resistant to the very changes needed in acquiring new family members). Too little time between marriages can be quite confusing for adults as well as children. It is difficult for a family to go from being a traditional nuclear family to being a single-parent family to being a stepfamily, in relatively short order. Obviously, people who divorce will progress in different ways. If one were to give an estimate of the length of time needed between marriages, a range of two to five years would seem to be indicated (Hetherington, Cox, & Cox, 1978, 1979, 1982, 1985; Wallerstein & Kelly, 1980). This period gives people the opportunity to grieve, date others, adapt to a new life-style, and come to terms with the past.

Even when couples cohabit and their relationships progress successfully, there are no guarantees of success. Cohabitation and marriage are very different. Cohabitation has never been a successful antidote to divorce: the system surrounding cohabitation, including the lack of legal commitment, is much different from the institution of marriage (Martin & Martin, 1985, 1992).

When adjustment in the stepfamily is proceeding adequately, the inherent confusion and chaos will dissipate. If the

stepfamily experiences difficulty moving through its developmental progressions, then parents and children alike will probably have trouble. According to Goldner (1982, p. 201), "Crises
that paralyze remarried families are ultimately rooted in fundamental questions of family identity that can be traced back
to fundamental problems with family development."

The Vision of a "Perfect" Family

When courtship moves toward marriage and companionship becomes commitment, adults believe the new family will be a win-
win situation for everyone, and that everyone will live happily
ever after (Visher & Visher, 1988). The new family is viewed
as a healing mechanism for a previously failed family. The biological parent thinks that the stepparent will rescue the children
from the excesses or inadequacies of the ex-spouse. A new partner will be someone to share the burden of parenthood. At the
same time, the stepparent's rose-colored glasses see a nurturing
biological parent who wants help and support in forming a caring family. The stepparent also envisions adoring stepchildren.

The Vision Becomes Reality

The happily-ever-after dream quickly fades. Stepparents, strain-
ing to join the intimate biological parent-child unit, find themselves assaulted by unexpectedly powerful and negative feelings —
jealousy, resentment, confusion, and a sense of inadequacy.
Despite genuine efforts, they are unable to join the rhythm of
the firmly established parent-child relationship. Far from wel-
coming their stepparents, children may reject them outright
(Martin & Martin, 1985; Visher & Visher, 1979). At the same
time, stepparents observe that their spouses are more intimate
with their children than they are with them as marital partners.
    Papernow (1984) finds that the stepfamily begins with the
stepparent as outsider to a biological subsystem that contains
much shared history and many unfamiliar rhythms, rules, and
ways of operating, which have built up over years of connection and are often intensified in the single-parent stage. This

biological subsystem includes an ex-spouse (dead or alive) with intimate ties to the children. The resulting structure—a weak couple subsystem, a tightly bonded parent-child alliance, and potential "interference"—would signal pathology in a traditional nuclear family (Minuchin, 1974; Minuchin & Fishman, 1981); it is the starting point for normal stepfamily development.

Loyalty Conflicts of Biological Parents and Children

In the next stage of integration, the "outsider" stepparent triggers loyalty conflicts for his or her spouse, the noncustodial biological parent, and the stepchildren. Children experience loyalty conflicts in two ways.

First, they feel their relationship with their custodial biological parent threatened by the stepparent's efforts to join the family. In the single-parent household, they probably formed tight bonds with this person and may have often felt protective of the parent, beyond what was appropriate to their age. With remarriage, these children are expected to relinquish their adult-like roles and return to typical childhood roles (Martin & Martin, 1985). Instead, they experience jealousy and resentment over the intrusion of the stepparent.

Second, children face loyalty conflicts in connection with the noncustodial parent. They may feel that the stepparent's efforts to become an "insider" are actually efforts to replace this person, and that is frightening to children. They may receive messages from the noncustodial parent that any affection shown to the new stepparent hurts the "real" parent. That puts children in a dysfunctional position, where growing intimacy with a stepparent is translated into sorrow and disappointment for the noncustodial biological parent.

Another stress on the newly formed stepfamily is the custodial biological parent's loyalty conflicts surrounding the children. Therapists must realize that these parents are protective of their children. Extending the bonds of intimacy to include the new spouse may prove rather difficult (Visher & Visher, 1988). This hesitancy to include a stepparent as an equal parent is understandable, but it causes guilt in biological custodial parents. They feel torn between the tight relationships they have with their children and the perfect marriages and families they want to have.

The enormity of the task of integrating an outsider to form a healthy, vibrant family is often oppressive. Within the first two years, stepparents become disillusioned with the continuous cycle of rejection from stepchildren and the disparity in intimacy on the part of their spouses. As a normal defense to ease discomfort, stepparents begin to withdraw (Bray, 1988). At this stage, they also begin to suspect that they have made a mistake. Biological parents are sensitive to the withdrawal and frightened by the prospect of failure and loss.

The critical question at this stage, approximately two to three years after remarriage, is whether the biological parent-child subsystem will continue to function as it has done or begin to change its structure (Bray & Berger, 1990). Martin and Martin (1985) have found that the stepparent typically initiates the crucial process of loosening the boundaries around the biological subsystem. Essentially, stepparents raise the issue of meeting the children's needs versus meeting the couple's needs. Even couples able to handle differences in other areas of their relationships find this conflict polarizing. Therefore, the first three to four years of stepfamily life seem to be a critical period in which the family either makes it or breaks apart (Mills, 1984).

Restructuring

This is the action stage, where the marital partners are finally ready to begin functioning as a unit to resolve family differences. At this point, the marriage partners begin to redefine their relationship to meet their needs first and the children's needs second (Bray, 1988; Bray & Berger, 1990). In effect, they are building a new organizational system and restructuring the family. This reorganization includes the creation of new rules and rituals. The partners also define boundaries for themselves as a couple, stepparent/stepchild boundaries, and family boundaries, emphasizing the difference between the stepfamily and the ex-spouse's family. By setting these boundaries, the partners move the children out of their marital relationship and the custodial biological parent out of the stepparent-stepchild relationship (Martin & Martin, 1985).

Experiencing Stepfamily Life

At this late stage, family members begin to experience the benefits of stepfamily life. Patterns of nurturance are established in steprelationships—that is, a level of intimacy is achieved. There is increasing quantity and variety of one-to-one contacts between step subsystems (Martin & Martin, 1987).

Along with the emergence of these patterns of nurturance, another benchmark is the solid definition of the stepparent role. Waldron, Ching, and Fair (1986) find that the successful restructuring of the stepfamily is inextricably intertwined with the definition of this role. Stepfamily members also describe many differences in details of the workable stepparent role at this phase. Nevertheless, Visher and Visher (1988) indicate some points of agreement.

1. The stepparent does not usurp or compete with that of the biological parent of the same sex.
2. The role includes an intergenerational boundary between stepparent and child.
3. The role is sanctioned by the rest of the stepfamily, particularly the spouse.
4. The role incorporates the special qualities that this stepparent brings to this family.

Resolution

The last stage is reached when norms have been established and history is built. The family now has a reliable rhythm of cycle completion in which all members can join. Issues of inclusion and exclusion occasionally appear as biological ties remain more intense than steprelationships, but these issues are mostly resolved. The stepparent is now solidly established as an "intimate outsider"—intimate enough for children to confide in, and outside enough to talk or interact with in areas that might prove too threatening to biological parents (Papernow, 1984).

This stage is also marked by a sense of loss and by the realization that there is still another biological parent. For both the custodial biological parent and the stepparent, sharing a child with an ex-spouse is difficult. Visitation is understood and expected but accompanied by the longing for a different reality. Letting go of children is a regular occurrence in most stepfamilies, however, and will continue as joint custody becomes the norm.

The absence of societal guidelines and visible support systems for stepfamilies seems obvious (Martin & Martin, 1985). The absence of legal or kinship bonding between stepfamily members, as well as the apparent inability of stepfamilies to establish their own rituals, may lead to more chaos than necessary. Therapists and stepfamily members alike need to learn how to deal with problems and crises when they arise.

Many stepfamily members entering therapy do sincerely want to face their problems, and they demonstrate the high levels of motivation, awareness, and energy necessary for working through their dilemmas. They may show a strong resolve to succeed in this new attempt at family life, because of the pain of the past. Stepfamilies like these want answers and guidelines that they cannot find in our culture. They look to the therapist as someone who has a strong theoretical and practical base of knowledge for facilitating change. Of all the types of families who seek help, stepfamilies need immediate reassurance and the confidence that someone understands how "different" they are. Good therapists can provide the input and help that stepfamilies deserve.

2

Examining
Stepfamily Systems

In the mental health field, it has been established that stepfamilies are not "unhealthy" families, nor are their members at greater risk for psychiatric disorders. Reviewing the literature, Visher and Visher (1988) conclude that while separation and divorce are major life stressors, associated with physical and emotional disorders, these events must be viewed in a larger context. Certainly, there is transitory disruption and difficulty for adults and children involved in divorce (Wallerstein, 1990). Under certain conditions, however, there are individuals for whom the stepfamily environment provides opportunities for growth (Martin & Martin, 1983). Just as certain aspects of married family life (for example, conflict-ridden relationships) are pathogenic, it is the quality of the emerging stepfamily, rather than the past divorce, that determines the mental health of family members. As a stepfamily continues to take on the functions, roles, and responsibilities of the traditional family, it continues to process growth for its members. It copes with family problems and crises, and it plans and carries out routine events and social occasions. While divorce generally requires families to alter the ways they handle these basic functions, it does not necessarily result in disintegration of family functioning.

Based on the view that the stepfamily is essentially a viable, healthy unit, this chapter identifies those processes and patterns that are normative or common to stepfamily treatment, as well as those that result in successful adaptations for family members. The therapeutic implications of this information are also articulated. Since one major problem confronting therapists who work with stepfamilies is the absence of a conceptual framework to guide their work (Goldsmith, 1982), a paradigm based on general systems theory is presented.

In sessions, therapists can quickly ascertain that stepfamilies are different from intact nuclear family systems. Their developmental stages and tasks are different from those of traditional families. For example, stepfamilies have to learn how to integrate many relationships (such as with biological parents) both inside and outside the home. Members of stepfamilies feel the difference between their own grouping and that of traditional families, and they experience social alienation. They see other people as not understanding stepfamilies. Rules and boundaries seem unclearly defined. Human service systems and social institutions do not know what to do with them. Pathology surrounds them, and expectations of others are often unhelpful. Certainly, patterns in traditional nuclear families may be dysfunctional and disruptive, but seldom to the extent entailed in the daily challenges that stepfamilies face. Therefore, the treatment goals for stepfamilies are quite different from those for traditional family therapy. Even if the issues seem similar to those in nuclear families, the structural differences in stepfamilies mean that therapists must look at these issues from an adjusted perspective.

We believe that it is usually the better choice, as the major therapeutic modality, to work with the entire stepfamily unit, when possible, rather than treating subsystems or individuals. We recognize that, unfortunately, this is not always feasible for some human service professionals, but for therapists who must work with individuals and not families, at least knowing how stepfamilies operate will help, from an intervention perspective. In fact, some of our interventions can be useful with individuals in stepfamilies, but we believe that most are more effective when therapists work with the stepfamily as a unit.

Stepfamily Systems

In general systems theory, the stepfamily is viewed as a "system" whose members are the components and whose relationships bind the system together. Every part of the system, by definition, is related to its member parts, so that a change in one member will cause a change in all and in the total system. In this sense, family members are interdependent (Becvar & Becvar, 1988). Stepfamily systems have the property of self-regulation — that is, any input to the family (for example, change in one member) is acted on and modified by the system itself, through the mechanism of feedback. Family stability or equilibrium is generally maintained through negative feedback mechanisms; change (learning, growth, or crisis) is maintained and increased by positive feedback (Becvar & Becvar, 1988). The stepfamily system is also nonsummative: while the characteristics of individual family members partially determine the characteristics of the family system, the total system generates a unitary complexity and an emergent quality, or "style," that cannot be accounted for by the sum of its individual members and their attributes.

Within the family system there are subsystems. These are smaller groups (for example, the parents) defined by boundaries that establish who will participate, and how. Subsystems possess all the basic properties of a family system.

Stepfamily treatment results in changes in the original family system. When parents begin a new spousal relationship, the child-rearing structure changes, and the stepfamily system needs adjustment; the attributes of the system and their inherent relationships have to change. The family system is not dissolved but altered. Despite these structural changes, the tasks facing the stepfamily remain the same. Changes that occur in the system generally focus on redivisions of labor — who will do what tasks — and on new methods of organization. For example, from the systems theory perspective, when the noncustodial parent continues to be involved in child rearing, it is helpful to include this person as part of a treatment plan, in keeping with the idea that even distantly involved family members are included in the ongoing stepfamily system. All the original family members affect and are affected by the presenting problem. Sessions with a noncustodial parent may be conflictual if the ex-spouses do not agree on parenting or if their past issues are inhibiting the development of their child(ren).

In these sessions, integration is a primary focus, and it includes integration of the past family unit into the developmental stages of the remarriage. Such integration must also embrace any problems that have occurred in the evolution of the stepfamily, as well as an understanding of the recent context of the child(ren)'s behavior. Involving all family members (particularly former spouses) in therapy requires ingenuity, flexibility, and perseverance, since family members are often quite resistant to such an approach (Goldsmith, 1980). The recommendation that all original family members be included in assessment and treatment planning does not mean that all members should be seen together all the time. Once the overall system has been evaluated, subsequent sessions may be undertaken with subsystems and ex-spouses may or may not play a prevalent role.

There are four basic units that one is apt to see in therapy (Visher & Visher, 1988):

1. A woman with a past marriage who has children and marries a man who has no children
2. A man with a past marriage who has children and marries a woman who has no children
3. A remarriage in which both spouses have children from past marriages
4. A single parent who has children and whose ex-spouse has remarried

It is important to develop a structure for each session, reflecting the particular problem being addressed while supporting clear boundaries between subgroups (Goldsmith, 1980).

Visher and Visher (1988) discuss goals in working with stepfamilies. Most are derived from issues that concern the previous marriage, the divorce, the single-parent experience, the remarriage, society, and the bringing up of children. Because the boundaries in stepfamilies are so permeable, children usually move in and out of separate families. This movement necessitates freedom and individuation, coupled with cohesiveness, normally not demanded of the nuclear family. Development of strong, caring relationships among family members is necessary before stepfamilies can function effectively.

Composition of the Stepfamily

To improve family functioning, subsystems and boundaries must be delineated. In fact, each former subsystem has been found to be critical to an understanding of the new stepfamily system, because many problems in remarried families stem from continuing difficulties in the relationships among original family members (Visher & Visher, 1978). Determining whom to treat is often a reflection of boundary issues. For example, stepfamilies may enter therapy because of a misbehaving child, who is the "identified patient." Should the therapist see the custodial parent and the child? All persons living in the same household? All the original members of the remarried family? The stepfamily often has a two-household formation, in which children move from the custodial to the noncustodial parent (Katz & Stein, 1983). Sometimes there are three or more households, when previously married parents remarry, or only one household, when one biological parent has died. These circumstances explicitly or implicitly determine the methods by which therapists define stepfamilies. These are critical determinations, for the structure of therapy shapes the therapeutic process.

> Susan, a fifteen-year-old, found her stepfamily impossible. "I can't seem to get a straight answer out of anyone," she said. "Nobody wants to make a decision when I ask where I'm going or what I'm doing. It just gets to be a royal pain, particularly with my stepmom and my mom. They fight all the time. They're constantly putting each other down. The funny thing is, I don't dislike my stepmom; it's just that I don't see her giving me space to do what I need to do. Lately, I've just said to hell with it! I do what I want, and they fight so much that they don't even know the half of where I'm going. Maybe it's better that way."

Adolescents like Susan are good at bringing families into counseling. They push family boundaries and unity. If the family is dysfunctional, extending boundaries produces chaos and crisis.

The family members begin to realize that they cannot function successfully without help. Some stepfamily boundaries must be permeable, however. Members need to move freely in and out of different types of family settings. One difficulty for therapists is determining which boundaries are effective and which keep negative or hurtful feelings going. Movement between families may cause conflictual motion, anxiety, jealousy, anger, sadness, and rejection. Cooperation among adults is important but is frequently difficult to achieve in stepfamilies. If the adults cannot discuss the issues that concern their children, then it becomes the children's task to find ways of maintaining a healthy self-concept in the midst of disruptive relationships. When parents, whether biological or stepparents, act in a self-serving manner and consistently put their own needs first, boundaries are probably ineffective. Adults who closely examine the needs of their children are more likely to set effective boundaries.

Subsystems

A family system "differentiates and carries out its functions through subsystems" (Minuchin, 1974, p. 52). A subsystem is composed of any subgroup in the system, including individuals, dyads, triads, and so on. The sanctity of the subsystem is protected by the boundary, or invisible dividing line, that is established between the subsystem and the rest of the family. The "boundaries of a subsystem are the rules defining who participates and how" (Minuchin, 1974, p. 53). A clear subsystem boundary, preventing interference from other subsystems but allowing for contact with other family members, is necessary in order for a subsystem to fulfill its functions.

Helping family members develop relationships, respect, and reasonable boundaries can be the key to moving stepfamilies toward functionality. It may be comforting to assume that all stepfamilies have universal characteristics, but this is untrue and makes therapy challenging. There are some typical issues, however, and the therapist must address them while looking at the context of therapy. Becvar and Becvar (1988) mention several processes to be identified in examining family structure and subsystems:

1. Clear parental authority that establishes appropriate rules with consequences for misbehavior, acceptance of failure, and positive reinforcement
2. Positive language that builds self-esteem and appropriate emotional expression including regular physical holding and touch
3. A consistent agreed-upon parental philosophy as well as established rules for keeping the marriage healthy and vibrant
4. Ability to respond openly to problems and adapt to both developmental issues and crises

Beyond counseling for all the involved family members in therapy, there are also ways that the therapist can help subsystems. Because children often seem to be the source of family problems and are living with stepfamilies most of the time, remarried couples frequently seek therapy. Sometimes the therapist may see a couple with a child. If problems are due to marital difficulties, it may be appropriate to see the couple alone. Sometimes with a remarried couple, children are brought into therapy to be given a different viewpoint on how the couple functions.

It may be helpful to involve an ex-spouse when a newly remarried couple is stuck, which frequently occurs when one spouse is reluctant to engage in the new marital relationship and remains attached to his or her ex-spouse. Such issues can be understood through seeing the ex-spouses together, seeing the couple and the ex-spouse, or seeing the ex-spouse alone. Of these combinations, we have found that sessions with the ex-spouses together may be the most fruitful.

> Juan Miguel, a six-year-old, was referred to us because he was very physically aggressive with classmates and verbally abusive to his teacher. His mother had recently remarried, and while the marriage had some difficulties, it was stable. In the course of several interviews, we discovered that Juan Miguel's biological father, after years of little contact, had recently begun to phone his son. This

man was a substance abuser with a history of violent, inconsistent behavior toward his son. Juan Miguel's mother, who felt guilty about denying contact between the father and the son, would talk to her ex-spouse when he called. She did this even though her ex-spouse was becoming more and more abusive to Juan Miguel with each phone call.

Juan Miguel's dad, in an unusual move, was planning a visit within the next month, because of his son's birthday. Juan Miguel's mother arranged for herself and her ex-spouse to come to therapy and discuss Juan Miguel's problems. We had prepared the mother for this session, and so she began by asking her ex-spouse if there could be any connection between Juan Miguel's misbehavior and the increasingly abusive tone of the phone calls. With a faint smell of alcohol on his breath, her ex-spouse instantly told his ex-wife to "get screwed." She began yelling at him, and we intervened. As we attempted to calm them so that Juan Miguel's needs could be discussed, the father abruptly stood up, yelled several obscenities, walked out, and slammed the door violently on departure.

We quickly processed the session's events with Juan Miguel's mother. We talked about her reasons for protecting her ex-husband, and we challenged her to check the validity of her choices. She still carried guilt because she was the one who had left the marriage. She was afraid that her ex-husband would self-destruct without her, and that somehow it would be her fault. She also saw herself as a failure because she could not stop fighting with him. As the session progressed, she began to understand that her ex-husband's chemical dependency precluded any relationships with her. Furthermore, his actions were very damaging to Juan Miguel. We told her that her ex-spouse needed to determine his own choices while she made the best decisions she could for Juan Miguel.

Some therapists would debate the success of this session; nevertheless, Juan Miguel's mother did put a stop to the phone calls from her ex-husband unless he was sober. The father could not meet this condition. He kept calling, until the family eventually got an unlisted number. Meanwhile, with his father's abusive calls ended, Juan Miguel's maladaptive behavior abruptly ceased. He also developed a closer relationship with both his mother and his stepfather.

There may be other reasons to ask for the involvement of an ex-spouse. For instance, if a child is the "identified patient" in the family, it may help to get the ex-spouse's opinion of the child's difficulties or enlist his or her involvement in the solution of the problem. An ex-spouse centralizes the issue and gets more people active in the change mechanism; otherwise, the therapist's interventions may be dismissed by an ex-spouse who sabotages the new stepfamily's efforts toward healthy development.

When stepfamily members enter therapy, they may recognize only that their family is chaotic. Kaslow (1982, 1990) reminds therapists that every family needs a sense of mutuality, a clear and definite structure, openness to growth and change, and shared roles and responsibilities.

Establishing Family Boundaries

Stepfamily members' perceptions of relationships are often inaccurate. New spouses may not have fully terminated their past marital relationships, and they may have little understanding of themselves or others. Berg-Cross (1988) lists several questions that should be asked when relationships change and people establish distance from each other:

1. How do you feel about and react to separations in your family?
2. Do you act differently when faced with separation than when you were a child?
3. In looking toward the future, how will you prepare for separations to come, such as the death of a parent or spouse or the loss of friends?

Misconceptions can prevent or damage a stepfamily's cohesiveness. A common one is that the ex-spouse is more or less powerful and important than he or she really is. Idealizations may develop as people avoid coming to terms with past relationships. Children participate in such fantasies as they think about the past, hoping that their parents will reunite. Naturally, it is difficult, if not impossible, for the stepfamily to integrate and bond while some members retain such ties to the past.

To avoid confronting their own misconceptions, stepfamily members in chaos may look to their therapist to make rules and determine their boundaries: "You do it for us, since you are supposed to have the answers." Again, such avoidance counteracts cohesiveness. Whether therapists should initially make rules and boundaries depends on clinical judgment; most of the time, however, it is unwise to do so. For instance, some individuals are able to have amiable relationships with their ex-spouses. Other ex-couples are not so amiable, but they can parent their children effectively, and the noncustodial parents can have good relationships with their children, without causing or being subjected to great interference. Pushing such ex-spouses to be closer would not be helpful.

From a therapeutic standpoint, there are usually schisms in relationships when a stepfamily comes to therapy. The best decision on the part of the therapist is to engage all the parents so that the children can grow up in the least restrictive environment. Decisions should be made on the basis of what works best for the children. For example, if an ex-spouse or stepparent is an alcoholic and is abusive to the children, this relationship should be examined carefully. Likewise, if the custodial parent is neglecting the children, or if a noncustodial parent is visiting infrequently and causing more pain than joy by these sporadic visits, this situation must also be assessed. To examine the psychological health of the children is vital to success, and in so doing the therapist identifies the best decision-making process for the adults in the stepfamily.

Stepfamilies may also have an assortment of legal issues and may need rules concerning money, child support, and visitation. These conflicts may continue throughout the remarriage.

Many such issues are seen as double binds. For example, Sarah, in her early forties, complained that her husband earned a lot of money and yet was unwilling to share it with his biological children; his child support was minimal. Sarah was unwilling to take him to court, because she believed that she did not have enough money to pay for a lawyer and feared that the case would drag on. Therapists can help find legal resources for people in this situation; but Sarah, as it turned out, was more interested in keeping the conflict alive than in resolving the situation for the children's benefit. Therapists should examine this sort of behavior in the context of therapy: "What do you get out of complaining? How is it worth it to spend all this energy thinking, worrying, and talking about this particular person?"

Helping an individual like Sarah, a therapist may discover that the client has unresolved issues related to the divorce. People may be angry about being left. They may feel responsible for what occurred and be resentful that their ex-mates have moved on and found a better life. All these factors make it hard for people to get better. When ex-spouses seem to be successful, to have more fulfilling relationships, or to be more financially secure after a divorce, many left-behind spouses become angry; in some ways, they wanted their ex-spouses to fail. When visitation, custody, and support are made into conflicts, the ex-couple can be kept alive, and one ex-spouse has a vindictive mechanism for hurting the other.

Stepparenting issues are considered important by Katz and Stein (1983) in an understanding of the remarried couple and of stepfamily cohesiveness. Lack of parental authority, responsibilities, and clearly defined roles confuses stepfamilies. Discipline may be unstructured. Loyalty is a constant issue, and family members may have unrealistic expectations of one another. With children shifting back and forth between two family units, it is difficult to maintain order and clear boundaries. Stepparents may be resistant to becoming financially involved with stepchildren. Initially, this resistance may be accepted, but as the stepfamily unit strengthens, it becomes a less palatable solution.

Many other factors may undermine cohesiveness in stepfamilies, including extended grief from the death of a biological

parent and unwillingness to shift from the single-parent family
to a stepfamily. In the single-parent family, children and the
parent often become very close, and generational boundaries
may become blurred; children assume many adult responsibilities and believe that a stepparent is intruding, and so the new
stepparent stays uninvolved. This distancing presents obstacles
to healthy stepfamily development. If stepparents do not perform such parental functions as caring for the children, the family
will probably become dysfunctional.

In addition to these factors, most stepfamilies face the task
of establishing boundaries between households. Walker and
Messinger (1979) and Messinger and Walker (1981) have described the boundaries in stepfamilies as being more permeable
than those seen in nuclear families. In a stepfamily, "parental
authority as well as economic subsistence may be shared between the households in the system" (Walker & Messinger, 1979,
p. 186). This situation results in a greater degree of interaction
outside household boundaries than is usually seen in nuclear
families. One problem for stepfamilies is finding a way to acknowledge these realities and still establish clear and stable
household boundaries wherein each family member is treated
with respect and caring.

Families need to establish clear boundaries but also recognize that other household units, interacting on their own, may
be unwilling to change. When interactions become destructive,
steps must be initiated to force healthy adjustment, in order to
protect the children. Such adaptations require flexibility and the
recognition that interactions outside the household may have
significant effects on family life (Katz & Stein, 1983).

Sexuality may also become an issue that affects cohesiveness
in the stepfamily. Remarried couples, particularly when newly
married, may display intimacy in front of older children. It can
be difficult for children to understand. Incestual boundaries are
also weaker in stepfamilies than in traditional intact families.

Another factor for therapists to explore in assessing cohesiveness is ambiguity of the steprole, which may spawn difficulties for a stepparent trying to fill a role in the family (Visher
& Visher, 1988; Martin & Martin, 1992). The most dramatic
problem seen in stepfamilies is the stepparent being frozen out

of his or her role, but we believe that many other roles in the stepfamily also have potential for becoming ambiguous and conflict-laden; the ambiguous stepparenting role is merely the most obvious one.

Sam, a child of ten, voices a common complaint: "When I'm over at my dad's house, he's constantly asking questions about Jim, my stepdad. It seems like he's jealous of him, or he doesn't understand what's going on. I really like Jim. We do a lot of things together. He's a good stepdad. And I love my dad even though I don't get to see him as much as I'd like. Sometimes I feel I'm in the middle—that they're each competing against the other for my affection. It seems kind of weird, and I don't like it. Sometimes I'm not sure who's the child—them or me."

In the move from the nuclear family to the postdivorce family to the stepfamily, all family roles undergo dramatic changes. As soon as family members move out of a nuclear family setting, they lose their well-defined roles. Moreover, even though society's definitions of nuclear family roles are changing, there is an institutionalized standard by which to measure these changes. The basic roles in the nuclear family are the reciprocal, paired, and hierarchically organized roles of husband/father, wife/mother, daughter/sister, and son/brother. Family functions become elaborated from these basic roles (Katz & Stein, 1983).

In summary, therapists need to recognize three things. First, all role relationships in the stepfamily undergo change. The entire system is experiencing some sense of role ambiguity and lack of guidelines for proceeding. Second, it is important to assess how role ambiguity and conflict are recognized and negotiated in the stepfamily. Third, changing roles and relationships are developmental and, in many instances, predictable; stepfamilies need to be made aware of their developmental issues and forewarned of possible scenarios.

Stepfamily Adjustment

The stepfamily's ability to progress through developmental stages is important. By contrast with the situation in traditional nuclear families, stepfamily organization is not as discrete and is more variable. Issues for stepfamilies are different because of different life events. New issues become evident and must be resolved if the family is to develop. Avoidance and denial fail to resolve such issues; they result only in maladaptive, rigid patterns.

The stepfamily must incorporate major events of its life cycle into a developmental schema (Bray & Berger, 1990). First, "There are always overlapping stages of development in a stepfamily, because there are children who predate the marriage" (Katz & Stein, 1983, p. 397). The individuation of children in a stepfamily occurs simultaneously with other stages of development. This situation produces a high potential for both interference in children's individuation and interference in the integration of the stepfamily. Ex-spouses also have probable impacts on stepfamilies: one stepfamily may be dealing with an intrusive ex-spouse on a regular basis, while another may be more at peace. Therapists need to realize that the regular developmental stages for children are escalated in a stepfamily. There is more fragility because family structure is uncertain. Loss is a major issue, and integration of the remarriage takes several years. Stepfamilies may not have time to grieve before they are inundated by other developmental issues (for example, the birth of a new sibling).

Second, in the stepfamily system there usually are at least two separate households, each involved in its own development. When the households are at different stages, stress and conflict may cause problems for all members of the stepfamily.

Third, such life events as the birth of a child tend to produce more structural changes in a stepfamily than in a nuclear family. A nuclear family's development tends to unfold more gradually than a stepfamily's.

Fourth, stepfamilies tend to have higher levels of work to do at each stage of development than nuclear families do, and they have more issues to resolve. Their tasks require more energy over a longer time than tasks do in a nuclear family (Katz & Stein, 1983). Bray and Berger (1990), Katz and Stein (1983), and Visher and Visher (1988) discuss a total of six basic issues in the developmental process that must be addressed in therapy.

Issues Surrounding Divorce

While adults certainly have loss issues, we have observed that children may mourn for extended periods, particularly if parents are self-involved. In therapy, children need to process how a divorce was for them and identify the feelings that they still have. What looks like maladaptive behavior on the part of children may actually be mourning that has evolved into anger, and children strike out at those around them when they hurt.

Issues of the Single-Parent Household

New roles and different types of life-style patterns emerge. Children may be encouraged to adopt adult roles, with positive and negative consequences. In traditional nuclear families, children gradually move into roles of responsibility; in stepfamilies, roles fluctuate, and children become independent–dependent–independent or less responsible–more responsible–less responsible. This fluctuation contributes to disharmony and confusion. Children have many reactions to living in a single-parent family, and we will discuss these later in more detail. For now, suffice it to say that such families often have problems with money and discipline. Members of single-parent families may begin to adopt the attitude that only individual needs are to be met.

Issues of Remarriage

When the single parent remarries, family roles are disrupted again. The remarried custodial parent now has to learn to invest in the new marriage, maintain relationships with children, and help integrate a new parental figure. This is difficult. Children's ages can have an effect on the development of relationships and boundaries. Children may quickly sense any instability in a remarriage and push for security. Furthermore, the extended family may not accept the remarriage, and there may be schisms and difficulties with relatives. The closeness of the spouse to his or her extended family influences the extent of approval, disapproval, and schisms (Katz & Stein, 1983).

Issues Surrounding Child Rearing and Parenting

Children long for a sense of belonging in a family and may seek acceptance through maladaptive behavior if they do not receive it in the normal ways. Custodial parents may struggle with child-rearing dilemmas, and stepparents probably do not know how to become involved or where their boundaries lie with stepchildren. Establishing rules and family roles is an important task for the prospective family to accomplish before it unites, but most families hesitate until a crisis arises. Remarried spouses may have their own biological children, and this circumstance may affect the family positively or negatively — drawing members closer, or escalating their separation. The birth of a new child may help family members understand their roles better. It may also separate ex-spouses, because it symbolizes the remarried couple's commitment to the new family structure and a breaking free of the past.

Issues of Independence and Separation in the Stepfamily

At this stage, stepfamily members begin to define their roles. Parents examine what children need for healthy development. When stepfamilies are chaotic, children may regress developmentally because they are scared. They may not believe that they can master situations when their world is in chaos. In dysfunctional stepfamilies, the children and the biological parents may hope that the stepparent will become a stabilizing factor, a savior. Furthermore, if the single-parent family has been dysfunctional, the children have been responsible for tasks beyond their developmental levels. When poorly supervised, they become more easily enmeshed with peers and vulnerable to drug use, sexual promiscuity, and academic failure. Adolescents need the comfort of being able to separate from the family while knowing that they are supported emotionally. Appropriate boundary setting, initiated by parents and stepparents when adolescents display maladaptive behavior, is important. Therapists must identify the child who feels alone, isolated, and uncomfortable with making decisions that should be made by the parents. If children believe that they are not recognized or loved, and if their parents are too involved with themselves to set appropriate boundaries, then the children will demonstrate maladaptive behavior. If boundaries are established, then the next stage — the departure of children — becomes more satisfying.

Issues of Children's Departure from the Stepfamily

Adolescents may have difficulty leaving the stepfamily unit. They may move into and out of it over a period of years. Unable to succeed in the adult world, these children force the stepfamily to push them toward responsibility and individuation. Sometimes children drift between two households to find themselves. Therapists must remember that the departure of children from stepfamilies often means saying good-bye to more than one household, and so feelings may be confused. Children may not know where the biological and stepfamily boundaries lie, and those boundaries will have to be discussed, understood, and renegotiated before the children can separate successfully. Because stepfamilies may have children at a variety of developmental levels, some members may be leaving while others are entering. Stepparents mourn departure differently from biological parents, and there may be a variety of misunderstandings about such differences. An adolescent child may have been with a stepfamily for a brief period, and relationships may not have developed deeply. For other children, relationships may be close, and there may be mourning coupled with joy when these children move successfully into adulthood. A child's leaving signals a time for reflection. Have the parents done a good job? Are they happy? Therapists can help stepfamily members reassess experiences with departing children. Again, this work involves many people, and the therapist must help children on the threshold of adulthood connect with a variety of family members, so that they can have a strong sense of understanding and resolution of issues (Bray & Berger, 1990; Katz & Stein, 1983).

Stepfamilies live with change. They lose and gain members as children move back and forth between their biological parents. Roles, relationships, and rules are difficult to determine, requiring both flexibility and stability. If negative interactions become stereotypical, the remarried spouses may separate. One family we counseled illustrates several of these developmental process interventions:

> Bryan, a fourteen-year-old, was an intelligent child whose grades were going downhill. As a result, he distanced himself from school. He was living with his mother, Fran. The events that precipitated the family's entering therapy were not only Bryan's grades and avoidance of school but also his refusal to visit his biological father, Paul.
>
> Paul was a physician with an extensive practice in surgery. He had not been at home much while Bryan was growing up. He and Fran had been divorced for five years. It was a bitter separation, mainly because of disagreements over money.
>
> Paul had bouts of depression. He felt guilty that he had not given enough time to his son, but he made no changes in his behavior. After the divorce, he married one of his nurses. The marriage was very dysfunctional, and Bryan had difficulty connecting with his stepmother. The stepmother believed that she was reaching out to him, but Bryan saw her as self-centered. Soon after their marriage, Paul and his new wife had two children in two years, and this seemed to alienate Bryan even more. He saw Paul spending more time with these children then he had with him, and he became resentful and sullen.
>
> Fran's new marriage appeared to be more healthy. She had married a man who spent time with Bryan, playing baseball with him and encouraging him in sports. Nevertheless, Bryan's mother and his stepfather expressed frustration about his grades, and they seemed unable to get him to go to school or achieve. In the course of therapy, we discovered that Bryan's stepfather was refusing to

help Fran set limits on Bryan's activities or push him toward school. He believed that this was Paul's job.

When we gathered everyone for a session, the atmosphere was tense. People were polite to one another and showed concern for Bryan. After we began to understand the context of Bryan's problems, we engaged the family in discussing the past—how Bryan's parents got together, and why they had divorced. This discussion became particularly painful for Bryan, and at one point he said that he could not understand why they had ended their relationship.

Paul spoke up. He said that he had thought he needed to protect Bryan from his feelings during the divorce, and so he had not spoken about the problems in the marriage. He had been afraid to be honest. Fran also shared her impressions of how the relationship had deteriorated. Paul and Fran were angry at times, but we worked at reframing their communication more positively. Bryan needed to understand that sometimes relationships end, and that divorce may be the better choice for the parties involved. Each of his parents began to talk about their new mates, what they wanted from these relationships, and how Bryan could fit in their families.

At one point, Bryan poured out his frustration with Paul. He said that Paul had not been a true father. Paul began to see a connection between how he had treated Bryan and how his own father had treated him. In another session, Paul cried and said that he wanted to get close to his son, but he was unsure and afraid of how to do that, since Bryan was older now. It seemed easier to stay away than to become involved. This opened up some avenues for Bryan, and he reached out to his father, saying that he too wanted to be closer.

It also became clear to all the parents that they had different roles in connection with Bryan's behavior. From these discussions, they began to understand more about Bryan's need for structure. They made agreements with one another and established new behavior, so they could discuss what was beneficial for Bryan in each family environment. They also recognized that each of them had unique contributions to make to Bryan's development. We focused on capitalizing on all these strengths, to help Bryan grow and change.

Although Bryan did not agree with or like all the boundaries that were established, such as expectations about going to school and consequences for poor grades, he did respond to the boundaries in a positive way. Eventually, his interactions with family members improved considerably.

The Impact of Other "Systems"

A therapist helps the stepfamily define boundaries that are comfortable, even when these are boundaries that the therapist would not choose. Lessening a stepfamily's pain is a therapeutic objective. Relationships need encouragement to change, and family members must be taught to care for one another. Stepfamilies seem not to have the same potential for closeness that traditional nuclear families have, but this impression is false. Obviously, as therapists, we know that many nuclear families are not close. We also believe that all kinds of families have the potential for healthy relationships and overall success.

Unfortunately, subsystems (including extended families) may provide little support for stepfamilies. Our culture still has difficulty accepting divorce, remarriage, and stepfamilies. Too often schools also respond in traditional ways. Remarried women who have custody of their children may experience "identity separation" because their children must use the surnames of their biological fathers, even if their biological fathers do not pay child support (the legal process surrounding adoption or name change is complicated, and women have little say about their children's last names). Stepparents have no legal rights concerning their stepchildren, and thus feel they have no proper place. Stepfamilies may try to find others with the same problems, but more often they begin to isolate themselves. It is almost a feeling of "them against us." The label *stepfamily,* in our society, does not usually have positive connotations. A negative message is delivered from traditional families and from many institutions.

Helping stepfamily members predict and understand the issues they may encounter can be beneficial. Therapists need to use their skills, knowledge, and status in the community to help others notice the dilemmas of stepparents. They need to nurture stepfamilies' involvement with other systems, whether human services or schools, particularly when the rights of children are concerned. For example, stepparents are often not invited to school conferences, awards ceremonies, or other events. Working to promote change can be helpful, and in some regions of the United States progress has already been made. In other regions, the needs of children are still sacrificed to "convenience."

Therapists must examine their work from an ecological perspective (Becvar & Becvar, 1988). If stepfamilies are dysfunctional because of alcoholism, truancy, or maladaptive self-harming behavior, therapists need to interact with human service agencies, schools, and corrections personnel; each kind of subsystem has a distinct view of stepfamilies. These families provide opportunities for therapists to educate others, and because many systems affect intervention with stepfamilies, being aware of and examining their influence will be a useful guide.

3

Identifying the Special
Needs of Stepchildren

Stepchildren are children of loss, either through the death of a parent or through divorce (Keshet, 1980). When a remarriage occurs, many of these children are still mourning the past. They feel the pain of the tragic situation that has enveloped their lives (Carter & Leavenworth, 1985). They are conscious that their family has drifted from the cultural norm, the traditional American family. Stepchildren show a range of emotions, from fear and anger to enmeshed feelings of love and need for security. The key to understanding stepchildren is to be cognizant of the effects of the loss of a parent. Many children of loss, particularly boys, exhibit social incompetence and behavioral problems (Santrock & Warshak, 1986; Warshak & Santrock, 1983). Yet others adapt well to their situation and are socially, academically, and psychologically well adjusted (Wallerstein & Kelly, 1980; Warshak & Santrock, 1983). The ways in which children cope with conflict, with relationships with their custodial and noncustodial parents, with the relationship of those parents to each other, with the adjustment of each parent to the loss, and with the child-care and child-rearing practices of the parents lead to success or difficulties (Furstenberg & Allison, 1985; Martin & Martin, 1985, 1992). Therapists need to pay particular attention to issues that concern mourning, attachment to significant others, and the need for a secure environment and life (Poppen & White, 1984). While some stepfamilies are formed through the death of a parent, most

48

are created because of divorce. We believe that this type of loss has a special effect on the development of the stepfamily and is of clinical significance to the therapist.

Kalter (1990) discusses some of the dramatic changes that occurred in American society between the 1960s and the 1990s. He notes U.S. Census Bureau statistics that in 1980 one child out of three experienced his or her parents' divorce. For the 1990s, nearly 40 percent of all children in the United States will have divorced parents.

A prevalent stereotype of the divorcing family has included the view that daily married and family life before separation was characterized by considerable conflict, poor communication, and lack of cooperation (Kelly, 1988). Although this stereotype accurately describes substantial numbers of divorcing families (Emery, 1982), there is evidence of considerable variation in marriages that end in divorce (Kelly, 1988; Wallerstein & Kelly, 1980; Wallerstein, 1990). For example, couples may choose to divorce because of a gradual falling out of love or a growing apart in their life-styles (Furstenberg & Nord, 1985). Kalter (1990) indicates that high levels of anger, poor child-specific communication, and lack of cooperation are not associated with marriages that end for these reasons. Thus, children in such families will have experienced less conflict and tumult than those in severely dysfunctional families. Kalter likens divorce to social surgery. The benefits of this surgery are personal growth and fulfillment, removal from a physically abusive or damaging environment, and lessening of emotional trauma.

The risks of this surgery are great, however. Four significant problem areas are connected with children of divorce: anger and aggressive behavior, sadness and depression, poor academic performance, and difficulties with intimacy. Recent statistics (Visher & Visher, 1988) indicate that between 30 and 50 percent of children of divorce experience long-lasting (over two years) consequences that affect their views and behavior. Even larger numbers have adjustment difficulties for up to two years after the divorce process. Most overcome these difficulties after that period, however.

Stages in the Divorce Process

In working with divorced couples, it becomes evident that divorce is not an event but rather a process, one filled with conflict and pain. Therefore, in counseling stepfamilies, therapists need to assess whether dysfunctional behaviors are derived from the formation of the stepfamily or from unresolved divorce issues. We will summarize here the findings of Kalter (1990) and his major research project examining children of divorce. We will examine the stages in the divorce process and how that process may affect remarriage and stepfamily formation.

The Parental Coalition Disintegrates

For children, the period of a divorce is a fearful and confusing time because their world is disappearing. The parental coalition is the pivotal axis of family life and shapes much of how the family functions. The nature of the parental coalition primarily determines how well children adjust (Kelly, 1988). In our clinical work, we have witnessed children as young as five or six relating how angry parents can be. They tell stories of their parents yelling and screaming at each other, throwing objects, crying, and sobbing. Such intense behavior has a profound impact on children. Emery (1982) has found that such behavior affects children in intact as well as divorcing families. Unfortunately, many adults continue high levels of conflict after divorce. Studies consistently link continued parental conflict and lack of cooperation with personality and behavioral problems in children (Hetherington, Cox, & Cox, 1982; Wallerstein & Kelly, 1980; Guidubaldi & Perry, 1985). Furthermore, Crosbie-Burnett (1984) notes that continued high parental conflict has been associated with increases in psychosomatic problems and with loyalty conflicts among adolescents in stepfamilies. For therapists, "it is best to improve communication and reduce the polarizing distortions that inevitably exist when there is an acrimonious relationship between parents and stepparents. Such animosity is often a primary contributing factor to the psychological problems of stepchildren" (Gardner, 1984, p. 41).

Other youngsters get confused because their parents act friendly and demonstrate little conflict. These children relate stories of their parents spending the night together, despite a separation or divorce. While severe conflict is not helpful, children also need to see consistent behavior indicating that the relationship has ended, so that they can begin to process the divorce rather than fantasize that their parents will get back together. Sometimes children in stepfamilies still want their biological parents to reunite and believe that their parents will do so (Hess & Camaara, 1979; Visher & Visher, 1989).

Parental Capacity Diminishes

Kalter (1990) discusses phases of the divorce process that affect some custodial parents. Obviously, adults respond in a variety of ways to a divorce. For some, it is a positive time of personal growth and development. Others, however, may find themselves crying, sleeping continually, or exhibiting other behavior associated with grief and loss. They may not pay attention to their children's needs. They may be angry and irritable. When a parent does not eat regularly, there may be a corresponding lack of food preparation for the children. Adults may disappear into their work during this time and rarely be available to their children. During the marriage, one parent can shield the children from some of the negative actions of a spouse who has psychological problems or erratic behavior. If such a disturbed or neglectful spouse becomes the custodial parent, however, the children will probably experience serious deterioration in social, academic, and behavioral functioning (Wallerstein & Kelly, 1980). This decline often continues in the stepfamily.

Economic Difficulties Arise

Research by Santrock and Sitterle (1985) indicates that economic matters are of great concern to families of divorce. Many female single parents fall below the poverty level and must adapt to a life-style to which they are unaccustomed. Some mothers have been out of the job market for years, raising children.

Others may have worked only part-time. Entering the job market full-time after divorce may be stressful, especially if a woman has not remained abreast of changes in her field. Emotionally, she may not wish to work outside the home and may resent being forced to do so. Some women remarry only because of financial needs, and these stepfamilies soon experience crises.

Women gain custody of children more often than men do, and men are typically responsible for children's financial support. Seldom is anyone completely satisfied with these arrangements. This issue ranks high among those that appear to contribute to unhappiness in a remarriage and a stepfamily. Women often complain that child support is insufficient and sporadic. Younger children probably do not understand child support and its ramifications for the stepfamily. It is difficult for them to see themselves without luxuries (or, in some cases, necessities) while the father's new children or stepchildren have them (Kalter, 1990). The custodial mother probably shares their hurt and anger. Meanwhile, the father's new spouse and stepchildren may be jealous of funds sent to the former family. Hetherington (1981) reports that financial support is very important in the readjustment process of a single-parent household that has become a stepfamily.

Men may easily see child support as a burden, particularly when they are trying to care for two households. Finances for a noncustodial father are often a no-win situation; he is caught in the middle, unable to please anyone. New family members are looking to his income to help the stepfamily build its new life together, and they may resent that a portion of it is sent to a former mate and children. At the same time, he may feel guilty for abandoning his children. For some men, child support may mean that a remarriage is financially infeasible. Women usually experience reduced economic status because of divorce, and so may men, because of the amount of child support needed. Fathers may not be able to afford apartments for themselves, car payments, food, and so forth, along with child support. They may be forced into a significantly altered lifestyle, with accompanying anger, frustration, and resentment.

The Child-Parent Relationship Fluctuates

When divorce reduces strife and conflict, children report that reduction as a positive outcome of the family's disintegration (Kurdek & Berg, 1983; Warshak & Santrock, 1983). Conversely, the loss of contact with a parent is reported as the primary negative outcome of divorce (Hetherington, Cox, and Cox, 1982; Kurdek & Berg, 1983; Wallerstein & Kelly, 1980; Warshak & Santrock, 1983). Custody is typically awarded to mothers, and many fathers do not keep in contact with their children (Kalter, 1990). They see them irregularly, and their involvement may decrease over time. Divorce always affects the relationship between the noncustodial parent and the children because their time together is not only reduced but also altered (Hetherington, Cox, & Cox, 1978; Wallerstein & Kelly, 1980). Thus, fathers are removed from day-to-day interaction with their children. Wallerstein and Kelly (1980) have found that such limited contact creates intense dissatisfaction in children, especially among young boys. Reactive depressions in these children have also been observed (Kelly, 1988).

When noncustodial fathers and their children do have extended time together, they usually have to structure it around such activities as going to movies, having dinner, and so on. This means that fathers become removed from such day-to-day routines as chores, homework, and reading to their children before bed (Kalter, 1990). In short, fathers find that their relationships with their children are significantly affected by the "visiting" role that they assume after divorce (Hetherington, Cox, & Cox, 1979; Jacobs, 1983, 1986; Wallerstein & Kelly, 1980). This role also creates chaos in stepfamilies as they adjust to the visits.

Custodial parents, typically mothers, also may become more distant as they return to work or school and reestablish their social lives, including dating. This distancing may increase a child's sense of independence, but it also withdraws the close relationship that the child has been used to. Custodial mothers also have more difficulty with discipline than custodial fathers do (Hetherington, Cox, & Cox, 1982; Santrock, Warshak, & Elliott, 1982). To gain and maintain control, custodial mothers may turn to an authoritarian style of discipline, but they are usually more inconsistent and less patient than mothers or fathers in intact families. The authoritarian style that custodial mothers may assume has been linked to negative outcomes for children, particularly boys (Guidubaldi & Perry, 1985).

Children entering stepfamilies have been influenced in another way by their time as children of single parents. Nastasi (1988) studied the activities of children in traditional and mother-custody families. The findings indicate that children with custodial mothers spend less time in joint family activities than children do in intact homes. The children of single mothers do less homework, watch more TV, have irregular bedtimes, have less organized home routines, and spend more time with extended family members or babysitters.

Joint custody is increasing in popularity as a method for combating some of the relationship fluctuations involved in single-parent custody. One of the key advantages of joint custody is continued paternal involvement. Bowman and Ahron (1985) and Leupnitz (1982) have found that joint custody kept fathers more involved with their children one year after divorce, in three ways: they had more contact with their children, were more involved as parental figures, and shared more parental responsibility than noncustodial fathers did. In fact, noncustodial fathers abandoned their children with much greater frequency than did fathers with joint custody (Kalter, 1990; Martin & Martin, 1992.) As expected, parents who were attempting joint custody reported an initial period of awkwardness while working out the arrangements; within the first six months, however, most difficulties can be resolved (Ahron, 1980, 1981, 1983; Irwin, Benjamin, & Tracme, 1984; Leupnitz, 1982).

Sexuality Issues Arise

When adults date actively, children see the sexuality of their parents, and that may be confusing. Children, particularly adolescents, find it unsettling to realize that a parent wants to have sex with others (Kalter, 1990). When children are attempting to model the missing parent's behavior, the other parent's sexuality becomes even more of a problem. The custodial parent may find the children exhibiting sexual behavior, to compete with dating partners. Children may resent new dating partners and become aloof, because they feel that they are losing their place with the parent. Active dating and sexuality may convince the children that reconciliation between their parents is impossible. Confronting that reality is a major process for children and must be discussed openly, with a view toward healthy transition. Otherwise, children may transform their feelings into antagonism toward the parent's dating partners. If the parent decides to marry one of these partners, the children may feel that this person is responsible for the failure of the desired parental reconciliation. Such feelings — dashed hopes, and loyalty conflicts — are ongoing stressors in the development of a new stepfamily.

Dysfunctional Family Patterns Continue

Therapists also need to assess any maladaptive patterns that may have developed after the divorce. For example, some single parents may have become too close to their children. These parents may have their children sleep with them, rationalizing their behavior by claiming that their children are afraid of sleeping alone, or that the apartment is too small and has only one bedroom. Other children get caught in conflicts between their parents. Each parent may try to force the children to be his or her allies. These children are expected to serve as middlemen between two angry, hurt adults. They are supposed to present messages to each parent and report on the activities of the ex-spouse. Other parents shift responsibilities onto children that the children are not developmentally able to master. Some children may respond with competence, but most feel insecure about assuming parental roles, such as taking care of younger children, preparing all the meals, doing extra household jobs, and so on (Kalter, 1990).

A divorce may be drawn out because of a custody battle

and financial disputes. Long-term conflict and hostility between parents have a profound impact on children (Emery, 1982). In such cases, the spouses may be enmeshed in anger, to the point where they cannot truly separate. Other types of maladaptive behavior also draw spouses together. For example, one spouse may develop excessive neediness, illness, or financial ruin, to keep the other spouse involved. Still others refuse to let go of a relationship because they are deeply hurt and angry. They seek ways to punish. Such spouses behave in a manner designed to be difficult. They endlessly negotiate financial decisions, pay child support late, and fail to pick up the children. All such behavior on the part of ex-spouses influences the functioning of the remarried couple and the children.

From a therapeutic standpoint, it is imperative that therapists work to lessen overt hostility and end destructive processes in stepfamilies. Such therapeutic involvement may mean encouraging parents to pursue legal action while teaching them to defuse their hostility. Kelly (1988) believes that until the intensity of conflict is controlled, children in such families remain at serious risk for developing behavioral disorders. Children in families nearing divorce do not anticipate it; relief at the news is felt only when there have been extreme hostility and repeated acts of violence. Children typically react with anxiety about the future, reactive depression and sadness over losing a parent, inability to concentrate on schoolwork, loyalty conflicts, and hopes for reconciliation (Emery, Hetherington, & DiLalla, 1984; Kurdek & Siesky, 1980; Waldron, Ching, & Fair, 1986; Wallerstein & Kelly, 1980; Warshak & Santrock, 1983).

The Divorce Process: Influence on Children

In his extensive research, Kalter (1990) uses various developmental models to discuss the experiences that children have during divorce. We will explore some of Kalter's findings by age range and present their implications for stepfamily functioning.

One to Three Years of Age

The major stressor for children during this period is the absence of a parent or major caregiver for long periods. Children develop worries over the separation. At this age, they feel a need for predictability and for a caring family. Separation and divorce confuse them. They may exhibit temper tantrums and, in their own way, may replicate parental distress. An unpredictable schedule and exposure to continual conflict between ex-spouses may be particularly detrimental to young children. Parents often think that because children this young do not understand the cognitive basis of the argument, it does not affect them, but most therapists recognize that this is far from true. Because of their tender years, the majority of minor children live with their mothers after divorce, and some mothers may become excessively enmeshed with their children, with negative implications for a remarriage.

Besides recognizing the signs of depression in parents, the therapist needs to assess the behavior of young children, particularly if they are crying, refusing to eat, and having difficulty sleeping. These are often signs of an infant's withdrawal from relationships, because of fear. In response, the therapist may push the mother to resume a nurturing role. This type of situation also warrants increased involvement of the male parent. The father should be encouraged to spend more time with the child, to provide a more balanced environment.

There are other indicators that children are in distress during this time, from a developmental standpoint. They may regress behaviorally, by refusing to stand or walk. Their speech may also regress: children in distress may point to objects rather than name them. Such children are highly reactive to events and seem emotionally out of control and overreactive to situations. Their fear or anger is directly related to continued separation or withdrawal from a parent. Again, what such children are looking for is a secure environment, and in instances like these the parents need therapy.

In addition to experiencing changes in the relationship with the primary caregivers (typically the mother), children this age may mourn the loss of the relationship with the noncustodial parent. It is difficult for young children to remain close to a caregiver whom they see infrequently — and for this age group, even weekly visits may be insufficient (Kalter, 1990). At the same time, parents sense that their children are not close to them, and this feeling is uncomfortable. Whatever the motivation for a divorce, the sense of abandoning children leads to inner conflict and guilt, and withdrawing from children is a way to avoid the discomfort of facing these feelings. Therefore, these adults (typically fathers) may put their energies into other relationships and hobbies, or they may miss appointments and forget birthdays, in an effort to avoid emotional distress.

For young toddlers, remarriage may symbolize an opportunity to have greater stability and economic security. If the remarriage is healthy, then these young children return to a secure environment, where physical and emotional needs are met. Such an environment is certainly better for a child's development and growth, but this is often difficult for a depressed noncustodial parent to accept. Children in this situation are often the most responsive to stepparents. They are in the early stages of learning to develop attachments, and so they are open to a variety of relationships, particularly when the stepparents are loving and involved with children's daily care.

Three to Five Years of Age

Children between the ages of three and five are generally egocentric and have difficulty distinguishing between imagination and reality. They are prone to fantasizing about situations and to believing that their fantasies are reality. These children are struggling to acquire more independence as they move into nursery school. Preschoolers still need continual caretaking, supervision, and a supportive environment. More than toddlers, preschool children may feel the effects of a parent's discomfort. The great majority of mothers of preschoolers are employed full- or part-time, which means that day-care institutions play a major role in caring for these children (Kalter, 1990).

The loss of a father can be particularly damaging at this stage. Fathers tend to be more distant and playful than mothers. They help children develop separation and independence. Typically, they do not restrain children as much as mothers do when children attempt physical activities or other means of exploration. For girls, attachment to the father helps provide emotional support for separation while still allowing closeness to the mother. The absence of a male figure also means that they have no one with whom to test their femininity. A girl may become enmeshed with her mother when she lacks a relationship with her father. Lack of emotional bonding often appears in adolescence, when a girl has difficulty getting close to boys her age. For boys, masculinity is often developed through modeling fathers' behavior. They wish to look, act, and behave like their fathers. If a boy lacks a relationship with his father, he may be uneasy with other males and more secure around women, unsure of how to bond emotionally with other men as he grows older.

Preschoolers may feel uncomfortable leaving their mothers to visit their fathers. Because their fathers are the noncustodial parents, these children may not feel close to them. In fact, they may not experience them as fathers at all, especially if they live far from the children and do not see them regularly. According to Kalter (1990), these children may see their mothers as sending them to a stranger, and this perception may affect the mother-child relationship adversely.

Another problem, prevalent among toddlers, is enmeshment with mothers, particularly among little girls. A mother may be lonely or sad after separation and divorce. In enmeshment, she uses her children to fulfill her intimacy needs. She hugs and holds her children for comfort, more than another mother would. Little boys fight enmeshment because of their strong desire to be independent and because they are less socially verbal, but girls may be vulnerable to this type of arrangement. They are more in tune to their mothers' emotional needs and are more socially and communicatively adept. Enmeshment causes special problems in a remarriage, because the new parent will have to break through it to establish a relationship with the children. From a clinical standpoint, therapists can work to establish structures in the stepfamily system that allow the new stepparent to help separate the biological parent from the children. The stepparent role can also be used in promoting an appropriate level of independence for the children. At the same time, therapists must balance these interventions with others that encourage biological parents to fully support stepparents' efforts.

It is important for the therapist to remember that preschoolers develop a great deal — cognitively, emotionally, psychologically, and behaviorally — at this stage. Since their perceptions are often egocentric, they may blame themselves for a divorce and for what is occurring in their lives. They see themselves as unlovable. They may believe that they do not possess the characteristics necessary to being loved (intelligence, beauty, and so on). In a subsequent relationship with a stepparent, these overriding beliefs may cause tentativeness or, sometimes, overinvolvement to compensate for the sense of being unlovable.

Sometimes when parents remarry, preschool children show symptoms that they have been hiding. Louis is an example of this type of child:

> Louis's mother, Mary, and father, James, had divorced approximately a year before the family entered therapy. Shortly after Mary and James separated, Mary met Max. Despite the brevity of their relationship, they decided to marry. Louis had seemed to cope with the divorce fairly well, but no one realized that this was simply because his father had been regularly in the house; in fact, James had a key, and he could enter whenever he wished. This was not a problem for Mary because she spent most of her time at her fiancé's house. Until the remarriage, everything seemed agreeable.
>
> After the marriage, however, family structures changed, and Louis reacted. His father was not able to enter Max's house, which is where the new stepfamily moved. Louis was upset and moody. Every day, he cried for his father. James, because he missed Louis greatly, complained of being unable to see his child enough. He became depressed and withdrawn. Seeing his father sad made Louis even more upset, and the situation began to spiral out of control. When it started to affect Mary's new marriage, the stepfamily entered therapy. After a few sessions, James was invited to come to a meeting

where Louis's behavior was to be discussed. In this meeting, it became clear that James had not divorced himself psychologically from Mary, and he was too involved with his own issues to recognize the needs of his son. He agreed to individual therapy, however, and within several months his depression began to lift. Then, in coordination with Mary, he began to structure guidelines that enabled the father-son relationship to develop. Louis got the structure that he needed, and he was able to see his father in a healthier way.

In stepfamilies, structure and routine are crucial for children between three and five. If they see continued conflict between the biological parents or have lost their relationship with the noncustodial parent, difficulties are likely. Their parents need therapy more than these children do. If the youngsters can understand that their parents are getting help for their problems, then they are likely to adapt successfully to the changes around them (Martin, Martin, & Porter, 1983; Martin & Martin, 1992). A remarriage cannot solve all the problems of children in distress, but a healthy one is a good step in the right direction.

Six to Nine Years of Age

Children in the lower elementary grades need structure, just as younger children do. Loss is difficult for children at this age, and they may carry distress for a long period (Guidubaldi & Perry, 1985). They realize cognitively that the loss has happened because of the divorce, but they may also blame themselves. They too see themselves as unlovable and may exhibit depression or anger. The kinds of behavior most important to therapists assessing children in this age group are withdrawal or difficulty in school or in peer relationships, problems with sleeping, destructive fantasies, aggressiveness, hostility, sadness, and defensiveness. Severe parental conflict can be particularly damaging. If the conflict continues, these kinds of behavior may become ingrained, and the children may require intensive psychotherapy.

When young children are living in a stepfamily, several issues that may be initially evident. For example, parents who have encouraged overinvolvement on the part of their children may be surprised by how vigorously the children battle to maintain the enmeshed relationship. Furthermore, these children and their parents may resent stepparents' attempt to discipline or assign chores. To successfully adapt to the stepfamily, biological parents and stepparents alike need to spend time alone with the children. They also need to take time for family interactions. Above all, they must be supportive of each other. The biological parent must be committed to insisting that the stepparent be treated with respect and care while allowing that partner to develop his or her own relationship with the children.

Another issue is competition with the new spouse. Children of this age are afraid of losing their place with the biological parent. There may also be conflicts with stepsiblings or new children in the family, tension about parenting issues with the stepparent, and loyalty conflicts concerning the stepparent and the biological parent of the same sex. It is certainly our impression that children need time to adjust to the stepparent and to the new stepfamily.

Ideally, the children will have been given some preparation for a remarriage, but talk about it and the actuality of it are often very different. Preparation through discussion is worthwhile, however. If there has been no effort at preparation, then the remarriage will remind children of the divorce, which was probably also a surprise. This is not the best way to build a stepfamily. Children should be given time to get used to the idea of having a new parent.

Nine to Twelve Years of Age

Experiences related to divorce and remarriage for children in this age group may be very complicated. Unlike younger children, they have more understanding of the world about them, more cognitive development. Through a divorce, they become aware of legal issues and recognize that their parents' relationship has come to an end. Because of their level of sophistication at this time of developmental transition, they may manifest more complicated behavior that parents are unaware of or that parents and therapists may not quickly recognize (Kalter, 1990).

Children at this age may not appear to be as vulnerable as younger children, but they too are dealing with great loss and sadness. If the parents' marriage was conflictual and adversarial, these children experience deep pain over divided loyalties but are much more likely to be angry than to be sad. They pretend that they do not care, and at other times they act as if they know, understand, and accept what is going on when in fact they do not. These children often miss the noncustodial parent (typically the father), yet they may pretend that they do not.

Girls are usually very willing to help, as a way of gaining the mother's acceptance, because at the same time they are gaining some of the power associated with being an adult. An underlying theme for them, however, is that they feel burdened by all these responsibilities, and their grades often suffer. Warring parents are particularly damaging for girls because of girls' strong need to be loyal. Conflict continually brings up feelings of sadness and loss related to the divorce. These children can see no end to these events. Parents also place their daughters in an inappropriate power position when they use them as go-betweens. They must deliver messages, bring back messages, or talk about what the other parent has been doing. That role is a major stressor for girls in this age group.

Boys, while pretending that they do not care, may experience academic difficulties or become aggressive at school or at home. They are affected more adversely than girls by parental conflict (Santrock & Warshak, 1986; Warshak & Santrock, 1983). They may become hurtful toward peers and siblings by teasing or belittling. They will refuse to cooperate with the custodial parent, forget to do things, and complain about having to help out. Sometimes boys adopt the characteristics and personality traits of their fathers. These may be positive or negative traits, but in either case they are upsetting to mothers because they are obvious reminders of ex-spouses, and mothers may become angry with their sons for displaying these types of behavior (Wallerstein & Kelly, 1980; Wallerstein, 1990).

Boys, like girls, are good at hiding the emotional distress they are feeling because of a divorce. Rather than share with people around them, they are likely to transfer these feelings onto others (teachers, siblings, and so on). Thus they show anger by fighting, verbal aggression, and complaining. Parents may see these boys as hostile and explosive, and this labeling may lead them to adopt that type of personality. In other words, negative stereotyping of boys at this age, when they are adjusting to the divorce of their parents, may constitute a self-fulfilling prophecy.

Children in this age group may also be overwhelmed by responsibilities acquired while living with single mothers: these women frequently struggle to survive economically and may turn to their children because of this distress, asking them to assume tasks (Kalter, 1990). Obviously, assumption of some tasks may be appropriate for children. In this case, however, we mean assumption of so many family responsibilities that normal developmental activities are precluded. These children are stopped from gaining independence from the family and have few relationships with other children or adults outside the family unit.

For these children, a new stepfather brings up feelings of loss and divided loyalty. When parents begin to date, particularly custodial parents, issues surrounding the divorce process surface. Children may get angry with the custodial parent for neglecting them and not giving them enough time. These children fear that when a parent dates someone, there is less love to give the children. Sometimes parents send the message, through their courtship behavior, that this fear may come true. Such parents spend considerably less time with their children and show less interest in them. When a parent's dating increases the children's insecurity, they may become more uncooperative, angry, and sullen. At another level (more typical of adolescents), children beginning to recognize their own sexuality are confused by the parent's sexual activity. If the mother is involved in a sexual relationship, her children may believe that it is wrong. They may also distort it or pretend that it does not exist.

If older children find that they like the male partner whom the mother is dating, they are confronted with feeling disloyal to their biological father. If their mother and her dating partner become closer, these children pull away or withdraw emotionally. This behavior is an effort to reduce inner conflict and feelings of disloyalty. For mothers caught up in the bliss of romance, the withdrawal of children is disappointing and may make her angry. Issues of sexuality and disloyalty to a biological parent are more conflictual for girls than for boys. Boys have an inherent emotional distance from their mothers, and they are frequently hoping for a man to interact and identify with.

When dating becomes remarriage, children in this age group are frightened. They do not know what to expect. Sometimes they have to move to new cities and schools, make new friends, and live in new houses. These are children who have already been surprised by divorce; the new stresses of remarriage escalate old defense mechanisms. Even when a parent talks openly with children, the beginning of a stepfamily through remarriage is a tense, tough time for the children. They often react negatively to the new stepparent, even if they liked this person at the dating stage. Upon remarriage, older children may say that the new stepparent is overbearing, inadequate, and unsympathetic. Obviously, it is important for the therapist to see the purpose of such behavior. In most instances, stepparents will be more successful if they seek to work themselves gradually into the system. If the family is very chaotic, however, then the stepparent is often forced into a more active parenting role, which may evoke resistance from the children but may also decrease extremely maladaptive behavior. In such cases, it is crucial that the stepparent have the support of the spouse and the therapist.

Adolescence

Adolescents have the most difficult time adjusting from a divorce to a remarriage (Lutz, 1983). Intellectually, they understand such issues as dating, divorce, stepfamilies, custody, spousal support, and so on, but psychologically and emotionally they are still ill prepared to deal with trauma of this nature. Therapists need to know if the divorce was a surprise, how it was announced

to the children, if the marriage was conflictual, if there were
emotional fireworks, what types of behavior the children exhibited before and after the divorce, what types of behavior they
are exhibiting now in the stepfamily, and what their sources
of emotional and social support were. Adolescents' behavior can
be very difficult to understand, particularly when they choose
such dramatic actions as expressing anger at school authorities
or using alcohol or drugs. The dilemma for the therapist is to
determine whether these are divorce-related issues that have not
been resolved or whether they derive from the remarriage and
adjustment to the stepfamily.

Both divorce and remarriage send adolescents into a tail-
spin. They may have difficulty managing their impulses, may
doubt parental stability and love, and may lack trust in their
parents (Kalter, 1990). They may see their parents as self-
indulgent and dishonest. Because of their own developing sexuality, they may see their parents in a sexual light. There are
many kinds of behavior that are "red flags" to therapists, particularly denial mechanisms among adolescents and unwillingness to disclose their feelings. Often they move into what are
termed *action defenses,* to block their feelings. These include steal-
ing, aggression, fighting, sexual acting-out, substance abuse,
and conflict with authority figures (Kalter, 1990). The paradox-
ical dilemma for therapists is that the same people who are trying to help these adolescents—the parents—are key elements
of the problem. To complicate things still more, adolescents are
often seeking independence from parents during this time and
yet may also want comfort and reassurance, and so they find
themselves in a confusing double bind.

One critical factor with adolescents, as with all other children, is parental adjustment. Parents' continual fighting increases children's anger. Adolescents often see themselves as the
reason for battles over child support, custody, and visitation,
and they do not understand why the people they love so much
are so mean to each other. Obviously, acting-out behavior may
have more societal ramifications for adolescents than for younger children. Therefore, it is imperative that therapists help parents, teachers, and others coordinate efforts. All parties have

the common goal of enabling adolescents to externalize their feelings rather than internalizing them destructively. Direct and displaced communication techniques can be helpful.

Adolescents' typical dilemmas have to do with self-identity, but an adolescent boy faces increased developmental stress when he lacks a father figure. He may avoid peer relationships, stay at home, and play with younger boys rather than those his age. Some boys who have no father figures may do well in school and be liked by teachers; they do not cause overt problems. Others, who may be concerned about their masculinity, tend to be more challenging and demonstrate through their actions their need for assurance (Kalter, 1990). Masculinity issues may be escalated if a biological father, even with intervention and advisement, refuses involvement with his son. The trauma will increase if the stepfather also avoids involvement. Double rejection is difficult for young males.

Issues that start with parental dating often overflow into remarriage and the stepfamily. Although problems may be related to the current phase of the divorce/remarriage process, they may arise a considerable time after the divorce. Parents may not recognize the divorce as the source of such difficulties, because of the time lag. This is particularly true when adolescents have given the impression of going through the divorce without much trauma. Too often, parents do not sit down and discuss their own dating with their adolescents. They do not state openly that their intention in dating is to remarry. In our practice, we have worked with many remarried couples who had behaved as if their dating relationships were somehow illicit. They had chosen to date in secret, and that choice gave the marriage the atmosphere of an affair. It is as if these couples hoped that, by dating clandestinely, they could somehow cause the children to accept the remarriage without protest. But with most children, and particularly adolescents, secrecy fails. Adolescents will resent and react strongly against a surprise remarriage.

A stepfamily experiences the same types of difficulties if a new stepparent tries to issue parental edicts without taking the time to build a relationship with the children. Such efforts are ineffective with adolescents and may actually polarize the family, for any of several possible reasons. First, adolescents in general tend to challenge authority figures. Why should new stepparents be any different, particularly when their power base is not well established? Second, the original family and the subsequent single-parent family may have been ineffective or maladaptive, and the adolescent may be used to getting his or her way. From the adolescent's viewpoint, why should this change? Third, adolescents seek whatever they see as best for themselves, whether it is or is not. They are smart enough to pit biological parents against each other, or to position a parent against a new stepparent, to get what they want. Adolescents adroitly pick the most fragile period of a new relationship to display problems. Obviously, this adds a tremendous burden to a remarriage. Not only are couples dealing with one or both partners' past marital failure and often guilt, they are also attempting to renegotiate and reunderstand themselves in light of a new relationship. Adolescent acting-out quickly threatens stability. Parents may be tempted to drop their own fundamental issues and work together to aid an adolescent. As we have already explained, however, this is not an appropriate choice.

James Bray and Sandra Berger (1990) say that they were surprised by the findings of their research and their extended study of stepfamilies. Children who fell into younger age groups at the time of divorce and stepfamily formation may have exhibited no maladaptive behaviors, but a substantial group of them began to show problems when they reached adolescence. This may be because relationships begin to crystalize during adolescence, and these young adults found unanswered questions when they looked to the past for structure and guidance (Getzoff & McClenahan, 1984).

Another dilemma for stepfamilies, particularly for those with adolescents, is the birth of a new child. According to Hill (1986), many remarried couples tend to bear children just when the other children are launching into adolescence. This situation may present many difficulties. It is hard for any married couple, even with a good marriage, to maintain stamina for working through adolescent transitions. The added burden of an infant increases the complexity. The birth of a child into a stepfamily

confuses issues of adolescents' individuation toward independence and bonding for continued security. If the stepparent-
stepchild relationship is tentative, the adolescent will naturally
test that relationship, in an effort to determine her or his own
strength. When a new baby arrives, the stepparent has a biological child to whom he or she is naturally attracted, and this
relationship can be upsetting to the stepchild. The stepchild may
not understand why the infant needs so much time and affection. An adolescent may also be upset with a biological parent
who is pulling away and spending more time with the infant.
The biological parent's behavior may be seen as disloyal, and
the adolescent may withdraw even more.

Both the adolescent's stepparent and the biological parent may be confused by this withdrawal, because it appears that
the adolescent is seeking less time with both parents. In reality,
however, the teenager wants more stability and caring. Knowing that he or she can venture out of the family but still have
the security of parents who care and are supportive is very important to an adolescent. If the adolescent perceives the parents as too involved with the infant, then he or she may resort
to maladaptive behavior, which may create a crisis or be dan-
gerous.

Therefore, the remarried couple needs to have a strong
relationship before attempting to have children. Otherwise, there
is a risk of alienating older stepchildren. It is difficult enough
for a child to learn how to share a biological parent with that
parent's new spouse; to have those feelings compounded by the
addition of a new child may mean emotional chaos. If a remarried couple has not mastered the developmental tasks that all
families typically must accomplish, then it is not helpful to in-
troduce an infant into the family. Spouses must be in touch with
each other. They must already have worked through such issues as how much time they will spend with each other and with
the children. They must be demonstrating appropriate levels
of affection, adequately sharing economic resources, and resolving issues of parenting before they begin to think about involving themselves with a new infant. These types of issues must
be understood before the stepfamily can function adequately.

If the family is coping with its developmental issues and is adjusting, however, the birth of a new child can be a very positive experience. It can help the remarried couple come closer and help establish bonding between all the children, as well as between children and parents.

Intervention: Creating a
Healthy Environment for Children

There are several points that we believe are important in providing the best environment for the child and for the family. These are goals for our therapy.

Providing a Secure Environment for Children

Assess whether the children are showing signs of distress. If they are, intervene to structure a secure environment, at least temporarily. If a custodial parent is depressed or angry, it may be helpful for the noncustodial parent to seek legal permission to provide the proper environment for a child. It is imperative that therapists become involved for the sake of the children, to see that they do not suffer continually because of parents' inability to cope.

Helping Parents Develop a
Consistent Schedule for Young Children

If day care is involved, help parents get the best caretakers for their children. Remember that routine is important: it imparts a sense of continuity.

Removing Children from Conflict

Children of young age cannot verbalize their feelings effectively. Parents often forget that. Because children do not verbalize distress, parents may be lulled into the false belief that their arguing does not harm their children, but this is far from the truth. Therapists need to intervene to remove children from these battles. If the parents must fight, the therapist can work with them to arrange times and locations for arguments that will not affect the children. For example, some parents argue while one is delivering the children to the other's home. Therapists can get these parents to agree to remain physically apart at such times: one parent can stay in the car, while the other stays in the house. Whenever therapists are trying to create civil relationships between parents who despise each other, the interests of the children must come first. Unfortunately, there are always parents who refuse to set aside their hostilities for the sake of their children, and a therapist must then take direct action, either legally (with the assistance of one of the parents) or through the intervention of social services.

Urging Noncustodial Fathers to Continue Relationships with Their Children

In discussions with noncustodial fathers, therapists must recognize that these men may have hidden guilt feelings. They may be unable to sustain relationships. These males, rather than directly confronting their own sense of guilt, often experience their difficulties as anger at their ex-wives. As a result, children too often lose their relationships with their noncustodial fathers, unnecessarily. Therapists can work with these fathers so that they can have a comfortable level of involvement but still communicate caring to their children.

In some cases, joint custody may be a solution to some of these issues. To be successful, however, it requires the parents to be interested in a good coparenting relationship. They must have respect for each other and place their children's needs before their own. They must truly put aside their hurt, anger, and other personal issues, and that is not easy. Many divorced persons talk about being able to do this type of parenting, but fewer are successful at it, particularly those seen in therapy.

PART TWO

Guidelines
for Accurate Assessment
and Effective Intervention

The first two chapters in this section provide an overview of assessment and intervention processes with stepfamilies. Throughout this book, we have attempted to reflect our clinical and research experience with stepfamilies from diverse cultures and income levels. Nevertheless, readers may perceive a subtle bias toward lower-socioeconomic-level families. Much of our clinical work has been devoted to serving lower-income stepfamilies, who we believe are a vastly underserved population in the United States. We have found that families with few resources are frequently disregarded and not understood by bureaucratic systems. These stepfamilies are often chaotic and may present the greatest challenges to therapists. We have also had significant clinical experience with middle- and upper-income families, however. In this section, we offer processes that we believe can be helpful to stepfamilies regardless of socioeconomic level.

Our objective in Chapters Four and Five is to provide a framework for specific types of intervention, which is described in detail in the chapters that follow. Assessment is a continual process in therapy, and effective intervention is the product of comprehensive assessment. Chapter Four discusses in detail such areas as the parental coalition, communication processes, affect levels, coping abilities of the stepfamily, and the relative autonomy of children and other individuals in the stepfamily, in order to demonstrate the determination and development of adequate intervention. We provide specific suggestions and examples of how assessment can proceed. This discussion includes questions for assessing parental figures, members' communication patterns, behavioral sequences that are worthy of note, and feeling levels. We also explore the covert and overt structures of the various subsystems within the family, including power distribution, boundaries, cognitive abilities, and the therapist's bias.

One aim of Chapter Five is to help therapists define who is the client in working with stepfamilies. This requires both assessment and intervention. Another aim is to help therapists empower parents. This involves segregating those who are healthy from others who may be pathological or destructive. Again, the therapist uses assessment and intervention in a complementary way. Roles and boundaries are also examined — those that are helpful and those that are not. Finally, Chapter Five reexamines stepfamily structure from an intervention perspective and looks at a variety of problems that may be superimposed on that structure. That discussion leads to an outline of general guidelines for effective therapy.

Additional aspects of assessment that pertain to stepfamily subsystems are discussed in the chapters that follow. Chapter Six initially examines the marital couple. We believe that this assessment is the key to helping the stepfamily function effectively. We explore family-of-origin issues, issues related to past marriages, and specific dilemmas related to the new marriage. Chapter Six details couples' structural issues and some of the types of couples that therapists are apt to see as clients. We discuss some parenting philosophies that are helpful in intervention, as well as dilemmas that a couple may have with an ex-spouse. Reflecting the work of Haley, Minuchin, and other systems therapists, we investigate power issues and hierarchical concerns with the remarried couple and finally move into communication processes.

Chapter Seven elaborates on Chapter Six's brief presentation of dilemmas with the ex-spouse. The primary discussions concern the adjustment process after divorce and how ex-spouses help or hinder the development of a stepfamily. Using case studies, we present rules and interventions that we have found helpful when an ex-spouse impedes a stepfamily's process.

Chapter Eight examines the stepparent-parent relationship

and particular interactions between stepparents and stepchildren. Case studies are used to present specific dilemmas of stepmothers and stepfathers, and guidelines for improving those relationships are offered.

Chapter Nine continues this discussion by exploring the nature of interventive therapy with stepchildren and their stepfamilies. Children are often the "identified patients" in stepfamily systems. In our experience training therapists, they often initially see a stepchild alone, or a stepfamily with the child, as the major focal point of a dysfunctional family. To advance the therapeutic aim of creating healthier, more caring relationships, we probe many of the major boundary issues that concern children in stepfamilies. We also offer interventions that can be helpful to therapists exploring these boundaries. The last portion of Chapter Nine returns to the marital couple. The role of the couple in relation to the children is shown to be the major force for stepfamily stability and the major impetus for change in a healthy direction.

The characteristics of a healthy stepfamily are the topic of Chapter Ten. First, we look at the marital couple and review some of the motivations for remarriage. We also review some of the highlights of family functioning, such as roles, affect, power, and communication processes, particularly as they are evidenced in healthy stepfamilies. All family units face the dynamic of stress, and how families handle stress certainly affects their functionality. Therefore, we explore various beneficial approaches to stress, which therapists can incorporate into therapy. We also review some developmental processes related to healthy growth. Finally, we present some considerations for therapists seeking to work with stepfamilies. There is a need for therapists to carefully examine any personal issues or biases that may hinder therapy, and this portion of Chapter Ten pulls together and expands on thoughts presented throughout the earlier chapters.

4

Unique Components
of Stepfamily Assessment

A stepfamily usually enters therapy because one or more of its members is unable to function effectively. The family unit may be chaotic and disorganized, and it may contain members of the "original" families who are vying for a common role (Visher & Visher, 1988). Parental authority is not firmly established in the eyes of the children or the spouses, and family rules are vague. There is inconsistency in how members respond to one another, and they may lack caring and respect. Evidence of nurturing may be absent, and the family often has difficulty showing basic affection. It is not atypical, in questioning a stepfamily, to discover that there are few evident goals. Members are either estranged, pursuing their individual needs, or they are enmeshed in groups of two or three, separate from the rest of the family. These people have a history of personal and family crises: separation, divorce, death, remarriage, and vague integration of past families. Any of these crises, or a combination of two or more events, may bring the family into therapy (Martin & Martin, 1985, 1992).

Thorough clinical assessment is a continual process evident throughout treatment. Initially, the therapist needs to understand and identify the presenting problems of the family. Then, as therapy continues, the focus shifts to whether interventions are effective and how the family is healing, changing, and progressing through expected developmental stages. Nevertheless, an understanding of basic family assessment processes does not ensure success with the stepfamily.

Components Complicating
Dysfunctional Stepfamily Structures

The nature of stepfamily functioning defines distinct problems.
These problems may be familiar, but the reasons for the dysfunctions stem not from traditional sources but from stepfamily
structure. Stepfamilies have many of the characteristics of dysfunctional traditional families, but they are complicated by
several additional components (Henggeler & Borduin, 1990).

Weak Parental Coalition

Stepfamily members often join detouring coalitions, in which
the intent is to alleviate stress or attack others. Underlying anger
is a common trait of stepfamilies as they try to integrate two
established systems. There are no clear boundaries around
parenting and children's functioning, because the authority of
stepparents is frequently challenged. As a result, many stepfamilies have what structural therapists call *weak executive functioning* —
that is, the parents do not have enough leverage to help children
reach a more positive self-concept and function appropriately.
Whether or not this anger is disclosed and interpreted is an important factor in whether stepfamilies become close or maintain distance. Without conflict, there is little intimacy (Resnikoff,
1981). Obviously, too little or too much conflict fosters dysfunction. Families that interpret any hostility as an attempt to hurt
another individual are dysfunctional. Functional families look
beyond anger to its meaning, and they use conflict to help family members learn to care for each other. Functional families
know how to disagree (Satir & Baldwin, 1983). They can accept that other people have different opinions. Dysfunctional
families see disagreement as evidence of hostility and lack of
commitment and caring; conformity and the willingness not to
rock the boat are desirable behaviors. Brock and Barnard (1988)
believe that family members must have the ability to bring issues to closure. Dysfunctional families, however, move from
topic to topic and do not seek conclusions or attempt solutions
to issues. In fact, this process becomes quite obvious when a

topic has intensity and deep meaning for a dysfunctional family. Members immediately shift to a more comfortable subject or level of conversation (Henggeler & Borduin, 1990).

Closed Communication

In a dysfunctional stepfamily, there are few healthy agreements or disagreements, and there is lack of commitment, because family members do not feel free to share openly with each other. They need time to get acquainted and reorganize conflictual roles. Members of dysfunctional families have difficulty revealing their thoughts and feelings (Hampson, Beavers, & Hulgus, 1989). They also experience discomfort in having people listen to them and in making themselves understood. Dysfunctional families do not give clear, concise messages, nor do they have a sense of congruence among feelings, thoughts, and behavior (Wynne, Jones, & Al-Khayyal, 1982). There are frequent mixed messages and hidden meanings in what members say to one another. Their messages are not direct; they rarely use the first person. People are often critical, and they seek to find fault with others. Conversely, functional families have a more positive tone in their interactions. They use direct questions because they are interested in each member's intentions and actions. Family members use language that shows their acceptance of responsibility for their own lives (Huey, Martin, & Martin, 1987). Stepfamily members need to speak clearly to one another and develop a feel for how their messages are heard. Functional families handle this task well, but dysfunctional family members have difficulty sharing what they perceive so that others can understand them.

Misdirected Feelings

Affect in dysfunctional stepfamilies is closed and predominantly negative. Intensity may be dampened or heightened according to the mood of a therapeutic session and the stage of development in the stepfamily's structure, and so it may be difficult for the therapist to assess the family's affective levels accurately. Healthy families have mastered a variety of emotions and display them in a therapeutic relationship (Walsh, 1982). Dysfunctional families have mastered few emotions and find it difficult to display them appropriately. They often express extreme emotional distress, such as depression, anger, or apathy. Do members feel good about each other? Do children attack or provoke their siblings? In unhealthy families, individuals who exhibit protective mechanisms tend to distance themselves from conflict; they do not identify with the family unit, and they view peace of mind as an elusive ideal (Henggeler & Borduin, 1990).

Lack of Coping Ability

Members of stepfamilies are undergoing integration, role definition, and turf battles. They often seem to be passive-aggressive or to be attacking others while working through their anger in a situation. In functional families, members have the freedom to make individual choices for their lives for selecting from a variety of alternatives (Brock & Barnard, 1988; Walsh, 1982). They know that family members will support their choices, even when those others believe that these choices are not the best ones. The security afforded by being part of a stable, healthy family does not change as members grow and develop in their lives. Dysfunctional families, however, do not enjoy such healthy security; stability comes at the price of imposed rigidity (Becvar & Becvar, 1988). Therefore, individuals are not so free to choose from available alternatives without guilt and anger. One major difficulty affecting dysfunctional families is their insistence on repeating the same mistakes over and over. They fight learning new information and analyzing their mistakes because newness threatens their perceived stability. The healthy family wants to stop ineffective patterns and replace them with more comfortable and successful behavior; correcting mistakes enhances stability and frees members from the harmful effects of past models, and in healthy families harmful behavior is weeded out. Children gain enough self-esteem to evaluate the messages they receive and make good choices. Parents and spouses clearly see what has not worked in the past, and they make efforts to avoid those patterns in the present. Members of dysfunctional families, however, often have trouble discerning the messages from their families of origin or from other influential models. They persist in family patterns of substance abuse and physical, emotional, and mental abuse. Functional families have the ability to share explicitly (Martin & Martin, 1987). Disagreement is tolerated well, and individuals are committed to one another whether they agree or disagree. Dysfunctional families lack clarity and cannot share effectively; disagreement is a threat to perceived stability because members lack the skills to resolve conflicts.

Nonautonomous Children

There is lack of definition in children's roles and in how they will function in the family. Children may act as surrogate parents, while the adults display incompetence and indecision. Myopic vision is a trait found in unhealthy stepfamilies: people in these families refuse to listen to other family members, and so they are unwilling to look objectively at their own behavior. They function from a state of denial. In a functional family, vulnerability enhances intimacy (Satir & Baldwin, 1983). Each member can trust others for commitment, support, nurturing, and encouragement. Family members who believe they cannot trust others in the unit must seek to protect themselves. They do not share their vulnerability; instead, they use such protection mechanisms as denial, abuse, infidelity, and lying, and the members of these stepfamilies certainly do not take stands with significant others on important issues. Dysfunctional family members may demonstrate lack of commitment to one another when there are parenting problems, such as when adolescents are learning to individuate from the family (Grunwald & McAbee, 1985).

Traditional definitions do not fully explain stepfamilies, and the standard instruments prove inadequate. For example, when a child's risk in school is examined with family interaction scales, responses are typically generated from a common family history, but a stepfamily may not have been together for an extended period, and so respondents may have little material to draw on. The picture may be distorted even more because biological family members may understand the communication patterns of the past, but their understanding in the present circumstances may be faulty. Stepfamily members may attribute an entirely wrong motivation to certain actions because they do not know the meaning of a message.

In assessing stepfamilies, we have determined eight basic areas that present an overview of stepfamilies' issues, presenting symptoms, problem solving and possible intervention strategies (Martin & Martin, 1992). (See Table 2.)

Table 2. Initial Assessment.

Category	Observation	Tasks
Outward appearance of the stepfamily	Observe family for 15 minutes without therapist interaction; examine family position and body language.	Assign tasks to strengthen family structure and parental coalition (e.g., setting consequences for a child's misbehavior, planning family meals, increasing parental time with children).
Communication patterns	Observe how messages are communicated; examine affect levels with messages; determine style of communication of each family member.	Label double-bind communications; audio- or videotape sessions and categorize communications; help family shift from masked to clear communication by modeling, role play, etc.; list clear rules for communication in family ("I" messages, listening skills, permission to interrupt).
Dysfunctional behavioral sequences	Observe defense patterns used in creating or continuing a "stuck" situation (denial, blaming, placating, "one up" stances, etc.); define sequence stages by steps, in detail.	Videotape or chart sequences; label behaviors and teach communication skills; replace defensive behavior with "connecting" skills

Table 2. Initial Assessment, Cont'd.

Category	Observation	Tasks
Affective levels	Identify affective responses of each member; determine family rules and messages about affective expression.	Use Epstein questions to identify feelings; help families reduce or increase affect, according to therapeutic need.
Subsystems and structure	Observe triangulation sequences among members; define family roles and relationships.	Reframe negative roles; help members share their relationship needs; interrupt and shift dysfunctional sequences by assigning tasks, directives, contracting, behavior rehearsal, etc.
Power distribution	Observe who gives and receives power messages; diagnose who is in control of family.	Help disperse power in family; strengthen parental hierarchy; remove child from "power" position by assigning parents leadership tasks (e.g., ask family about rules for dating, help parents determine limits).
Boundary formation	Assess bonding among members; determine individuation issues; observe over- or under-involved parents; examine for abuse or chemical dependency.	Reenact critical incidents (e.g., adolescent breaks curfew, father arrives home drunk); link responses to show mutuality; intervene in crisis situations; teach caring skills.
Problem-solving abilities	Determine individual and family developmental levels; assess needs of new family members.	Teach more family mutuality and less egocentric behavior; reassure children of place in family; assign tasks to help stepfamily members integrate into unit.

Outward Appearance of the Stepfamily

Initial observations are important clues as the therapist begins
data collection for assessment (see Exhibit 1, at the end of this
chapter). Sometimes the therapist's first impression may be of
some point where the family does not appear to be functional.
For example, a therapist may observe an adolescent son or
daughter who sits extremely close to one parent, indicating bonding with that parent and exclusion of the spouse. The "identified patient" (IP) in the family may be separated from the rest
of the unit or be overprotected.

Stepfamilies present a choreography, and it is the responsibility of the therapist to discern the dance from the first mo-
ment the members enter the therapeutic environment. This
choreography is typically executed by stepfamily members without specific, verbal directions. Lack of bonding is often apparent as a stepfamily walks through the therapist's door. The therapist can see whether biological family members sit next to each
other, as well as where the couple positions the children. Are
they between the parents, or on either side? Is the youngest closest
to the parents, or is the oldest? Distant family members will probably make it a visible point to stay separate from the others. The
therapist may be able to sense tension, anger, depression, or disappointment as the family enters. Who talks to the therapist?
Is it a parent or a child? Who sits nearest to the therapist? Is
it possible to sense why (protection, seeking help, an opportunity to share)? Many therapists, such as Papp (1980, 1984) and
Satir (Satir & Baldwin, 1983), purposely arrange families in order
to duplicate or intensify a psychological issue in physical form.

In rare instances, an ex-spouse may be brought into an initial session. The relationship between the adults — within the couples (both remarried and ex-spousal) — will be important to assess.
Do they get along? Are past marriage issues fairly evident? Is
it possible that a child is being used as a pawn while these adults
try to figure out their new families and levels of intimacy?

A stepfamily that we recently observed illustrates the use-
fulness of assessing outward appearances. After his divorce, the
father, a minister, remarried and had custody of his adolescent
son. When this stepfamily entered the therapeutic environment,

we immediately observed disappointment and overt hostility among the three family members by their seating arrangement. Each family member sat apart from the others, as far away as possible. The adolescent sat somewhat closer to his father and distant from the stepmother. As the session began, we watched the family interact for nearly ten minutes as each person accused the others of lack of commitment and misunderstanding. It was interesting to observe that as the family became more functional, the parents began to sit closer together in subsequent sessions. The family was given tasks that helped the members interact. For example, the parents set consequences for the son's poor test grade, and the son planned and prepared a family meal. Through these tasks, the parents became a more functional unit. Meanwhile, the son began a healthy individuation and, in the seating pattern, maintained closeness to the parents. The family clearly was becoming closer.

Communication Patterns

This is another area of assessment where the close observation of communication sequences, tone, and affect offers a wealth of insight. The sending and receiving of messages in stepfamilies will present a variety of difficulties for the therapist. Is communication clear or masked? Direct or indirect? Understandable, or muddled and vague? Messages must go to the people for whom they are intended. Does the family communicate in ambiguous ways? Do people interrupt one another? When listening to conversations, the therapist must focus on the clarity of the message's content and the appropriateness of the pattern (Gumaer, 1984; Epstein, Bishop, & Baldwin, 1982). Trying to make what is implicit become explicit, or the covert become overt, is often the family therapist's role. Family members must be able to understand one another and feel free to share openly, in order to be functional.

Stepfamilies in trouble have difficulty presenting a clear picture of the major issues facing them. Dysfunctional stepfamilies operate from a position of denial, and so they present a picture that says they are stuck and incapable of solving their problems. Furthermore, a stepfamily may contain hidden messages, with private meanings transmitted among biological family members. These messages follow the patterns of the past.

Members sometimes send each other several messages at one time. Not knowing which messages to respond to can make interventions confusing for therapists. For example, a child in a stepfamily may receive one message about the necessity for obedience and parental respect and another about the need to disregard a stepparent.

All communication also involves affect, and the therapist finds affective complications in working with stepfamilies. Because of the ease with which stepfamily members misunderstand roles, rules, and boundaries, their accurate interpretations of one another's affect is crucial for problem solving, but they may find it uncomfortable and awkward to share their feelings clearly and demonstratively. They may not believe that they know the newer members of the family well enough. They may be unsure of the extent of commitment and of the likelihood that the new family will survive. The therapist needs to be observant of metamessages and contradictory messages. For example, when a message is given and is received dysfunctionally, the receiver may act either inappropriately upset or apathetic.

There are four basic styles of communication to observe in stepfamilies and other family units (Epstein, Bishop, & Baldwin, 1982). The first style is *clear and direct*. A family member delivers a message that is understandable to another member, who then receives the message appropriately. One important goal of therapy is for the therapist to help family members talk clearly and concretely to one another. (Unfortunately, the three other styles of communication are more likely to be seen in stepfamilies.)

In the second style — *clear and indirect* — the message is clear, but the receiver is not hearing. These messages involve generalizations: "Children never listen." "Men don't care for anyone but themselves." "All women like to do is spend money." Such statements may be intended for children or adults.

In the third style — *masked and direct* — the receiver of the message is active, but the content of the received message is ambiguous. The therapist may observe such communications on the part of parents who want control and power over children. These parents' statements clearly tell the children that their behavior is displeasing, but they fail to furnish sufficient information for the children to take corrective action. For example, Bill's stepmother, Rhonda, would get upset at him, and yet she could not get him to change his behavior. Her communications with him were global, negative statements: "You never help out." "Don't treat your sister that way." "Don't talk to me that way." Bill complained that he knew Rhonda was mad at him, but he could not figure out exactly what to do to make her happy. From her messages, he was unsure of how to change his behavior, and that made Bill vulnerable to Rhonda's control and anger.

The fourth style of communication is *masked and indirect*, and it is the most dysfunctional pattern. In these messages, both the content and the reception are unclear: "People should know what I mean." "Life never seems to work out." Besides the obvious problem of ambiguity, another difficulty with these messages is that they tend to elicit similar responses from other family members, and the stepfamily becomes stuck in a morass of muddied conversation. On the communication continuum, the greater the frequency of masked and indirect messages, the more dysfunctional the stepfamily will be (Epstein, Bishop, & Baldwin, 1982).

Some stepfamilies display overt hostility and anger in initial sessions; others may be fearful, disguising issues from the therapist in initial assessments. In either case, we have discovered that a stepfamily can be so chaotic and emotionally overburdened that members may leap into anger in a matter of moments when discussing a volatile situation. The therapist must be prepared for emotional liability and heightened affect. By establishing rules for communicating in therapy, the therapist enables stepfamily members to back away and look more clearly at their situation, without the distortion of their overriding affect.

Dysfunctional Behavioral Sequences

Stepfamilies inherently lack rules and boundaries and members' commitment is uncertain. As a result, members' efforts to protect themselves or seek closeness may take the form of dysfunctional sequences. A typical sequence may involve a stepparent who refuses to parent the children when the biological parent is absent. The children know this and escalate the issues by indulging in obnoxious behavior. Through their efforts, they are attempting to involve the stepparent in setting rules and making decisions (that is, demonstrating a commitment to the relationship). If the stepparent makes the choice to get involved and sets a rule, the children may fuss and disagree, but ultimately they will do what the stepparent says. Too often in this sequence, however, the biological parent comes home and actively sabotages the stepparent's effort. The biological parent may openly disagree with the stepparent in front of the children and then permit the children to continue the obnoxious behavior. Such nonproductive behavioral sequences are destructive for all stepfamily members, and they begin to fragment the newly remarried couple. To the therapist, this is a definite sign of unhealthy alignments (Martin & Martin, 1992).

In counseling dysfunctional stepfamilies, we have discovered that one basic method members use to solve a problem is to accentuate the same behavior, just as a car stuck in the sand spins its tires faster and faster while the hole becomes deeper and deeper. One difficulty for the therapist is that a stepfamily may not come to therapy until it is already buried in the sand. Because stepfamilies learn overt conflict, family members may be resistant to sharing and working through issues. They may prefer to blame one another, act irresponsibly, placate one another, and make excuses for their problems (Henggeler & Borduin, 1990). Unless they perceive some potential for success, they are likely to terminate therapy quickly. Families born of grief and loss are used to despair. Reframing problems positively is helpful, as is encouraging family members to forgive one another rather than see "hurtful" acts as deliberate. Most clients do not intend to hurt other family members; but they are confused and angry, and because of their poor communication skills their messages may be received as hurtful.

During assessment, the therapist needs to determine the particular or major defense patterns that a stepfamily employs (such as avoidance, denial, blaming, and placating). In assessing these sequences, the therapist must be certain that the information received about them involves a step-by-step process, leaving out no detail. The therapist can feign ignorance or confusion, in order to encourage family members to describe each action thoroughly. It is crucial to be persistent in getting complete, accurate information before choosing an intervention and a plan for change.

Affective Levels

The therapist must examine the quantity of affect and determine whether it is relevant and appropriate to the family situation. The family must learn to reframe its anger. Even for therapists, assessing this aspect properly is difficult, especially if they are not from stepfamilies themselves. Epstein, Bishop, & Baldwin (1982, pp. 120–122) pose a number of questions, which may be helpful in working with stepfamilies:

> How did you feel then or now?
> What else did you feel?
> How does that feel inside?
> When you have a problem like this, how do the rest of you feel (other stepfamily members)?
> What are the similarities about how you feel and the differences?
> How have others allowed you to feel or blocked or suggested you feel another way?
> When have you seen yourself as feeling more intensely than you believe is reasonable for a situation?
> Which feelings does your family experience?
> Which feelings in this family are now allowed?

The therapist must examine the basic emotions of the family (love, kindness, anger, depression, sadness, anxiety, fear, hurt, hate, rage). How does each of the stepfamily members respond to these emotions?

The therapist is likely to see more affective dilemmas and dysfunctional responses in stepfamilies than in traditional families. Helping members get past their anger so that they can hear one another is an important first step. Attempts to reframe anger more productively can help. The therapist can try to give people a positive reason for their behavior, particularly in "stuck" family sequences. For example, a mother may complain that she is not getting help from the stepfather with the rearing of the children. The therapist needs to reframe the mother's critical, destructive anger with her spouse. Her behavior can be seen as an attempt to get love, affection, and a sense of caring from her spouse. The stepfather's withdrawal can be reframed as fear of intimacy and closeness, so that the perception of his unwillingness to help discipline or do child-rearing chores is now allowed to stand.

Other phenomena common to stepfamilies must be considered during assessment. Does the stepfamily show different levels of affect? Are the various levels appropriate to the situation? Does the stepfamily demonstrate only one mood (such as anger or hurt), or do members exhibit a variety of moods? The therapist must examine both the quality and the quantity of feeling responses, observing whether family members experience the full range of emotions as individuals within the family structure. One thing that complicates the assessment picture is the fact that stepfamily members have emotions that society says are forbidden. Grief is an example. Throughout the lifetime of a stepfamily, memories keep bombarding individuals. Spouses remember ex-spouses. Family events remind people of the way things used to be, and children mourn the loss of the life they used to have, even if it was dysfunctional.

For example, Ben, a fifteen-year-old, told us in one session that on most holidays his biological father used to drink nearly a whole bottle of whiskey in the early morning hours. Ben's father blamed his wife's family for not understanding or accepting him, and yet Ben knew that his father was an alcoholic who would use any excuse to drink. When Ben recalls these incidents, he feels the anger and disappointment of the past. He wonders why his dysfunctional biological father could not have been more like his new stepfather, who is caring and thoughtful.

Most people mourn for the "idealized" parent, and step-families accentuate this tendency. There is loss and deep emotion (whether anger, hurt, sadness, confusion, or anxiety) for those involved in stepfamilies. Members live with a whirlwind of loss characterized by continual changes, negotiation, double binds, and sometimes double crosses. Most such behavior is engaged in because family members are trying to protect one another or themselves from pain. Paradoxically, however, avoidance of pain creates more pain. Members of dysfunctional step-families must learn to commit themselves to one another. Assessment of this inherent lack of commitment is one of the major processes that therapists undertake in examining stepfamilies.

Often, instead of insufficient affect, stepfamilies exhibit excessive affect. Children in stepfamilies typically visit non-custodial biological parents, and there may be significant emotional reactions for those involved. Such visits can foster instability in the stepfamily while promoting stability for the child as he or she works through the grieving process. This situation can be particularly difficult for custodial parents and stepparents. Should custodial parents commiserate with their children? The answer is that they probably should, but with the assumption that the feelings of loss will disappear after a reasonable time. If these feelings are reinforced too strongly, they may not disappear and may become more overt.

Therapists need to determine whether children's behavior is authentic. Is a child feeling sadness? How can he or she express it in healthy ways? A child's sadness over the loss and change of familial relationships is justified; if the noncustodial parent is being seen on a regular basis, however, how much loss or pain does the child need to express, and for how long? A few minutes? A few hours? A few days? Until the next visit? How is the grief of the child hooked to the noncustodial parent's needs? Is the child really feeling grief, or is it the parent's grief? Are there messages of guilt, or messages of sadness? How should the stepparent react? Assuming that the mother has custody, should the male stepparent commiserate with the child? Is he angry because the biological parent is intruding? Is he more comfortable not getting involved? The therapist will have to scrutinize the stepparent's behavior in terms of overall assessment and the behavior's impact on the stepfamily.

From a therapeutic standpoint, it is helpful if all family members learn to deal with separation. The child will have to deal with separation anyway throughout his or her life. Without intervention, a child may return from a visit with the noncustodial parent and grieve for days, leaving stepfamily members confused and angry. Successful separation involves appropriate caring and sharing and is one goal of therapeutic intervention. Good therapists seek to widen the affective responses of individuals and assess any misinterpretation of messages that may be contributing to inappropriate affect. Brock & Barnard (1988) describe the most functional families as having a full range of responses; these feeling states are the "music" that accompanies a family's words.

Subsystems and Structure

Remarriages involve struggles: fights with ex-mates, difficulties from past marriages, past agendas, and a variety of family-of-origin issues brought in from previous marriages. Spouses in a remarriage keep one foot in the new relationship and one foot out while they test the durability of the new marriage. Therapists need to assess the levels of subsystem development because triangulation in a dysfunctional stepfamily is routine (Imber-Black, 1989; Huey, Martin, & Martin, 1987). Between a biological parent's enmeshment or neglect, children struggle for identity. Stepparents act confused and appear unwilling to make sacrifices for and commitments to children who are not biologically related to them.

Relationship development is integral to a family's survival. The therapist needs to determine whether stepfamily members show a genuine interest in each other, a willingness to be involved and care. For example, sometimes a family functions as a kind of boardinghouse, where members come in and out and remain relatively uninvolved with one another, sharing few interests. Sometimes in stepfamilies the parents are overinvolved in their work and careers, and the children have no parental guidance. If the children are self-motivated, they may be able to make it through school without many difficulties. In most such families, however, the children rapidly begin to display symptoms and push the parents to become more involved. The symptoms may include truancy, poor grades, drug use, and sexual promiscuity. The children become scapegoats or identified patients in their families. They may be the "reason" for the divorce of the biological parents, or "thorns in the side" of the stepfamily. Without comprehending the patterns of their behavior or its harmful effects, former IPs may continue these patterns when the stepfamily forms. Stepfamilies who bring in children from several families may present a varied assortment of IPs, who are vying for this unique position in the stepfamily's structure. Stepparents may feel rejected when they try to intervene in a parental role. In a destructive sequence of this kind, a biological spouse may reinforce a child's misbehavior. When this occurs, the stepparent continues to withdraw, and the IP gets "worse" and pushes for commitment on the part of other family members.

Sometimes a child who lacks affection may be a pleaser. He or she may seek love from a parent. For example, a stepfather named Tim liked his stepchild, Marie, and rewarded her by paying attention to her when she was willing to work around the house, do his laundry, or perform other chores. He was happy with Marie's servicing, and his wife was pleased when she returned home from work and found the house clean. Marie, in her desperation, was willing to take whatever affection she could get, even if it meant that the only time she got attention was when she did things for Tim. Marie's mother, Linda, assumed that Tim and Marie were doing the housework together. It was not until this arrangement was discussed in therapy that Linda realized what had been occurring for several years. She became very angry with Tim, while Marie simultaneously expressed her affection for him. Tim had trouble hearing these messages. He became defensive and could not understand either reaction. After deeper exploration, Tim began to see his self-involvement and its impact on his life, in his family and in his marriage.

Power Distribution

Power is inherent in most communications. Walsh (1989) has developed a useful diagram for assessing power balance in a family. She points out that families are likely to change if a "power member" can give up some of his or her power to other members, with all members operating less at the extremes of power and anxiety, sharing and re-owning these qualities.

The therapist must assess who gives and who receives power messages in the stepfamily. How the family faces power issues must also be observed. For example, Lou was given custody of a child he had believed to be his legitimate daughter. Shortly after the child was born, however, he discovered that his wife was married to another man. The woman was an active alcoholic, and a judge ruled that she was psychologically too unstable to care for her daughter. As his daughter grew older, Lou became close to her, replicating a husband-wife coalition. Eventually Lou remarried, but the stepmother and the daughter had trouble caring for each other. The family was referred to therapy because the 12-year-old girl was exhibiting problems at school, including unexcused absences, poor grades, and disrespect for her teachers. She had been suspended from school for bringing alcohol onto the school bus. Within the first five minutes of the initial therapy meeting, the family members began yelling at one another. The daughter screamed that she was misunderstood and "picked on." The father complained that he could not force her to do anything and had whipped her on many occasions, with little success. The stepmother whined about how much she loved both the father and the child and felt left out. She put her hand over her chest and said that she believed she could not do anything in this family because no one respected what she had to say. As the assessment session progressed, it became clear that the child had assumed a powerful role and was unable to handle it. She wanted her father and her stepmother to take control and provide some guidance. From an outsider's point of view, it seemed as if the father and the stepmother wanted this power, but they did not seek it. The therapist's job was evident: balance the power in the family until the spouses were functional enough to fulfill their proper roles.

The people with the greatest power in a family may also be the most dysfunctional and disabled. They often "appear" to be weak. Because stepfamilies tend to have poorly functioning rules, boundaries may be broken, and such extremes of behavior as abuse and incest may occur. The therapist must be careful to observe who truly is powerful in the stepfamily. While watching a discussion of a sensitive issue, the therapist should note how conflict is resolved. This process typically reveals who wields the most power.

Boundary Formation

Are stepfamily members separate thinking and feeling human beings? Is there overbonding between parents and children? Sometimes two significantly different family units join to form a stepfamily. The remarrying individuals may both believe that they will be happy with their "opposite." For example, a person from an enmeshed family may want to be with someone from a disengaged family. The enmeshed, overinvolved mate is pleased, believing that the union will help the disengaged person feel close to others. Sometimes this works. Often, however, family members begin to resent the "differences" they were seeking. This remarriage pattern becomes more complicated in stepfamilies because there are more people involved. Issues arise when a disengaged family of a spouse with children joins an enmeshed family of a spouse with children. Conflict ensues as family members soon become alienated from one another. If adolescents' issues of separation and individuation are involved, the problems will escalate (Henggeler & Borduin, 1990).

Symbiotic relationships present an extreme example of enmeshed, affective involvement (Minuchin, 1974; Minuchin & Fishman, 1981; Brock & Barnard, 1988). These are more pathological than simple enmeshed involvement and are marked by units of individuals in stepfamilies who respond *as one*. In such cases, there are few boundaries between parents and children or between spouses. The most frequent scenario involves a biological parent and child who are so bonded that the stepparent has little opportunity to become close to either person. We have seen this pattern in families where a biological parent has abused a child and the other parent has assumed or been granted custody. The custodial parent is prone to becoming over-protective of the child, to prevent further pain. When the step-parent is a caring person, deep understanding of the past abuse can free both the custodial parent and the stepchild from the symbiotic relationship.

Another pathological stepfamily subgroup concerns the overinvolved or overprotective custodial parent who will not per-mit other family members to develop their own individuality. This pattern is particularly troublesome between parents and adolescents, who normally seek individuation. If a stepparent tries to break through this overprotection, the biological parent may dismiss the stepparent's views as unimportant. Even though the biological parent may be caring, his or her level of over-protection can lead to hostility and to abandonment by other family members.

The healthiest types of relationships involve stepfamily members who have strong emotional involvements with one another and display their concern and caring. Members demon-strate love and support for one another even when the issues of one member may not be directly pertinent to others. Seem-ingly insignificant events can allow members to demonstrate car-ing, and the careful therapist will note such responses.

> Fiona and Tom related an incident that occurred after they had been married for about a year. Fi-ona came home from work one evening and an-nounced that her company had filed for bankruptcy and terminated her job. Fiona and Tom had re-cently bought a house, under the impression that both their jobs were secure. This crisis sent their relationship into a "tizzy" as Fiona described it. Fi-ona's and Tom's children were scared and worried that the stepfamily would not have enough money to survive. They were also afraid that they would have to move and would not be as close to their biological father as they now were. During this crisis and the subsequent transition, Fiona said, Tom be-

came even more caring than she had expected him to be. "My former husband would have been all over my case," she said. "He wouldn't have understood and would have thought that I was a failure. In fact, he often told me I was a failure. Instead, Tom just talked to me and held me and helped me work through my grief. Tom was visibly shaken the day I came home with no job, and my self-concept wasn't very good then either. He understood that, and he was willing to work through it with me."

Tom not only supported Fiona but also had discussions with his stepchildren and his biological children about their behavior and the need to stick together.

"It shows our worth as a family," Tom said. "Life had presented a negative situation to us, and we needed to take chances as a group, to turn it into something positive. It was a risky time, but I thought we could become stronger and closer from it. I told Fiona that I thought the best move I ever made was leaving my marriage and finding her. This was my chance to be happy, and I wasn't going to quit now. We ended up relocating because Fiona found the type of job that she wanted. Then I worked hard to find what I needed, too. In the end, it's been worth it, but it hasn't been easy. She's the most important person in my life, and I wanted to convey that to her and to the kids."

Empathic involvement is demonstrable and measurable. For example, therapists can record or simply point out the number of negative statements made in a ten-minute period during a session. Having members share their hurt and pain constructively helps create empathy rather than the angry blaming that produces distance. Stepfamilies often enter therapy when they are chaotic or in crisis. Many of their issues stem from their inability to commit themselves to one another. This lack of commitment and the inability to show caring escalate the crisis. Helping stepfamilies move toward empathic involvement is a difficult but crucial job for the therapist.

Problem-Solving Ability

One of the complexities of working with stepfamilies is the variety of issues related to the life cycle. There may be adolescent children and younger children from previous marriages, and remarried parents may go on to have children of their own. Dismay and confusion may arise. Children need a place in a family. In fact, being fairly egocentric, they think that their place should be the most important one in their parents' lives. Children do not like sharing parents. From a therapeutic standpoint, however, we believe that learning sharing and caring with other stepfamily members can teach children a variety of skills that will be of benefit in later life. Too often, a stepfamily appears to be led by its children. If their every demand is not met, they create or cause crises.

Obviously, stepparents looking at problem-solving approaches need to be flexible, because they may have children spanning a variety of age levels. If they do not learn to be flexible, they will often fail. At the same time, the balancing of a variety of developmental levels also makes unusual demands on children (Becvar & Becvar, 1988; Martin & Martin, 1992). They may have to become more involved than they wish. For example, the older children of one spouse may have to integrate with the younger children of their new stepparent. Again, stepfamilies need to address issues of nurturing and separation, and these will have to be faced directly and overtly.

The Effect of the Therapist's Bias on Assessment

Stepfamilies have a knack for causing confusion among therapists. Therapists from traditional families are as vulnerable to confusion as those from dysfunctional stepfamilies. It is very important that therapists examine the family's actual needs, rather than imposing their own philosophies and values. Sharing personal reactions is certainly beneficial (Martin & Martin, 1992), but therapists need to be creative enough to look at different types of interventions and philosophies that can help the stepfamily.

Therapists also must understand their own family-of-origin issues if they are to be successful in therapy with any kind of family. In a clinic for at-risk families, we train therapists by using videocameras, in-session help via the telephone, and extensive case discussion and review of videotapes. Time and again, a major hurdle that we have seen for neophyte therapists is their inability to integrate family-of-origin issues into a healthy conceptual framework for therapy. For example, one trainee was twenty-five years old, unmarried, and involved in no intimate relationships. Her mother was divorced, and this trainee drove several hours every weekend to console her and "keep her company." All this traveling kept the trainee from spending time in relationships with others, even though she openly said that she wanted to marry and have children. Ironically, the remarried couple that she was counseling in therapy replicated her issue. The partners were afraid of commitment, and the wife felt guilty about her ex-spouse's depression, which had "resulted" from the divorce. This couple spent little time together as the wife continually counseled her ex-husband. The trainee therapist was unable to work effectively with this couple until she herself received counseling and chose to become involved in an intimate relationship. Our bias is clear: you cannot ask clients to do something that you will not attempt. Authenticity is a major requirement for therapists working with stepfamilies.

Stepfamilies enter therapy in pain and with the perception that they have few resources. They need guidelines for coping. Too many of their relationships are immobilized, and they are unable to make sense of their problems. It takes time for them to learn new behavior, develop boundaries, and demonstrate mutual respect. Intervention into such complexity and chaos is never easy, but adequate assessment enables therapists to increase the chances that a stepfamily will ultimately attain healthy outcomes.

Exhibit 1. Family Assessment Interview.

Referral Information

Family name _____

Family members referred, their names, family positions, and ages

_____

Couple/family type: ___ spouses ___ spouses and children ___ extended family
___ nuclear ___ single parent ___ step ___ other _____

Referred by _____

Reason for referral: ___ assessment/evaluation ___ treatment/counseling
___ other _____

Presenting problem, chief symptom, critical incident, and date

_____

_____

_____

_____

Family schematic: # male   o female   * child

Demographics, Social History, and Personality — Adults

Name	Sex	Age	Family Position	Education	Occupation
1					
2					
3					
4					

Career Stability	Income	Place of Birth	Geographical Mobility	Ethnic Background
1 H M L			H M L	
2 H M L			H M L	
3 H M L			H M L	
4 H M L			H M L	

Source: Martin, D., Martin, M., and Medler, B. (1983). *The Marriage and Family Interview Technique.* Dallas, TX: Wilmington Press. Reprinted with permission.

Exhibit 1. Family Assessment Interview, Cont'd.

Religion	Religiosity			Military Service		Police Record
1	H	M	L	Y	N	
2	H	M	L	Y	N	
3	H	M	L	Y	N	
4	H	M	L	Y	N	

Marital History — Adults

Male name _____ ___ husband ___ father ___ stepfather
___ boyfriend ___ other _____

Dates	Spouse's Name	Status				Children's Names and Ages	Custody/ Visitation
1		M	SEP	D	W		
2				D	W		
3				D	W		
4				D	W		

Chief reason given for divorce _____
_____
_____
_____

Female name _____ ___ wife ___ mother ___ stepmother ___ girlfriend
___ other _____

Dates	Spouse's Name	Status				Children's Names and Ages	Custody/ Visitation
1		M	SEP	D	W		
2				D	W		
3				D	W		
4				D	W		

Chief reason given for divorce _____
_____
_____
_____

Exhibit 1. Family Assessment Interview, Cont'd.

Appearance, Personality, and Behavior — Adults

Name   Description

_____   _____
                       _____
                       _____
           Mood:_____ Intelligence: H M L

_____   _____
                       _____
                       _____
           Mood:_____ Intelligence: H H L

_____   _____
                       _____
                       _____
           Mood:_____ Intelligence: H M L

Demographics, Social History, and Personality — Children/Adolescents

Name	In Home	Age	Sex	Grade	Grades	Custody/Visitation
	Y N		M F		H M L	
	Y N		M F		H M L	
	Y N		M F		H M L	
	Y N		M F		H M L	
	Y N		M F		H M L	
	Y N		M F		H M L	

Appearance, Personality, and Behavior — Children/Adolescents

Name   Description

_____   _____
                       _____
                       _____
           Mood:_____ Intelligence: H M L
           Development: ___ Normal ___ Problematic

_____   _____
                       _____
                       _____
           Mood:_____ Intelligence: H M L
           Development: ___ Normal ___ Problematic

Exhibit 1. Family Assessment Interview, Cont'd.

Name   Description

Mood:_____ Intelligence: H M L
Development: ___ Normal ___ Problematic

Mood:_____ Intelligence: H M L
Development: ___ Normal ___ Problematic

Mood:_____ Intelligence: H M L
Development: ___ Normal ___ Problematic

Mood:_____ Intelligence: H M L
Development: ___ Normal ___ Problematic

Family Health History

Physical health — adults (major diseases, disabilities, hospitalizations)

Physical health — children _____

Mental health (counseling, psychiatric hospitalizations,
    institutionalization, psychoactive medications), who

Substance use (drugs, alcohol, cigarettes), who and frequency

Exhibit 1. Family Assessment Interview, Cont'd.

Couple/Family Structure

Couple/family developmental stage: ___ beginning ___ infant
    ___ preschool ___ school-age ___ adolescent ___ launching
    ___ postparental ___ aging
Appropriate developmental problems: Y   N

Milestones (plot along line)

___ (Event) _____
    (Year)

Organization: H   M   L _____
Unity: ___ Disengaged ___ Connected ___ Enmeshed
Leadership and decision-making process _____
_____

Family boundary guard _____
Family news reporter _____
Family myths _____

How often does extended family visit, and on what occasions and where
_____

Cherished values _____
_____

Couple/Family Process

Alliances (who gets along with whom) _____
_____

Antagonisms (who does not get along) _____
_____

Traits: Closeness: H   M   L   Openness to each other: H   M   L
        Openness to others: H   M   L   Reality contact: H   M   L
        Expressiveness: H   M   L   Affection: H   M   L
        Sensitivity to each other's needs: H   M   L

Accommodation (responses to problems) _____
_____

Mood and tone: ___ Optimistic ___ Pessimistic ___ Skeptical ___ Hostile
Parenting styles and skills:
    Parent name _____
        ___ Permissive ___ Moderate ___ Strict ___ Consistent
        ___ Inconsistent
    Parent name _____
        ___ Permissive ___ Moderate ___ Strict ___ Consistent
        ___ Inconsistent
Unit strengths _____
_____

Exhibit 1. Family Assessment Interview, Cont'd.

Unit weaknesses/conflicts _____
_____
_____

Stressors — Couple/Family

External _____
Internal _____
Individual _____

Problem Areas — Couple/Family

Area of Concern	Severity of Impairment			Area of Concern	Severity of Impairment		
___ Communication	H	M	L	___ Friendships	H	M	L
___ Physical health/ personal habits	H	M	L	___ Household responsibilities	H	M	L
___ Affection, intimacy	H	M	L	___ Drugs, alcohol use	H	M	L
___ Sexual behavior	H	M	L	___ Violence/acting out	H	M	L
___ Child-rearing practices	H	M	L	___ Values	H	M	L
___ Discipline	H	M	L	___ Cultural educational background	H	M	L
___ School experiences	H	M	L	___ Careers	H	M	L
___ Financial well-being	H	M	L	___ Recreation	H	M	L
___ Religious practices	H	M	L	___ Other _____	H	M	L

Couple Descriptions

How does each partner describe his or her relationship with mate?

Female:
- ___ equal
- ___ rational
- ___ parallel
- ___ passionate
- ___ romantic
- ___ compassionate
- ___ tender, caring
- ___ childlike
- ___ companionate
- ___ distant

Male:
- ___ equal
- ___ rational
- ___ parallel
- ___ passionate
- ___ romantic
- ___ compassionate
- ___ tender, caring
- ___ childlike
- ___ companionate
- ___ distant

Exhibit 1. Family Assessment Interview, Cont'd.

Female's description of mate _____

Female's self-description _____

Male's description of mate _____

Male's self-description _____

Family Diagnoses

_____
_____
_____
_____

Treatment Plans

Couple/family goals _____

Individual goals (if different) _____

Motivation for help: H   M   L
Therapist's rapport with couple/family: H   M   L

Therapist's strategy and recommendations _____
_____
_____
_____

Prognosis _____
_____

Couple/Family Rights

___ Informed consent to evaluation and treatment
___ Informed of duration of services and charges
___ Informed re: confidentiality to others in family
___ Informed re: confidentiality to third-party persons or agencies
___ Informed consent to discuss individual family members in group sessions
___ Permission to tape/videotape sessions
___ Release-of-information signed
___ Informed of likely treatment outcomes
___ Necessity to warn—dangers to members or others

Exhibit 1. Family Assessment Interview, Cont'd.

Completion of Evaluation

Date ____/____/____   Goals achieved _____

Report to _____

Follow-up appointment _____

Referral to _____

5

Basic Intervention
with Stepfamilies

Typically, a stepfamily enters treatment because the children have pushed boundaries between the biological parents and the stepparents. They are attempting to clarify issues of roles and responsibilities in those relationships. When therapists assess stepfamilies they are seeking, in a limited sense, clarification of many of the same issues. It is as if the children function to bring a stepfamily's problems into the open and then pass the ball to the therapist, who, it is hoped, will successfully continue the investigation and provide solutions. Assessment is the ongoing investigation, and intervention is the effort to the solution. In this chapter, we consider some of the basics of the intervention process.

Who Is the Client?

Deciding whom to treat in a stepfamily is difficult for the therapists. We try to include as many family members as possible in the initial sessions. This enables us to gain a more accurate understanding of the family and to plan interventions. We recognize, however, that having all family members at sessions is sometimes impossible. Sometimes we must settle for whoever will come. The children are in distress, and this requires a smooth, reasonably quick resolution of the initial conflict and crisis.

Initially, we examine caretaking activities with the children, siblings' interactions, and parents' interactions with each other and with the children. Having the whole family present is an advantage, but the therapist needs to be observant and not feel overwhelmed. He or she must also be able to assess interactions and recognize differences between old, biological family systems and new, stepfamily system interactions (Pasley, 1988). To understand how to proceed, most therapists ask a variety of questions:

- What is the stability of the remarriage?
- Is the couple intimate? Are the spouses sexually active and caring with each other?
- Do the spouses share issues with each other?
- How do the adults get involved in parenting the child?
- How do the parents cope with conflict?
- Is there parenting agreement between and among adults?
- Do biological parents sabotage the stepparents, and vice versa?

Beyond the cultural mythology of "honoring" biological parents, the therapist begins to assess who are the most functional parents, and who can make a significant contribution to the children and help them become psychologically healthy. In dysfunctional stepfamily systems, one or more parents may be unfit. If so, the therapist needs to assess the following areas:

- How do I proceed if one of the biological or stepparents is pathological, has limited parenting skills, or is emotionally unstable?
- Should the children continue a relationship with a neglectful parent?
- At what level should conflictual relationships remain?
- What about issues of loyalty, if one or more children feel protective?
- Are children protecting a disabled parent?

In the collection of parents in a stepfamily system, some will be more capable than others. The therapist needs to utilize the resources of the most competent parents. Sometimes therapeutic decisions are complicated:

Saundra was recommended for family therapy after she was released from a drug treatment program
at a neighboring hospital. She was fifteen years old
and had been using drugs for the past several years
with her mother, Mary, who was in her early thir-
ties. Mary had now been free of drugs for two years,
but her previous personal life had been virtually
destroyed by the use of cocaine. Her husband had
left her and stolen most of their personal property.
He lived an hour away but rarely visited or saw
Saundra and refused to pay child support. A year
before we saw Saundra, Mary met Bob, her second husband, at a Narcotics Anonymous meeting,
and he helped her remain abstinent. In fact, Bob's
nonuse of almost a decade was a strong influence.

When we saw Saundra's family, it became
evident to us that Mary was too involved with her
rehabilitation and personal struggles to pay her
daughter the kind of attention she needed to develop self-esteem and stick with her own abstinence
program. Bob was concerned about Saundra, however, and was willing to become more involved in
his relationship with her. Saundra had a history of
being hurt in a series of relationships, including
those with her biological parents, and so she was
resistant to getting close to Bob. She treated him
rudely.

Initially, Mary supported Saundra's view of
Bob. She too saw him as too demanding and too
vigilant over Saundra's friends and life-style. We
directed Mary's attention to Saundra's history and
to her refusal to make new, "abstinent" friends after being released from treatment. In our view,
Saundra was a time bomb, set to explode unless
someone was able to get involved and place boundaries around her destructive behavior. Fortunately,
Bob, probably because of his own treatment experience, was able to put up with these intense reac-

tions from Saundra and remained firm when setting rules. Bob also began to tell Mary that he would not stay in the relationship with her unless she supported him in disciplining Saundra. This frightened Mary, and she began to work with Bob instead of against him. At that point, Saundra developed a closer relationship with Bob, even though she did not agree with his rules.

A therapist may feel overwhelmed and confused in working with stepfamilies because they are so complex and often do not fit traditional patterns. We recommend breaking the stepfamily unit down into subsystems. Rather than seeing these subsystems together, it may be more comfortable for the therapist to see each subsystem without the others. In counseling, material presented to one system must be open for sharing with others. Thus, if one sees biological parents with children, or siblings together, information must be shared all around, as appropriate. Therapists may assign subsystems to share with one another.

Defining Boundaries

The most difficult process in the assessment of stepfamilies is recognizing the boundaries between parents and children. Brand and Clingempeel (1987) maintain that the boundaries of stepfamilies are more permeable than those of nuclear families. Stepfamilies lack the common household residence of natural parents and a common household locus of parental authority. Dysfunctional triangulation is typical in stepfamilies. Therapists need to help children negotiate with parents, and vice versa, so that parents can understand the situation rather than simply overprotect the children. Children may be moving among households and attempting to figure out how to live in several families. They need to understand that different rules operate in different families.

Children as well as parents may use one family unit, or membership in one family, as a means of controlling or threat-

ening other individuals. Comments like these are not unusual
from parents: "You don't act like this with your dad's family."
"If you don't behave, we're going to throw you out or send you
to your mother." Children may give similar messages, particularly when they are not getting what they want and perceive
the family environment as unjust or too demanding: "I don't
have to do these things with Mom." "I'm leaving to go to Dad's
house if you continue to treat me this way." "They treat me so
much better over there. I don't know why I have to stay with
you." This negative communication creates bitterness and in-
hibits each family from developing its own identity. Therapists
face the challenge of establishing clear, firm boundaries around
stepfamily units. Stepfamilies live in denial by not recognizing
who they are, the assets and abilities of all their members, and
what family members have to give to one another.

Empowering Parents

Therapists have to empower parents to do what is right for their
children and provide an environment where growth is nurtured.
Sager and others (1983), Boss and Greenburg (1984), and Visher
and Visher (1988) see discipline as one of the thorniest issues
for stepparents, and Lutz (1983) has found that stepchildren
share this perception. Discipline is certainly a source of conflict
in all families; as Visher and Visher (1979, 1988) point out,
however, a prerequisite of effective discipline is trust and caring between children and adults. Because it takes time for these
conditions to evolve, stepfamilies often have problems in this
area during the first two years.

Stepfamilies have few boundaries, and that fact contributes to lack of identity and diffusion on the part of the children.
Sometimes, in a state of mutual pseudocooperation, family members deny previous losses in their lives (Bowen, 1981); they have
not established boundaries within which individual subsystems
of the multifamily system are able to establish their identities
(Berman, 1988).

New spouses who are also new stepparents may become
angry about their impotence in the family. They begin to pull

away from both the family and the marriage. A remarriage may disintegrate, and the families faces the threat of additional guilt. The therapist must recognize that the remarried couple and relationships with children will be growing and changing at the same time. The development of the *marriage* must be the primary focus of the family. A couple can talk endlessly about the children, ex-spouses, in-laws, and all the other people surrounding the relationship but fail to confront issues inherent in the marriage. Children provide an excuse for not facing the anxieties of remarriage. This concern for others may cause the marriage to fail, leaving children and others to struggle through another divorce.

As Visher and Visher (1988) point out, custodial parents are drawn to bond with their biological children, and without adaptation this bonding also causes problems in boundary formation. Children from single-parent homes are frequently in caretaking, nurturing, or economic roles beyond their capacity. These roles must change and be reassigned when a stepparent enters the picture. A custodial parent needs to spend time alone with his or her new spouse and must work to form an appropriate boundary for that subsystem. The stepparent needs time to bond and form boundaries with the stepchildren. If time, space, and money are allocated as in the past, the stepfamily will never form fully. Instead, two separate households will be attempting to share one roof, and there will be conflict.

Change in one part of a subsystem typically changes the entire stepfamily. A family will react to any movement or change by seeking a new balance, or homeostasis. Stepfamily members may be so angry when they enter therapy that the therapist may be tempted to see an individual, instead of the family or a subsystem, because the therapist has difficulty with the levels of anger and may not be able to control the session. On occasion, we see a stepfamily member individually, but only if material in these sessions is allowed to be shared with other members. If we are not allowed to share the information, we are making a pact with one family member against others, and this is usually detrimental to the therapeutic process. Change in stepfamilies is more significant if we can encourage and promote healthy interactions and provide support for stepfamily members to continue change.

Understanding Ex-Spouses

Therapists need to identify instances when ex-spouses have not divorced each other psychologically. Many people retain anger and bitterness toward ex-spouses. Children, caught in the middle of these battles, are used as tools to attack an ex-spouse. Of the many problems that therapists see in stepfamilies, this is one of the worst. The everlasting bond of anger between two ex-spouses who are still wedded psychologically can destroy couples and children. Angry ex-spouses are a formidable obstacle to therapists (Berman, 1988).

Another type of dysfunctional divorce involves at least one ex-spouse who is still in love and wants to continue the past relationship. Sometimes a new spouse brings a remarried couple into therapy because he or she cannot get the ex-spouse out of the marriage:

> Vonda, recently remarried, was angry when she and her husband, Jim, first came to counseling. Vonda said that Jim spent more time with his ex-spouse, Mary, than with her. Jim said that he felt in a bind and did not know quite what to do.
>
> "I divorced Mary because I got tired of taking care of her. She was so helpless. Either she was physically or emotionally sick or tired most of the time, and she just couldn't seem to handle things well. I know she could have done better, but I still feel guilty that I left her. I tried to get custody of my son, but I couldn't. So he ends up staying with her and taking care of her. I don't like putting him in that role, and so I feel like I have to help her. I'm drawn into it."
>
> Vonda disagreed.
>
> "I think we need to teach both Jim and his son to stop taking care of Mary. I think then she'll

learn how to do it herself. I think she can. It's just that they do everything for her, and she's learned how to manipulate them. It's crazy. I don't think it's healthy for them or for her. Something's got to give here. I feel bad for Jim's son, but I feel worse about our marriage because Jim spends half his time over there, checking on her and seeing if she's okay and getting things for her and picking up medicine. It's a constant fiasco, and I'm tired of it."

When we brought Jim's son Bob, age fifteen, into therapy, he acted very much as his father did. Bob felt guilty that his parents had divorced, but he could understand his father's point of view. He was not spending much time with his peers. He spent most of his time taking care of his mother. Interestingly enough, as we helped remove Bob and his father from their caretaking position, Mary's health seemed to deteriorate at first, but then she became better. At the same time, Jim's and Vonda's marriage took a similar course—troubled with intimacy at first, but arriving at a more balanced state as time progressed. This "getting worse before it gets better" scenario is not unusual in stepfamilies.

Helping with Role Definition

Role simulation, evolving through a process of conflict, is typical in stepfamilies, but steprelationships have potential for intimacy and closeness that can parallel the closeness in biological relationships. Unfortunately, roles may stay peripheral, according to the needs of family members. One difficulty for therapists is determining whose needs are being voiced, and whether they can be met or not met without the creation of a "leadership vacuum."

Katz and Stein (1983) talk about power vacuums in stepfamilies; Jim and his son Bob exemplify this phenomenon. When there is a power vacuum, a family member, or a coalition or subsystem in the family, has an unequal share of power and exhibits control over other family members. Inequality of power creates instability and dysfunction. It causes guilt, resentment, anger, and frustration on the part of stepfamily members.

Coalitions are also typical in traditional nuclear families, but the structure of the stepfamily lends itself more to power alliances because people are seeking control, in their insecurity and need for stability. Effective family roles are what make a family functional. In stepfamilies, new roles are added, and so is confusion. If both ex-spouses remarry, there may be combinations of many roles. Certain roles also have more power (for example, the biological parents). The new roles are defined by people's efforts and commitment, rather than by society's prescriptions.

Our society stereotypes the stepparent's role as confused or detrimental, although this view is completely unfounded. Hetherington, Cox, and Cox (1985) investigated the effects of stepfathers on children and found few negative consequences. Lutz (1983) has found that children are more comfortable with a stepfather than with a stepmother, presumably because mothers are more involved with parenting. Weingarten (1980) notes that both remarried parents find their parental roles in a stepfamily more difficult than in the first family. Given the challenges, that difference is understandable. They may face great obstacles, but most stepparents do not mean to be hurtful.

In counseling stepfamilies, our foremost concern is to protect and help children. They suffer and have little control over their environment, particularly when their parents are destructive or hurtful. When a divorcing adult deliberately removes himself or herself from a relationship with a child, with no explanation, the child feels intense pain. Children who experience this distancing frequently choose maladaptive behavior to express their hurt. They learn to protect their feelings in many ways (avoidance, denial, use of drugs, poor grades, or other avenues). Therapists are apt to see the children's pain because children have fewer defense mechanisms, and their behavior is usually overt (Buwick, Martin, & Martin, 1990).

Delineating roles and understanding the nature of relationships are primary tasks of therapists working with stepfamilies. In understanding roles, it is important for the therapist to maintain an open mind and not be biased by cultural or therapeutic stereotypes. Children have a tremendous capacity for love, and they can care for many adults in their lives if the environment is creative and if the adults involved understand and support their needs. If a biological parent or stepparent refuses to care for a child, then this behavior needs to be addressed in therapy.

Distancing

Stepfamilies are evolving units whose members have differing developmental needs. In understanding these families, it is crucial to understand the need for distancing. Stepfamilies often include adolescents, who need to individuate. Parents may allow children to go their own way but also exclude them from family activities, when the true need is for a supportive family strong enough to accept individuation. Exclusion is not a viable or effective solution, but it is a trap that therapists unwittingly may help to set. If a stepfamily is too rigid, an adolescent will rebel and break the rules; if boundaries are too permeable, the adolescent will angrily defy the parents. It is paramount that therapists be aware of effective parenting processes in order to help stepfamilies. Families with adolescent members are often the most chaotic stepfamilies that therapists will ever counsel. As adolescents struggle with attempting to define rules, their peers may side with them in their efforts to seek freedom. There is a precarious balance in helping adolescents individuate from stepfamilies.

Limiting the Influence of Destructive Parents

Biological parents who are psychologically and emotionally destructive to their children create difficulties in stepfamilies. Children attempting to compensate for a maladaptive parent may idealize the parent. The stepfamily may want to disengage the children from this destructive parent. This bind is complex for the therapist. To help a child understand a destructive parent and be able to make healthy choices in the relationship requires assistance from the family. At the same time, however, the therapist cannot condone a child's closeness with a parent if the parent is abusive. Intervention requires directness and clarity from the therapist, who must recognize the children's need to idealize and defend an incompetent and possibly hurtful parent. The therapist must also help the children heal the relationship. Without intervention, children do not usually choose to disengage from one of their parents; their natural desire is for reciprocity in relationships. Planning interventions by which the children actively attempt to engage the inadequate parent (going to a baseball game or to a park) is helpful: inadequate parents usually fail to follow through. The experience will be painful for the children, but this process of clarifying parental misbehavior can be freeing for the children and can minimize their feelings of guilt.

Integrating Children into the Stepfamily

Even young children will develop a special attachment to a parent, particularly to a single mother who has custody of the children (Visher & Visher, 1988). A mother may be trying to maintain the bond with her children while balancing the demands of a new remarriage and a new spouse. The great clue to the therapist who is attempting to evaluate the successful integration of young children into the stepfamily is this: Has the noncustodial parent adjusted to the divorce, and does he or she support the remarriage? If the noncustodial parent is angry or destructive, he or she will sabotage the new family by using the children.

Overinvolvement of ex-spouses is more difficult to change than their underinvolvement. The stepparent may be willing to assume some of the roles of an absent biological parent, but if this stepparent maintains distance, then the noncustodial parent may assume a more prominent place and push the remarriage toward deterioration.

Children, particularly younger children, create a sense

of belongingness in a family. Parents may be torn between their old and their new families, and stepparents may be stuck between their roles. In either case, children push for integration.

During counseling, these issues may intensify. The therapist should observe and intervene to help family members maintain flexibility in their roles, and to create opportunities for them to help one another. The treatment of stepfamilies is complex. They have weak boundaries, confused organization, and unresolved developmental issues that have escalated into crises (Sager and others, 1983). The therapist must seek to understand the family and reframe its conflicts positively. Family members can comprehend that their presenting problems are part of the whole family and do not belong only to the identified patient.

It is not unusual for a therapist to see an individual or a "problem child" from a stepfamily. It is possible to be successful with such a child if the therapy uses family system concepts. As the child changes, his or her growth causes problems in the family, and there are reactions. For example, adolescents may present their parents as uninterested, uninvolved, and unwilling to undergo therapy, but the parents may indeed be seeking involvement. They may be reluctant to enter therapy and may perceive their own issues as more important than those of their children, but having the parents present does make intervention easier. Adolescents may not present a clear picture of what is occurring in a family, and they may distort the truth, particularly if they are chemically dependent.

When a family member is seen individually, and the rest of the family refuses to enter treatment, the therapist needs to recognize the family's reactions and observe how the family is joined. A stepfamily's structure may aggravate individual differences, and if other members are not involved, issues will surface. By bringing other family members into treatment, the "isolated" individual can benefit. If the stepfamily chooses to remain uninvolved, then the isolated individual believes that he or she is unlovable. One needs to establish a framework: this individual is willing to engage with other family members, provided that they are willing to commit themselves to a nurturing relationship.

When family members wish to remain isolated from the "problem person," but this individual begins to improve, they may also enter therapy. They must then understand that the focus will not be on the isolated member but rather on all the members and their contributions to the family's problems and loss of direction. If the family is unwilling to accept this foundation for therapy, then it is unwise to continue working with them.

Treatment Philosophy

Whether seeing individuals, subsystems, or an entire family, the therapist should have a philosophy and a rationale for treatment, influenced by the family's developmental problems and structural dilemmas. The therapist can then determine when to confront a crisis immediately and when to delay issues for later sessions.

Issues directly related to a family's chaos and disengagement must be addressed, as must those that obstruct the family's unity. It is not always easy to define one clear problem; several issues are often intertwined. For example, many remarried couples are very active sexually. This situation may have a particular impact on adolescents, who are seeking to understand their own sexuality. If an adolescent girl is brought to therapy for promiscuous behavior and overt sexuality, the therapist may wonder whether the parents also have issues of sexual identity. Should the therapist assess the couple's sexual needs? Focus on the child's sexuality? As the therapist talks with the parents, the family's general level of sexuality is seen. Sometimes a couple does not put sufficient boundaries around a daughter's behavior because the partners believe that this boundary would restrict their own behavior, but the lines around a marriage and around a teenager's behavior are very different.

Sometimes issues are much clearer:

> Buddy came into therapy with his wife, Lucille, because she complained about his lack of involvement with her two children. Both boys were very young— three and six—and they quickly became attached

to Buddy during the courtship. The couple had been married for six months. The boys' biological father was minimally involved and lived far away. He rarely called the boys, and he saw them for only two weeks during the summer.

Buddy had two children from a previous marriage, and he spent a lot of time and energy on them. Although he liked Lucille's children, he said that he had too much to do with his own children and really could not care for her children at this point.

In a very painful session, the two stepchildren talked about how much they loved Buddy. As they cried and said they liked to be with him, Buddy began to reveal his own pain. We discovered that Buddy was afraid to get close because of all the pain he had caused his own children. In truth, he was not sure whether his relationship with Lucille would survive, because of his inability to commit himself to anyone.

"I don't want to hurt any more people than I have already," Buddy said. "I just can't figure things out, and I'm tired of hurting other people."

We then began to examine Buddy's past: his father had been married four times, and Buddy himself moved in and out of relationships. He had lived with several other women before his first and second marriages.

Lucille's presence in sessions with Buddy gave her a chance to understand him. Lucille also had issues with commitment and was scared that the relationship would not continue. As the spouses began to reveal their vulnerabilities and lack of certainty, a bond developed, and Buddy drew closer to his stepchildren and to Lucille.

Sometimes, rather than facing the marital issues, it is easier to help the stepfamily by joining with the couple and assisting in parenting. The remarried spouses may admit that they have marital problems but be resistant to doing much about them. Parenting dilemmas are much harder to ignore, particularly if children are maladaptive and causing problems at school or in the community. Determining whether to confront the marital issues or deal with issues surrounding the childen can be a complex task. Parenting issues are generally less threatening to couples; if the couple is resistant to helping the children, however, then it may be important to discuss the marital issues, because they are getting in the way.

The Lewis family is an example of a stepfamily that had difficulty evolving after a catastrophic loss:

> Sybil's first husband had died three years before we saw her in therapy. Their only son, Timothy, who was now fifteen, was in trouble and aggressive at school. His grades, once high, had dropped to D's and low C's. Sybil had since remarried Phil. This was his first marriage. He and Timothy seemed to get along well. Phil was in his early thirties, approximately ten years younger than Sybil, and Timothy seemed to think that Phil was understanding.
>
> Sybil's and Timothy's relationship had worsened after Sybil's remarriage. Timothy was arrested with both marijuana and amphetamines in his car when he was stopped for driving under the influence. The judge was lenient, and Timothy was put on probation. Sybil and Phil did not discuss Timothy's drug use, and Timothy's problems escalated until he began failing in school during his senior year. The school counselor called Sybil and said that Timothy would not be able to graduate. Because of the counselor's strong recommendations, the family entered treatment.

A case like this can present many dilemmas. Should the therapist focus on Timothy's chemical dependency? Should Timothy enter an inpatient treatment facility that emphasizes family therapy? Have Sybil and Timothy grieved the death of Timothy's biological father? What about Phil's issues, and the difficulties of becoming an instant parent? Do Phil and Sybil communicate about Timothy's issues? What is stopping them from intervening? Who is siding with this child? What stopped the family from dealing with the drug use when it first occurred?

In our first meeting with the family, we discovered that Sybil was abusing alcohol, and that neither she nor Timothy had faced their grief about her ex-husband's death. They both felt that they had contributed to his death because he had to work so hard to support them, and that his heart condition resulted from overwork. Phil's role, as stepfather, was to be a rescuer and enabler, keeping the family together while two chaotic individuals were depressed much of the time.

As the family's functioning became clearer, we began to focus on several major issues. First, we approached the issue of chemical dependency. Both Sybil and Timothy were referred for inpatient treatment and told to attend Alcoholics Anonymous meetings regularly. Second, Sybil and Timothy began to face their grief, their guilt, and how they felt they had let each other down. Third, Phil learned ways to stop being an enabler, and this helped reduce the distance but increased the conflict among Sybil, Timothy, and Phil. He began to stop doing too much (cleaning the house, cooking meals, doing Tim's homework or chores) and providing for everyone else while ignoring his own basic intimacy needs. Fourth, Phil and Sybil began to develop stricter, clearer boundaries around Timothy's behavior, and rules were established for socializing, schoolwork, and responsibilities around the home. There were consequences when he broke the rules. For example, Phil and Sybil met with Tim's teachers and talked about his deficiencies. They developed strict guidelines for studying on weekdays and weekends. We supported Phil and Sybil in determining a "no electricity" (stereo, Nintendo, TV, and so on) and "no car" rule until Tim showed improved behavior. Fifth, Phil and Sybil began to understand the reasons why they had chosen each other. They began restructuring their relationship in a healthy direction by agreeing on parenting rules, determining spousal maintenance tasks, and spending intimate time together. They also worked on sharing dilemmas openly, rather than hiding disappointment and becoming overtly angry or passive-aggressive.

Diagnosing Family Emotions

It is important to engage the marital couple and to help the partners become an effective parental hierarchy. If the therapist is unable to increase parental responsibility, leadership, and caring, then the family will probably continue escalating its dysfunction. Individual family members' emotions and feelings affect their behavior (Martin & Martin, 1985). Stepfamilies exhibit high levels of emotion, and it is important for therapists to address feelings. In addition to anger, there are guilt, remorse, loss, mourning, and fear concerning loss or the breakup of the previous family, as well as feelings of liking and love, which are often mixed with loyalty conflicts.

There may be many hidden agendas in stepfamilies, which must be discussed in the initial sessions. Some of the most significant ones that we have encountered with families are extramarital affairs, suicidal behavior, child abuse, incest, substance abuse, and sexual addiction. It is important in initial interviews to ask as many specific questions as possible. Nevertheless, it is not unusual for family members to disclose important information only when they trust the therapist, and that may take some time.

Integrating Two Households

In determining whether to cross the larger boundary of inviting two households in for therapy, the therapist must be sure that all the parents involved are willing to get beyond their past differences and see one another in a more understanding light. The adults must be willing to patch up their differences for the sake of the children. The two households often have the same dilemmas in raising the children. These issues include inability to communicate effectively, inability to fight productively, unresolved and frequent conflict, and failure to give appropriate feedback about feelings or needs. Family members get angry with one another but do not say so. They have difficulty caring, and they cannot comfortably demonstrate their positive feelings in relationships. There are issues of commitment. Other issues revolve around such dilemmas as money problems, differences in discipline between the two households, acceptance of a parallel parenting model, visitation rights, celebration of various holidays, and how summer visits will be arranged if biological parents are geographically distant. There are also loyalty issues and alliances from the past.

At some level, the stepfamily is always questioning what it is. Members try to hold on to old rules or alliances, and this creates high levels of tension and animosity. The therapist must remember that stepfamily members are often fearful. They are afraid of getting close and of what relationships mean, and they do not want to hurt other people. There must be freedom to love in stepfamilies, but when some members begin to show affection, others may become confused or jealous.

Structural Issues

We have already examined the stepfamily's structure from the perspective of developmental stages and assessment, and we will examine the structural subsystems in detail in subsequent chapters. A few more considerations belong in an overview of the intervention process.

Superparent/Superchild

The symptomology of the superparent or the superchild, who tries to live beyond or make up for past family problems, is discussed by Visher and Visher (1979). The superchild wants to be very lovable and keep the family together. He or she engages the stepparent. The superparent wants to make up for the deficiencies of the other biological parent and to give the child everything that he or she needs and wants in a relationship. This is a heavy burden, and these individuals often have unrealistic expectations.

Children may believe that they caused the original divorce,

and that if they are not careful they will do it again. Some step-parents believe that they cannot be as good parents as biological parents or have a significant place in children's lives. These misguided beliefs may be expressed when family members are sharing their feelings. In our therapy sessions, children may cry and discuss how lonely they are. Parents may say that they feel separated from other members of the family and feel alone.

Stepfamilies may believe that conflict is not good. Without conflict, however, there is little intimacy. Most stepfamilies do not know how to resolve conflict. They continually discuss the same issues, without understanding. They have not learned how to work toward resolution, so that people feel understood, with mutuality and a sense of closure.

Reducing Aggression

Because divorce is a painful and adversarial process, it is extremely common for therapists to see ex-spouses who are critical and angry, resolved to have little communication except for matters that involve the children, and despondent about money matters, visitation problems, and custody arrangements. These individuals evoke destructive sequences, particularly in the initial stages after divorce, but these may diminish with time as they learn to change their lives and establish more satisfying intimate relationships. Stepfamilies tend to become separate units, and biological parents establish parallel parenting styles rather than joint parenting approaches. Some therapists are dismayed by these choices and try to unite ex-couples for the benefit of the children. But these families have failed, and such therapy fails, too. Couples that disagreed about parenting when they were married generally find it even more difficult to agree after they are divorced.

An ex-spouse may demonstrate pathological attachment to a former mate, either through anger or through efforts to make the ex-spouse's new marriage fail:

> Samuel entered therapy with his new wife, Sonia.
> He constantly complained about his ex-wife's in-

trusion on their marriage. Samuel had experienced bouts of psychosis in the past, and he felt guilty when he was not taking care of Ellen, his ex-wife. Ellen was devastated by the divorce and called Samuel at all hours of the night, to tell him how much she and the children missed him. Sonia said that Ellen had also talked to her in a grocery store, saying that she missed her husband and that Sonia was a lucky woman. Ellen told Sonia about past mistakes, for which she just could not forgive herself. Sonia felt sorry for Ellen, but she was also getting angry about Ellen's intrusions.

Meanwhile, Samuel's two little girls, four and five years old, were having problems at school. They defecated in their clothing, and they were so aggressive that if either of them did not get her way, she would have crying spells or fits of rage. Sonia said that she did not think their marriage would work, and that it might be better if Samuel went back to Ellen.

Samuel acted confused in therapy. He saw himself caught between two relationships. He moved back in with Ellen, to test his love, but he was able to endure only one day with her before he came back to Sonia, saying that he had "seen the light." When he returned, Sonia set some boundaries regarding their relationship. She insisted on his making a commitment to her and breaking his emotional ties with Ellen. He agreed, and he and Sonia began to have a more structured relationship with the children.

When a therapist senses that an ex-spouse is still a hindrance to the development of a remarried couple's relationship, it is helpful to involve the ex-spouse. In many of the couples with whom we have worked, one partner in a new marriage may still be romantically involved, on a periodic or regular basis, with an ex-spouse. For example, the two ex-spouses may have a strong sexual relationship but believe that they cannot live together. If either partner in the new marriage is unable to make a commitment, the partners often separate. Sometimes an individual rebounds from a divorce by quickly marrying someone else, without understanding the past marriage. This can have devastating consequences for everyone involved.

If the ex-spouse's influence is undermining the remarriage, that issue must be confronted (Berman, 1988; Martin & Martin, 1987). The decision about whether to bring the ex-spouse into therapy must be weighed carefully against the fragility of the new marriage. The ex-spouse may have pathological interactions with the children, and the role of the therapist may be to help separate the children from the ex-spouse:

> Kathy had married a Navy career man. He had bouts of depression, drank heavily, and hit her on several occasions. They had two young sons, but he had not abused them. Eventually, the couple divorced, and Kathy married Frank, a good stepfather with a stable career. He was very supportive of her and the children.
>
> There were times when Kathy's ex-husband would visit and buy presents for the boys. He would promise to see them and not show up, or he would promise to bring them a variety of gifts but not deliver. Sometimes he would give one boy more than the other and create havoc in the household. He requested that the children spend extended time with him during the summers, but during their visit the children accompanied him to bars or were left alone as they tried to find him, while he went to various pubs around town. He asked the children not to discuss what they did with him, because he felt it was none of his ex-wife's business. When they came home from these summer vacations, or when their father visited them, the children became depressed and upset for weeks at a time. It became more and more difficult for Kathy and Frank to accept this behavior.

In therapy, this pact between the boys and their father was discussed. Through mutual support, Kathy and Frank established boundaries for the children regarding her ex-spouse, to protect them from his erratic behavior.

Marital Issues

Remarried couples have trouble separating themselves from their children so that they can spend time together and develop a closer relationship. Too often, a remarried couple becomes overinvolved with the children. The partners feel guilty and defensive when the children do not agree to the remarriage. These couples enter their relationships with fears of rejection, doubts about their sexuality, and concerns that the dysfunctional patterns of one or both of the past marriages will recur. Visher and Visher (1979, 1988) list several stressors for marital couples, including differences in life-style, preexisting parent-child bonds, relationships with ex-spouses, financial difficulties, discipline problems, and the divisiveness of stepchildren. External pressures increase the complexity of a stepfamily's existence. These include issues of moving into the partner's neighborhood, negative responses from in-laws, and lack of recognition from community institutions where the stepparent's role is concerned (Carter & McGoldrick, 1980).

Ruby, remarried for about two years, appeared anxious and overwhelmed in her initial session. She had two sons in their twenties, who were living by themselves. The elder, Tyrone, was twenty-six and a successful computer programmer. Richard, twenty-three, had a history of problems, including a poor school record and several juvenile arrests. He had recently lost his job and returned hom to "stay for a few weeks." Contrary to her husband's wishes, Ruby had allowed Richard to stay for nearly eight months, despite her suspicion that he was using drugs. Ruby had been raised in a severely dysfunctional family and had been married

several times. Her current spouse, Willie, was by
far the most competent of her husbands. Unfortunately, both her marriage to Willie and her relationship with Richard were being shattered.

Intervention in this case took several months and focused
on two general themes: helping Richard face his drug abuse and
seek treatment for it, and reconnecting the marital partners while
strengthening their ability to deal with Richard. Recognizing
that Willie was a key to effective therapy, we actively encouraged
him, through phone calls and letters, to come to therapy with
Ruby. He agreed after Richard hit Ruby one evening. In that
incident, the police were called because Willie "pulled a gun on
Richard and was about to shoot his ass." The police gave Willie a warning; Ruby protected Richard:

> Throughout several sessions, Willie said that he was
> going to leave. Ruby began to realize that she would
> be alone with her drug-abusing, violent son, but
> that realization did not affect her behavior until Wil-
> lie actually left. Richard became worse and began
> bringing friends over for drug parties. We actively
> encouraged Ruby to talk with Willie about return-
> ing, with the stipultion that there would have to
> be certain conditions for the relationship to con-
> tinue. We told Ruby that we believed we could help
> her and Willie.
>
> Willie returned, and Ruby agreed that she
> and Willie had to provide structure for Richard.
> Working as a couple, they told Richard that he had
> to stop using drugs and go into therapy. He had
> to find a job — any job — and would have responsi-
> bilities in the home, a curfew, and the obligation
> to pay rent. If he did not abide by these rules, he
> had to move out.
>
> We told Ruby and Willie that Richard would
> not comply, and that they would have to throw him
> out. That is what happened. Through therapy,
> however, we were able to prepare Ruby and Willie

for Richard's behavior and help them understand the nature and course of chemical dependency. Our hope was that Richard's condition would deteriorate to the level where he himself would seek treatment. Ruby and Willie continually offered Richard help in obtaining it.

Six months later, after a "driving under the influence" arrest, Richard did enter treatment. Although he has struggled in an up-and-down battle with drugs for over two years, Richard is now free of drugs and has a full-time job in a tire factory. Ruby and Willie are still married and have moved two hundred miles, to the same community where Ruby's older son, Tyrone, lives.

We have found that a variety of issues may surface in couple therapy, including those related to the divorce, to single-parent dilemmas that are now evolving in the new setting of the stepfamily, to postdivorce problems, and to children's beliefs that they are becoming less of a priority than they were in the former family. It takes extra effort to be in a stepfamily while recognizing the needs of others. The biological parent may be the communicator or "powerbroker" in the stepfamily, and that position must be changed. Individuals should be encouraged to choose positions where they can be free to develop relationships that are healthy for everyone involved.

Guidelines for Effective Therapy

The treatment of stepfamilies requires tolerance for lack of clarity and ambiguity. Because these families are often quite complex and there are few guidelines for effectively treating them (Katz & Stein, 1983), we offer the following:

1. Therapists need to be aware of systems theory and of developmental processes for marriages and children. They must understand the special nature of stepfamilies and their developmental stages and structure.
2. The therapist must base his or her work on nontraditional families, not on the traditional nuclear family.

3.   The therapist needs a clear understanding of the stepfamily (Giles-Sims, 1984).
4.   The therapist needs to be flexible, working with parts of a stepfamily and seeing dilemmas as individual issues. At the same time, she or he must recognize the basic family processes that develop within stepfamilies.
5.   The therapist needs to help with communication skills and foster understanding of family dynamics (Katz & Stein, 1983).
6.   The therapist should be aware of his or her own issues, including personal resolution of and involvement in family-of-origin work. An understanding of past marriages and current family living is vital. If the therapist lives in a dysfunctional relationship or has not resolved past problems, the stepfamily, in its conflictual state, may expose the therapist's issues, and the family may be impeded in its struggle for health.
7.   Therapists need to recognize when therapy will be of benefit to themselves while they are working with stepfamilies.

It cannot be overstated that therapists must be familiar with the complexities of stepfamily functioning. For example, a child in an intact family may be acting out to keep the parents united, by having them focus on her or his maladaptive behavior. In a stepfamily, the same behavior may have the opposite goal: disintegration of the relationship between the parent and the stepparent. Without an understanding of such issues, the therapist may do even greater harm than the stepfamily is already doing to itself.

Despite the complexities, the confusion, and the challenge, stepfamilies often present positive opportunities for individuals. We have found that the strengths of remarriages often go unnoticed (Martin & Martin, 1992). The advantages of remarriage include opportunities for midcareer changes that may support personal growth; greater maturity, knowledge, and skills; and, often, improved finances for women and children. When a biological parent has been destructive or refuses to continue involvement with the children, a stepfamily provides a chance for the stable, secure, and caring environment that all children need.

6

Working with the Couple

A comprehensive assessment of the remarried couple is important in understanding a stepfamily and helps the therapist develop appropriate interventions. During assessment, therapists evaluate such issues as power and control, nurturance, intimacy, and the decision-making process of the couple. The couple's psychological health is key to a stepfamily's survival, since the couple is the executive unit in charge of the family. Couples face many challenges as they try to balance the development of intimacy, family responsibilities, parenting dilemmas, socialization of children, and their own needs. Most want to form a healthy and successful family (Kim, Martin, & Martin, 1989).

Understanding the dynamics inherent in remarriage and helping the couple become closer as a unit are integral to success in therapy. Marital therapy typically involves helping couples become flexible, teaching them how to compromise, and helping to establish a way of relating between the partners so that they feel they are gaining by the relationship. When working with remarried couples, we find that the following basic issues need to be examined:

1. *Family-of-origin issues:* By examining family-of-origin issues in therapy, couples seek to gain an understanding of the types of families they grew up in, what they learned about marriage from their parents, and an idea of what their parents' marriages were like.

2. *Couple structure issues:* Each spouse needs to understand the path that he or she has taken to process divorce or widow-

hood, including the conflicts involved, a look at the past
marriage, issues related to any children, and issues related
to the ex-spouse.
3. *Relationship issues:* The couple should assess the present relationship, focusing on such issues as power conflicts, independence and dependency needs and struggles, parenting problems, and struggles around intimacy and closeness.

Dilemmas with the Family of Origin

Spouses who enter therapy have ineffective ways of relating to
each other. They probably learned these ineffective patterns in
their families of origin and past marriages, and they have solidified these patterns over years of numerous sequences and interactions. Changing these repetitive cycles takes time, initiative, and support on the part of the people involved.

Effect of Parents

One part of getting married is introducing one's intended spouse
to the family of origin. That is not always a simple task, but
it is more complex when remarriage is involved. In-laws may
not be accepting of the remarriage. Parents of children who are
becoming married for the first time may see marriage to a
divorced person as detrimental. Such parents see their child entering a complicated situation, one marred by past failure, or
taking a nontraditonal step that may be uncomfortable for them
as parents. Kathy relates that this happened with her parents:

> I think it's kind of amusing that my mother was
> so resistant to my marrying Phil. I had gone out
> with lots of guys and lived with several, but Phil
> was the first one I ever seriously thought of marry-
> ing. I had just turned thirty, and it seemed the right
> time for me. Phil was twelve years older, and this
> particularly bothered my mom. Dad was his quiet
> self, as usual, but I could tell that he didn't like the
> age difference either. Plus, Phil had three children

from his previous marriage, whom he saw quite frequently. I had a good relationship with the children.

As the wedding approached, my parents weren't very enthusiastic about what was happening. I had to talk to them about it. It took a lot of guts for me to share with them my disappointment in their position, but I didn't want to head into the marriage while they were so reluctant about Phil. I said that they were putting me in a position where I had to choose between them and Phil. I told them that really wasn't going to be much of a choice, because if they put me in that position, I would go with Phil. When I told them that, they kind of backed off a bit and began to see that this wasn't an easy decision for me, and that I needed support. It was almost as if they didn't want me to grow up. I was always going to be their little girl.

Divorce Residue

Sometimes the divorced person has issues with his or her parents regarding the residue left from the first marriage. Bob's parents' reactions to his divorce and eventual remarriage shocked him:

My divorce was a painful process. I was in therapy several months. I wanted some understanding from my parents of what I was going through. I had been married for over ten years, and my wife and I were just drifting apart. I guess I looked at it as my growing and changing and her being stagnant. I had gone for an advanced degree, switched jobs, and started doing the things that I liked to do while she continued selling real estate and grew tired of her job. She complained all the time, but after a while I stopped commiserating with her. I eventually found Karen, whom I knew from several of my classes. I just got tired and decided to leave. The kids were young, and I felt very bad about what was occurring.

Actually, at one point I think I went on a psychotic break; I just hopped on a plane and left New York to see my parents in Washington. I showed up at their doorstep, talking about needing their help and being confused. Instead of giving some understanding or sympathy, my mother pulled out the Bible and started reading various passages to me about how I needed to stay in the marriage. She quoted me verses about how it was my job as provider to take care of everyone, and she basically told me that I was crazy for what I was doing. What was ludicrous to me at that time was that my mom was not a religious person. I had never seen her read the Bible, so this looked almost like an out-of-body experience to me. I tried to control my anger, but I began to realize that this was crazy and that I would probably have to do it alone.

As the divorce went along, everybody sided with my ex-spouse's cause. They thought that I was going through this midlife crisis and that I was just this terrible, awful human being. This didn't sit well with me, and I felt very isolated, but there is also a part of me that is strong and goes for what I want. At some level, the reaction made me even more desirous of getting out of the relationship. After the divorce, my relatives, my mom, and her sisters would still talk to my ex all the time and involve her in what I was doing. It was like they were trying to get us back together again. I thought this was really bizarre, but that was their way. Eventually, though, it reached the point where I couldn't take any more.

One instance was particularly crucial. Because of our custody arrangement, I had the kids for the entire summer because they were so far away. My ex-wife didn't like this, but she reluctantly agreed. Well, behind my back she flew in for a surprise visit one weekend. My relatives put her up in their house and made all these arrangements, like she was some big goddess coming into town. These are my mother's sisters who did all this arranging. I went bananas. They also had children going through divorce, and they never would have treated their own children's ex-spouses like this. It's not that I didn't want her to be comfortable. I just thought that they should be on my side rather than her side. When she came, I sat down with my relatives and told them that they had to make a choice. If they wanted to be involved with my children, they would have to side with me. I told them I was not going to have them continually sabotaging what was going on in my life and doing things without my permission regarding my family. It was interesting that after that they left me alone. In a way, that was okay with me.

Dealing with Young Children

Therapists must often focus their efforts on helping a newly remarried couple assist young children in the family. In-laws and older children obviously also have an impact on the development of a remarriage. It is important that boundaries be developed quickly. We frequently find that couples who come into therapy are in crisis around boundary formation. One cornerstone is that couples must repeatedly emphasize to those around them the importance and primacy of the marital relationship. Through this action, couples make the statement that if others try to put them in the position of choosing between family members and their spouses, they will align with their spouses:

> June and Ken entered therapy shortly after Ken's twenty-six-year-old daughter moved into the house with them. She had been living with a man but decided to end the relationship. June said there were problems with Sarah in the house. From her viewpoint, Sarah was coming between Ken and herself.

She felt that Sarah continually belittled her and was not very friendly toward her. In addition, Sarah teamed up with her older brother, who would visit, and the two of them berated and belittled June, particularly when Ken was not around. Ken said that at first he had ignored what was going on; since Sarah had moved in with them, however, he was beginning to see June's point of view. When June described several situations, it became clear to both us and to the couple that Sarah had crossed the boundaries and was being offensive to June. She was pushing Ken into an uncomfortable position, but he did not want to alienate his daughter. Our suggestion was to bring Sarah to the next session, where they could all discuss their issues in an open but protective environment.

When Sarah came, we were surprised at how overtly depressed and angry she was. She appeared confused about the direction of her life. In our discussions, it became evident that she was jealous of her father. He had left a bitter relationship with her mother, and Sarah could identify with the conflict because she had also argued heavily with her. Now he seemed happy, but she had been unable to find that joy and stability in her own recent relationships. When June began to understand Sarah's anger, it opened communication between the two of them. Sarah began to see that June could help her and be a friend to her in a time of sadness.

Ken also shared his feelings of stuckness between the two of them. We helped Ken separate his role with each of them and to identify clearly his relationship with each. Ken realized that if Sarah continued to belittle and degrade June, he would have to ask her to leave. This would be done in a caring manner and without escalation of tone or conflict.

Over the next several weeks, Sarah, instead

of seeking a mature, healthy relationship with June and Ken, behaved almost like an adolescent. June, however, sensing Ken's support, was assertive and dealt openly with Sarah. As a result of this boundary setting, Sarah began to respect June, and their relationship began to evolve into one of more sharing. Likewise, Ken began to see another side of his wife as she interacted with his child. In retrospect, Ken said, actions that initially had seemed to separate them became means toward a more stable, united family in the end.

Resolving Family-of-Origin Dilemmas

There is a tenuous quality to the marital relationship in the early years of a remarriage. Marital bonding may be threatened by strong and lasting attachments to children, in-laws, or parents. Individuation and separation are vital and constitute a major task for the new couple. This does not mean alienating and rejecting parents or children: but if a strong bond does not form between the mates, there will be problems. Our philosophy is that it is better to have close extended-family relationships *after* the development of a strong marital partnership. If couples focus on children, in-laws, or parents in the early years of the remarriage, they are sending the message that these people are more important than the marriage (Peterson & Zill, 1986).

Spouses need to realize that in-laws may feel resentment because of the changes taking place. The more enmeshed spouses are with their families of origin, the more likely that family members will have high levels of anxiety, will label boundary setting as disloyalty, and will become angry or resort to overt ostracism. Nevertheless, as therapists work with couples, to unite them against intrusive family members, they must also be alert to the possibility that couples may use such conflict to disguise their own unresolved issues. In addition to assessing the marital couple, therapists should include an examination of family-of-origin relationships in making a stepfamily assessment. Are the members close or too far away? How does each partner feel with the other partner's family — comfortable, uncomfortable, angry, indifferent? Do the partners agree on how much time to spend with families? What do they do during the holidays? Who goes where? What are the loyalty issues between the spouses? Does either one feel pulled between spouse and family? Since the marriage, has the relationship with in-laws improved or deteriorated?

Unless they exercise caution, therapists can get caught up in believing that their clients' dilemmas are related only to past marriages, ex-spouses, or issues with children. We have found that these individuals do intrude on remarriages, but these conflicts may also hide family-of-origin issues that probably were not resolved in the past marriage and are now rearing their heads in the new one. Balancing loyalty to biological children with loyalty to stepchildren and loyalty to a new spouse is difficult enough without also trying to balance family-of-origin involvement. The observant therapist will find, however, that newly remarried couples frequently bring their parents into their new marriage.

Beyond emphasizing the primacy of the marital relationship and communicating and defending healthy boundaries, the therapist should use other methods to resolve family-of-origin issues. The following suggestions are offered.

In-law Rivalry

In a remarriage, there is an inherent potential for confusion in relationships, because of the numbers of parents and children often moving among a variety of in-laws. Jealousy may easily strike these in-laws, but couples must avoid playing that game.

Positive Assertion

Therapists need to teach couples how to be assertive in a positive manner. In most instances, couples should avoid arguments, yelling, or being put in the position of defending their actions. We tell couples that once they get put into a defensive position, the conversation must be ended.

Relationship Definition

Therapists also need to help couples determine who is important to them—the people in whom they will invest their energy. With the number of people surrounding remarried couples, the spouses will not be able to spend time with everyone, nor will they want to. Again, the therapist reinforces the idea that the immediate family is the major priority. Newly remarried couples should not lose track of spending time together.

Family Balance

Another method for resolving family-of-origin issues is to maintain a reasonable balance between the families of both spouses. One spouse's family should not be placed above the other spouse's family, and neither one should be placed above the immediate stepfamily. In a one-up/one-down scenario, one spouse is on the defensive about her or his family—an uncomfortable and destabilizing position. Yet every family has assets and liabilities, and therapists need to assist spouses as they determine what they want the balance to be, and what boundaries they must set to accomplish their choice.

From Single Parenthood to Remarriage

Another set of problems may arise when there is a switch from single parenthood to remarriage. Grandparents may have been very involved in helping out with or raising the children of a single parent. In fact, it is not unusual for some single parents to go back home to live for a time. Such bonding can be helpful to single parents. With remarriage, however, grandparents must address separation from their own children. They have also been acting as parents to their children's children and will have to abandon that role as well; if they do not, it will be hard for new stepparents to become involved with the children. Typically, grandparents create a schism in a new stepfamily by complaining about the parenting skills of the stepparent. This forces a boundary definition on the part of the biological parent, so that he or she can give support to the new spouse as a stepparent. Of course, the grandparents may get upset and angry.

Enmeshed Families

In other cases, parents may be too involved with their children:

> Mark said that he could not get time with his wife because his mother-in-law was always around. Her husband had died a few years before. She spent considerable time at their house and talked about full-time residency, even though she was physically able to live independently. Susan, Mark's wife, felt torn between her mother and her new husband, trying to please them both. Mark clearly stated that he thought his mother-in-law's moving in with them would not be good for their marriage, particularly since it was only six months old. Susan let her mother move in anyway.
>
> When we talked to Mark and discussed his family of origin with him, we learned that he did not have a nurturing mother. Mark missed Susan's caring for him and was acutely aware that her caring was going to her mother rather than to him. He was jealous, and Susan's mother was lonely. Both were stuck, and Susan's efforts to make each party happy were to no avail. In therapy, Mark talked directly to Susan's mother, and each of them began to understand the other's needs. Mark did insist that she move out, however, and eventually she complied for the sake of the marriage.

In working with a family-of-origin issue, ostracism is not healthy, but intrusiveness is also not helpful. Therapists can help couples work toward treating each other respectfully and sharing their feelings directly with each other, whether these are pleasant or unpleasant. Spouses can be taught and encouraged to take actions that demonstrate care for the extended family and to cultivate positive relationships with relatives. A healthy relationship with relatives entails compromise and efforts to find alternatives. Couples need to show their families of origin what types of relationships they want with them. By their actions, couples demonstrate how they want to be treated. To be effective, spouses must present a united front.

Couple Structure Issues

According to Wald (1981), there can be eight possible combinations of marital status in heterosexual remarried couples: divorced man–single woman; divorced woman–single man; divorced man–divorced woman; widowed man–single woman; widowed woman–single man; widowed woman–widowed man; divorced man–widowed woman; and divorced woman–widowed man. Obviously, in each case at least one partner has been married before and divorced or widowed. Assessing this history is part of the task for the therapist, since past relationships will affect the present marriage. There may also be problems inherent in some of these combinations.

Widowed Partners

Working with widowed individuals is demanding for therapists. Clinical sessions often reach a high level of emotional intensity and require affective receptivity on the part of the therapist. The death of a loved one is perhaps the greatest pain humans endure. If both spouses have been widowed, they can share an understanding of past pain. This may help with the couple's emotional bonding. A never-married person wed to a widowed individual may lack an adequate frame of reference for comprehending the partner's loss and grief.

Issues around widowhood are complex, and yet the couple may ignore them. Grief issues can prevent adequate bonding. Limits between the new spouse and the deceased spouse are not defined. The messages of a dead spouse can be influential, especially if the widowed partner believes that he or she had something to do with the death or could have prevented it. The widowed partner may also cherish this grief because others reinforce such behavior. In our culture, we see someone who fails to show grief as callous; we believe that there is never too much grief over losing a spouse. This grief can keep a widowed person emotionally stagnant, however, with no sense of purpose or direction in life:

> Al, a widower, came to therapy about six months after his remarriage to Betty, who felt the marriage was stuck. Each had brought a daughter into the new stepfamily, and Betty was two months pregnant. According to Betty, Al seemed to withdraw shortly after she was confirmed as pregnant.
>
> "It's not that he isn't caring or understanding," she said. "It's just that he seems withdrawn, depressed, kind of indifferent. We certainly don't argue a lot, and it's not that I think he isn't a nice man. I guess I'm just confused. I don't seem to understand."
>
> Al said that his work as a computer salesman was becoming more stressful. He felt tired after putting in long hours at the office.
>
> Al and Betty agreed that the two girls got along well. They were both about five years old and actually enjoyed playing together.
>
> In initial discussions, Al could not explain his depression and withdrawal from the relationship. When we asked Al about his first marriage, we began to understand his pain, distancing, and withdrawal. Neither Betty nor the children had heard Al's story.
>
> Al's wife and son had died in a car accident. On that particular night, Al was working late, and he was to pick up his daughter from a piano lesson. The family was planning to meet at a local restaurant, but his wife and son never made it. Al described how he thought he was at fault, because he should not have been working late that evening.

If he had been home, he would have been the driver and perhaps could have avoided the accident.

Al also said that he was having dreams about them and could not seem to forget. The bad dreams had become more frequent and severe since his remarriage. He felt guilty, as if he were betraying his deceased spouse. He felt that he should have died, too. Al told us that he had married Betty because she had pursued him. She seemed like a caring, loving person who would be a good mother for his daughter. He was no longer sure that he had made the right choice, however. Al felt that he was not being fair to Betty.

During this session, we intervened to help Al bring his memories to the surface. We gently pushed him to disclose his feelings and sense of guilt concerning his past and present relationships. We also helped Betty to understand the impact of Al's pain. We aimed our interventions at convincing her that she did not need to feel bad about herself. She also did not need to perceive that she had pushed Al into marriage.

Over the next several weeks, Al and Betty talked at length about his previous marriage. Al experienced relief through being able to talk about it. Gradually, his depression began to lift. As therapists, we could now begin to help them with the issues in their relationship.

Divorced and Never-Married Partners

Another potentially troubled combination is the divorced person wedded to a never-married individual. The dissimilarity in their prior marital status affects the partners' ability to empathize with each other, and tension results from the lack of shared experience. Disagreements over parenting often occur. The divorced partner has already been parenting children, and the never-married partner may feel inferior about parenting: his or her opinion may not be valued because it is not based on experience. There may also be disagreements over money. The divorced individual is probably either sending money to support children or receiving money for child support. Money issues may occur with the ex-spouse, and the never-married partner may have a difficult time defining his or her role in those transactions.

The previously married person may act as if he or she has an advantage in the relationship because of the experience from the previous marriage. At the same time, the never-married person seeks bonding and the formation of a new family while trying to avoid behavior similar to the ex-spouse's. Such inexperience may mean that the never-married spouse has difficulty determining an appropriate relationship with the ex-spouse. A never-married individual may see a relationship with an ex-spouse as the same as one with an ex-boyfriend or ex-girlfriend because the dynamics of marriage are not clear. The never-married person may also complain, justly, about the previously married spouse's overinvolvement with the ex-spouse. These are only some of the possible ramifications of the divorced/never-married combination. Therapists also need to assess all emotional and legal ties that remain between ex-spouses and their children. These usually affect the remarriage, particularly the sense of equality in the newly remarried couple.

Past Marital Issues

Our practice and research have taught us that divorced individuals frequently relive the same issues as in their previous marriages. They tend to repeat the same behavior patterns and thus trigger the same problems. Remarried spouses are different from some other newlyweds. Many have had sexual intercourse with their new spouses before the remarriage. They may have vacationed together or shared household responsibilities or expenses before the wedding. Sometimes, because of these joint experiences, they believe that marriage will not alter their relationship. Soon after the remarriage, however, they begin to see that life does change. For some couples, the changes are for the better, and the partnership becomes closer. They feel more in love. Others, including those we typically see in therapy, have less desirable experiences.

It appears that the legality of marriage heightens commitment and therefore intimacy issues. A couple realizes, because of past marriages, that remarriage brings complex and binding legal considerations. Some couples in therapy present their remarriages as simply a matter of convenience or of one spouse's feeling obligated or forced to marry the other. Marriages entered into because of obligation or convenience typically present clinical trouble.

When people marry, they are following in their parents' footsteps. Patterns inherent in parents' relationships appear. In remarriages, feelings arise that many people have not connected with since childhood or since a past marriage (dependency, deprivation, aloneness). For some couples, remarriage is a chance to work out conflicts and issues from the past.

Shapiro (1984) has found fear of permanence and closeness in remarriage. Spouses are afraid. They know that the cost of getting out of a relationship is great, both emotionally and financially. Many have one foot in marriage and one foot out. They are not sure if the relationship will work, and they want some protection in case it does not. For others, the pain of divorce was overwhelming, and they desperately want the new marriage to last. As a result, they lose sight of their independence, become too dependent, and increase the chances that the relationship will end.

Unfortunately, people spend more time talking about buying cars or houses than they do about their marriages. Entering therapy, they have doubts about the people they have married. Why have the feelings changed? Why do they feel so alone? Remarried couples in trouble typically believe that no one can understand their problems. Because of that mistaken belief, they isolate themselves. When people remarry, they are usually looking for a fresh start, and they get scared when things do not work out as they hoped. Sometimes they panic, believing that they have made a big mistake. They may be torn between divorcing and staying married. As therapists, we focus on their

attitude toward their problems. We reinforce their determination to work their dilemmas out, and we teach spouses that they
need to reaffirm each other every day.

Issues Surrounding Children

Children are a concern of many remarried people. In a traditional nuclear family, parenthood may be delayed and given
a chance to evolve as the marriage grows. In remarriage, parenthood may be immediate. Remarried couples face issues of separation and individuation from the family, closeness with a mate
in the middle of others, facing aggressive tendencies, and sex
in a family setting. There is also a need for acceptance and approval from the new mate. As therapists realize, how mates see
their partners influences how the partners see themselves.

When individuals get married, they are hoping for a romantic time when they can learn more about each other, experience joy in the new union, and find some stability and security. They want to believe that, as new stepparents, they will
have an instant relationship with children, and that the group
will become a close-knit family very quickly. This fantasy often
remains one. Children may have obvious residual anger and
hurt over parents' divorce or death. Loss and resentment easily
surface when a parent remarries. Children may also be uncertain and anxious about being accepted and having a place in
the new family.

We re not saying that couples cannot be happy in remarriages that involve stepchildren. They must realize, however,
that there is competition among all members for attention, nurturing, and so on. Remarriage that involves children forces individuals to face not only marital concerns but also issues related
to parenting skills, philosophies of parenting, religion, balancing career demands while raising a family, and so on.

Parenting

Children simply add complexity to the already muddied waters
of remarriage. It can be surprising just how few couples talk

about arrangements for custody and child care before remarriage. Most act as if problems will not occur, yet they almost always do. When we work with couples, we discuss the following ideas about parenting with them.

Attention

Children require a great deal of attention. They push the boundaries of relationships, disobey, and see whether parents are willing to discipline and set consequences for misbehavior. Children are also good at aligning with one parent, thereby pushing both parents to fight with each other over the children. This game of "you treat me so badly" often tugs at parents' guilt as children demand that their feelings be immediately assuaged and taken care of.

Giving Children Time to Adjust to a Remarriage

Like all other human beings, children get scared or anxious and experience loss when they are in new situations (Visher and Visher, 1989). Parents must demonstrate that children are important and valued and must determine appropriate boundaries.

Teaching Respect

Family members should address each other clearly, with face-to-face contact and proper voice tone. Listening skills are important when a family gets together; people need to understand that they are being heard. Of course, this does not mean that they will always get what they want, but their messages will be heard and considered.

Talking About Raising Children

When mates disagree, it is important that discussions take place in private rather than in front of the children. If children are aware of disagreements, they will see them as opportunities to divide and conquer. When spouses come to feel comfortable as a couple and secure about their parenting skills, it is possible to discuss differences in front of the children. Therapists can help individuals learn to share their feelings and anxieties about what it means to parent, as well as the insecurities involved. Here, we sometimes see the "I'm always vulnerable/I always have to be strong" games that ensure a one-up/one-down parental match.

Private Time with the Biological Parent

Remarried couples should discuss how time is going to be allotted with their children. Obviously, children have a natural bond with their biological parents, which should be permitted to continue growing and developing.

Special Time for the Stepparent-Stepchild Relationship

Stepparent-stepchild relationships must be developed. Through behavior and commitment people get close (Martin & Martin, 1983; Visher & Visher, 1989). Activities that people can perform together, no matter how simple, should be developed. It is the time spent together that is important, not what is done.

Letting Children Express All Their Feelings

This is very different from letting children be disrespectful or yell at and belittle a parent. There should be times, meetings, or situations for sharing feelings. Children need to be taught how to express their concerns respectfully, so that they can be heard. Letting someone scream or act inappropriately just reinforces this behavior and distances others from the screamer.

Fostering Vulnerability and Support Between Spouses

As we have seen, the togetherness of the couple as parents and as spouses is vital to the success of the remarriage (Visher & Visher, 1989). Spouses must learn about each other's insecurities and weaknesses. Some of these certainly involve parenting, an anxiety-provoking process that includes many fears that children will not be successful or happy. In disclosing these vulnerabilities, people can cry and laugh together as they experience the woes and joys of raising children. Remarried spouses are stuck in a paradox of parenting: they cannot expect too much too soon, and yet they must quickly provide appropriate, clear boundaries. These boundaries reinforce suitable behavior and allow relationships to develop.

Dilemmas with the Ex-Spouse

One of the more difficult issues for a remarried couple is dealing with the ex-spouse and with that person's effects on the remarriage. Biological parents share their children, and ex-spouses may still be in love with their former mates. For both reasons, old relationships may remain active and often problematic. One remarried spouse soon realizes the difficulty of attempting to build a new relationship while his or her mate is still tied to a failed previous marriage. Many people have told us how angry their ex-spouses continued to be after their remarriages, and how they continued conflicts. Our impression is that conflict and anger are ways to continue intimacy and involvement. We help couples draw and set boundaries in these relationships, to prevent them from being constantly pulled into situations where anger reigns. Joan told a familiar tale:

> I can't believe Clark's wife is the way she is. She still calls me on the phone, complaining about her ex, my husband, and what he is not doing for their children. What can I say? Certainly, I want to defend him, and I am tired of hearing this stuff. Sometimes I feel bad for her. It's crazy. What annoys me the most is when Clark's child comes to stay with us. She always tells me these mean things her mother says about me, and it makes me sick. I can't believe that Clark doesn't defend me when he hears his daughter saying these things about me. He tells me that it's his wife saying them, not his daughter.

> She's just repeating what her mother says. But I
> get the impression that the daughter likes these
> statements, and it's her own way of attacking me.
> I'm just getting tired of this, and I feel like an out-
> sider. Clark might as well go back with his old
> family.

Children in the Middle

Being pulled into the middle of biological parents' ongoing
conflict is not easy for children. They are forced to tell tales between these ex-spouses — who is doing what, who is going out
with whom, and other details. When therapists find ex-marital
bonds as destructive and chaotic as those between Clark and
his previous wife, then the couple must set firm boundaries.
Therapists can show these individuals that the ex-spouse is drawing them away from a healthy emphasis on their own relationship, and that this will prove detrimental to the remarriage. Of
all the questions the couple must answer, the first one is How
do we determine our relationship as the top priority in our lives?
Others include What do we do with phone calls and other behavior that intervenes in our marriage? and What do we say
to the child who carries messages between families? and How
do I talk to the ex-spouse, and what do we talk about? and If
my ex-spouse chooses to remain angry, what does this mean
for my remarriage and my children?

The Disabled or Helpless Ex-Spouse

Sometimes people play a disabled or helpless role to engage an
ex-spouse. For example, Jean said that after she left, her ex-
husband always seemed depressed:

> He would call me up, and I would listen to him
> talk for hours. I felt guilty about leaving him, but
> the reason I left is that it was so miserable being
> married to him. The phone calls just confirmed my
> misery. He also never got a job that he could keep

for more than six months to a year, and I was always the one with the steady job supporting him.
I got tired of doing it, and I figured I could do it
on my own anyway. What angered me is that I
never got my custody payments on time. They were
sporadic at best. Often he would miss months and
then show up at my house with a check, like it was
this huge gift, and I was supposed to be all smiling.

I was always trying to help him connect with
the kids. I felt bad that they didn't have a father
who wanted to spend time with them. So I would
call him up and arrange for him to meet with the
children. Most of the time I drove them to his
house. The funny thing is, after the kids got there,
he didn't spend much time with them anyway.

It wasn't until I was in therapy that I began
to realize that my behavior was a waste of time.
I was spending all my energy trying to keep this
man in step and in life. It was like I was still married to him. It wasn't until I began to realize what
I was doing that I could meet John, who did care
for me, and whom I eventually married.

In helping the marital partners deal with an ex-spouse,
it is important that they mutually develop boundaries around
their past relationships. It helps the remarriage when both people have something to say about their ex-spouses. Getting an
opinion from a new spouse about the partner's ex-spouse can
also open new avenues for discussion. If the new spouse feels
alienated, this will increase problems.

Children should be removed from the position of carrying tales. If information must be imparted, either between ex-
spouses or between an ex-spouse and a new mate, then the adults
themselves should pass the messages on. Children should not
believe that they have to carry messages. Some children use message carrying as a manipulative device however. Such behavior
should not be reinforced.

The partner must develop methods of conflict resolution

and establish an initial stance of noninvolvement with an ex-spouse. Therapists should tell remarried couples that their ex-spouses are adults and can be expected to take care of themselves.

The one time when ex-spouses should intervene in their former partners' affairs is when they believe that their ex-mates are neglectful or abusive to their children. This kind of intervention should be conducted with the help of a lawyer and social services. Too often, therapists are caught in the bind of hearing sad stories about how stepfamilies are stuck, and nothing can be done. This is not true. Therapists can teach members of stepfamilies and remarried couples to fight, and make enough noise to be heard. If a parent has a good enough case and wants legal advice, then the therapist should advocate change and appropriate actions. Sometimes this course may involve the therapist as an expert witness. As we have said, ex-spouses may trigger difficulties in their partners' remarriages when they still desire relationships with their ex-mates. The reverse is also true, and therapists need to be aware that an issue with an ex-spouse can indicate that one of the newly married individuals has an unresolved agenda from the past marriage. When problems arise in the new relationship, they may be attributable to this unresolved agenda.

Resolving Structure Issues

The missing, essential ingredient is the ability to communicate openly and constructively. Resolving dilemmas may involve issues pertaining to the following:

- The legal settlement, custody, visitation, and financial arrangements
- Family adjustments, household management, and new kinship relations
- Division of labor and responsibility for household finances
- Role relations between any children and the adults (stepparent's role as a disciplinarian and that person's financial contribution, if any)
- Parenting and parental structure

- What constitutes "a happy family life"
- Ex-spouses and adequate or inadequate involvement
- Visiting children and "before and after" effects

In discussing these issues, therapists need to help couples make every effort to communicate clearly. This process entails checking for feedback and ascertaining whether the meaning of a message is understood; separating assumptions, opinions, observations, and facts; and maintaining objectivity with regard to the speaker's personal agenda (Martin & Martin, 1985). Meanwhile, the listener of the couple must concentrate actively on the message being sent about these emotional issues. Each member of the couple needs to be aware of his or her personal agenda and any barriers or preconceptions that may distort a message. Difficult issues are often emotionally clouded. When therapists teach couples to take responsibility for their conversations, emotions and hostilities are lessened, and the hostile energy is diverted into the communication process (Martin & Martin, 1985). Thus, in the therapeutic environment, couples can be urged to practice these new skills.

Sue and Bill are an example of a couple constantly involved in conflict:

> Sue had left her first husband because, as she said, "He was a bum. All day he would sit around and drink beer and let the kids do whatever they wanted." She worked two jobs and had most of the housework and child-rearing responsibilities for two daughters, four and six years old.
>
> Sue saw Bill as the answer to her prayers. He was a hard worker and enjoyed having a good time with friends. Unfortunately, the marriage did not resemble the courtship. In our first therapy session, we could see that this was a couple in conflict.
>
> Sue said, "I'm in the same boat again. Bill is gone all the time. He teaches at the high school, is coaching three sports, plays cards, and is taking three night classes for his master's degree. This is

crazy. I never see him. I'm working two jobs and
raising the kids, who needs him?"

   Bill was caught in the bind of being a male
provider, promoting his career and avoiding his
wife.

   "I just think she's real bitchy. Always on edge
and bothering or reminding me to do something.
I'm sick of being yelled at!"

This type of marriage is difficult to counsel, requiring constant vigilance and interruptions on the part of the therapist.
Arguments begin within moments. Initially, we slowed the
process down and helped Sue and Bill hear each other's pain
and fear. One method we used for curbing arguments was to
talk to each other as co-therapists about the problems that we
saw Sue and Bill facing. We shared any ideas we had. Thus,
we slowed the communication process to a more reasonable pace
while also modeling good skills for Sue and Bill. This was particularly effective when we, as co-therapists, disagreed (sometimes deliberately). This slowing-down process also helped us
convey the frustration we felt as we tried to alter this couple's
constant belittling and argumentative style.

   In one of the early sessions, Sue said that she wanted the
marriage to work and wanted not to be alone. Bill told her that
he loved her but could not handle her anger. They had to do
things differently and attempt to leave their roles in the relationship: Bill as provider but incompetent, and Sue as demanding
and angry mother who took charge of everything. Structurally,
we helped the couple reassign responsibilities and arranged for
Sue to back down and for Bill to increase his involvement. We
insisted that major issues be discussed in therapy, and we helped
them talk to each other without attacking, by naming their disappointment and clearly stating what they needed. Once they
stopped hurting each other with their anger, they were finally
able to hear.

Present Relationship Issues

Even though they have been married before, new spouses have
trouble moving from courtship to marriage. In the aura of ro-

mance, people tend to idealize their lovers. They fabricate fantasies about their new spouses. Inevitably, this leads to disappointment as spouses begin to see each other realistically in the context of the remarriage. Yet individuals in remarriage have usually been hurt before, and they want to make sure that this time they will not have the same experience. If they see patterns in the new spouse that remind them of the ex-spouse, they may feel even more hurt, frustrated, or enraged. They project these emotions onto the spouse rather than recognizing the mutuality of the relationship. Some individuals move from marriage to marriage, never developing realistic needs and expectations or consistently choosing spouses with whom a marriage will inevitably fail. Some adults wish to see their spouses as adoring parents, the parents they never had. With this mindset, marital failure is imminent.

Marital Schisms

Complementary relationships, in which one person's qualities are essentially reinforced by the inability of the other, can lead to polarization (Martin & Martin, 1987). For example, a socially assertive person may bond with a shy individual. In time, the assertive spouse dislikes the shy person for not being involved with others. Meanwhile, the shy spouse dislikes the assertive person for his or her inattention.

As reality sets in for remarried couples, the partners move toward being critical of each other, to such an extent that it may be detrimental to the relationship. In working with remarried couples, it is not unusual for individuals to be critical of traits that they are either trying to rid themselves of or feel they cannot attain. This projecting can lock couples into continuing arguments:

> Samantha and Matt were fighting constantly when they came into therapy. They were afraid that the same patterns they had seen in their first marriages were recurring, but this time it bothered them more. Samantha said that Matt was too independent, and that he didn't tell her that he loved her

anymore. He would leave his belongings all over the house and expected her to pick up after him. She said that he was neat about his own appearance, and his closet and his bathroom accessories were always perfect; the rest of the house and his manners, however, were a mess. She always had to remind him to help around the house.

Matt complained that Samantha was too parental and liked being in charge. He also thought that it was Samantha's responsibility to make him aware when he needed to help out. This situation infuriated both of them. Matt felt that Samantha expected him to read her mind and figure out what needed to be done. Samantha was tired of Matt's playing stupid. She believed that after several years of marriage he did know what needed to be accomplished in the house, and that the truth was that he was willing to let Samantha bear most of the burden.

It was not until we investigated the families of origin that we began to see why the marriage was in trouble. Matt had grown up in a very disengaged family. His parents were hotel owners, and he rarely saw them. They never attended any of his sporting events in high school, and when he was seventeen, after Matt had been accepted into college, his father refused to pay his costs. Matt left home, never to return. He had learned that he could count on no one, and that he always would have to depend on himself. It was hard for Matt to get close to anyone, as demonstrated by the failure of his first marriage, by his inability to get close to his children, and by his current struggles with Samantha. Matt was looking for a family he could count on and somehow get close to.

In true complementary fashion, Samantha's family had been what could be described as enmeshed. She saw her parents as having a perfect

relationship, hardly ever arguing or showing conflict and continually expressing love for each other.

Samantha's mother was very traditional. She
did everything to make sure that her husband's life
was settled and that his environment was secure.
Torn between the example of her mother as a home-
maker and her own life as a career woman, Samantha did not know what to do. Inherently, she felt
that she had to take care of the household. She was
also recognized as an organizer in the community:
her church and several civic organizations often
volunteered her for activities, without her permission, and fully expected her to carry them out. Her
family accepted Matt as a long-lost son, and her
parents treated him royally, particularly her mother.

Because of her relationship with Matt, Samantha became more and more independent and
self-sufficient. She enrolled in college and completed
her degree, which she had put off for over fifteen
years. She was also intent on attending graduate
school. In some ways, marrying Matt had helped
her move toward the goals she wanted — self-suffi-
ciency and independence — but the cost, in loss of
her relationship, was high.

When Matt and Samantha became able to
state their needs in the relationship and say what
they had brought into it, the criticisms were less
frequent. We helped reframe much of their anger
into greater comprehension of what each was seeking from the other. Matt became more understanding of Samantha's desire to control her environment
and her need to please as a means of getting acceptance. He became more vocal in his apprecia-
tion and also more cognizant of what his family
responsibilities were.

Samantha became more assertive in dealing
with Matt and others regarding her needs. She
learned to set limits on what she was willing to do.

She also sat down with Matt and made some lists of relationship needs and family responsibilities. She pulled out of many responsibilties, and Matt and the children picked up a good number of them. This was difficult for Samantha, but she was rewarded by having more time to do other things, such as going to school.

Samantha and Matt began to appreciate their differences. They realized that these differences were helping their growth rather than threatening their individuality. They also learned that they might not agree on everything—that sometimes couples can disagree and not need instant solutions.

Dilemmas of Power and Decision Making

Remarried couples coming into therapy have problems with decision-making patterns. They know how to escalate or avoid conflict but not how to resolve it. Some spouses have partners who are unable to assert their own needs; others have difficulty balancing their own needs with those of a spouse. These people feel that they must retain power and control.

Adler (1964) wrote many years ago that the human drive for power is fundamental. Struggles over power come about when the needs of one or both partners are unmet. Adler believed that most married couples conduct themselves as if each party were afraid of the other: showing weakness implies vulnerability, and people want to protect themselves.

We have discovered that power struggles and issues of control begin not because one person wants to control another but because spouses are afraid of being controlled. Power issues are coming to the forefront in relationships as marital roles change in our society. The structure and responsibilities of marriage are not always clear today, and definitions of male and female roles are misunderstood (Madanes, 1984).

Power issues may also appear in remarriages because individuals step over personal boundaries. People come into a remarriage with a sense of who they are and the boundaries of

their personal domains. As they learn to live with their new partners, they try to sense which areas of decision making are their
own, which are the spouse's, and which represent a mutual domain. Often the determination of roles and the allocation of
power are influenced by parents' marriages. Sometimes spouses
have certain areas of expertise, and these may or may not be
recognized in the relationship. Whatever boundaries have been
established, when one mate oversteps the border and intrudes
on the other's space, conflict results.

Power Patterns

Several power patterns that individuals exhibit merit intervention (Katz & Stein, 1983). These include interactions along the
following lines:

1. *The passive-submissive spouse:* This is the dependent individ-
    ual who follows the other spouse's lead, no matter what.
    In a couple with a controlling spouse, there may be an un-
    healthy but stable balance; nevertheless, the passive-sub-
    missive spouse may go into crisis when he or she must solve
    a problem. This spouse may also suffer from a submissive
    type of depression.
2. *The passive-aggressive spouse:* This is the person who utilizes
    indirect manipulation. Sometimes such spouses agree overtly
    but sabotage at another level. These individuals are also
    good at triangulation (that is, pulling other people into
    conflicts). Their indirectness usually causes hostility in the
    people whom they manipulate, particularly as the latter be-
    come more aware of what is occurring. When their methods
    are illuminated, passive-aggressive spouses become quite
    angry.
3. *The passive-suffering spouse:* The passive sufferer generally uses
    a disability or an inability to face life as a method of get-
    ting another individual to take care of and control the fam-
    ily. This person may be a passive-submissive individual who
    has deteriorated emotionally. Even when this position is
    inevitable—that is, when an individual actually has a chronic

illness — the therapist can teach the couple methods that ensure the passive-suffering partner a role in decision making.

4. *The assertive-controlling spouse:* This is a person who uses assertion skills to control others and get what he or she wants. This pattern may be particularly effective with a passive-submissive or passive-aggressive spouse (Katz & Stein, 1983).

Ideally, movement away from these patterns will be toward healthy assertion and positions where individuals are comfortable exhibiting power but also comfortable relinquishing dominance or control. These are individuals who are able to determine what is important and what is not. Therapists need to remember, obviously, that power is not equal in a relationship all the time, nor would such constant equality be desirable. Couples need to determine what works for them and, in essence, what is healthy. When a spouse seems angry and overburdened with responsibilities or feels powerless, this is a strong indication that there is an imbalance.

Some individuals, after a failed first marriage, reach the point where they wish to negotiate everything in a remarriage. If negotiation does not occur, they are afraid that the remarriage will not be a fifty-fifty deal. These couples engage in the tedious process of constantly talking about every minor issue. They usually have long lists posted on the refrigerator: who does what, where, why, and the activities and chores to be shared every other day, or some other ridiculous system. To combat this tendency, therapists can help spouses talk about the areas where they would like to have more or less involvement from their mates. Spouses can learn how to share information without criticizing each other.

Spouses may also take advantage of their partners' weaknesses. For example, one spouse may make decisions quickly when he or she knows that the other needs or deserves more time. One spouse may not ask about the other's feelings before simply proceeding with his or her own plans. Therapists need to help these individuals determine what is influencing their behavior. When spouses insist on getting their own way, what are they afraid of compromising?

Many individuals are afraid of losing themselves if they do not win an argument. They feel threatened and alone. Others bring in a host of childhood issues when they examine the power balance in their marriages. Therapists help couples realize that they can take control of their lives. They illuminate influences from the past that are affecting the current relationship. For example, a spouse may be afraid because he or she lived with one dominating parent and one meek parent and overidentified with the meek parent. In such a case, the therapist should reflect to the individual how he or she is being controlled by the past.

Physical Issues

Issues involving space also affect power and decision making in a new stepfamily. For example, if family's house belongs to one of the spouses, the original occupant must try to find a balance between newcomers' need to feel at home and his or her own desire to keep the surroundings as they are. If stepchildren are involved, there is the challenge of trying to create a home where everyone feels comfortable. This is often impossible. Ideally, when this is economically feasible, it is better for the family to acquire neutral space by seeking a new place to live.

Realistic Expectations About Homemaking

Another factor in power struggles and decision making in remarriages is realistic expectations about homemaking. As couples examine the "shoulds" in their lives, they may get overburdened trying to be perfect. This becomes even more complicated when there are children to care for and the couple is committed to being more involved with their children than their parents were with them. Something has to give. Simply helping people realize that they do not have to have the perfect home to be happy can ensure better communication.

Money

Issues surrounding money may have a pronounced impact. With most remarried couples, money is either being mailed out to another family or is coming in from another source. In either case, the amount of money always seems to be too much or too little; we rarely hear remarried couples say that the amount or regularity of child support is satisfactory. People in remarriages usually feel that they were hurt financially in past relationships. They are very cautious about the use of money in the remarriage. Money may be used as a means of power and control in the relationship. Appropriate interventions may not always fit with a therapist's value system. For example, a therapist may not believe in joint accounts, but if a strong symbol of the partner's separateness is the maintenance of separate financial accounts and they are arguing over who is paying for what, then an appropriate intervention would be to have them share some money. This would give them the opportunity to learn to work out their differences.

In other instances, spouses may say that they deliberately keep money in separate funds, so that if the relationship does not work, they will be financially prepared to leave it. This is an unhealthy attitude, one not seen in many successful marriages. In contrast to people in first marriages, remarried spouses tend to be very specific about their spending habits and financial needs in the relationship. They need to negotiate whether they will have separate or joint accounts, who is responsible for what, and whether their money will be pooled. When the family is receiving money from a former partner, some spouses may believe that they "owe" the ex-spouses because of this money. Other people may bring large debts into the relationship, and this should be discussed frankly and openly.

In our opinion, money is another channel through which the spouses can share and get closer. If they choose to use money as a divider between them, they will probably argue about it consistently, and it will indeed be a divisive mechanism. If communication processes are effective, people can learn how to be honest with each other about money. We tell couples that having different attitudes about money is healthy. Contrasting opinions about the financial situation may be vital to helping the relationship evolve and change.

Competitiveness

In recent years, we have become interested in the clinical significance of competitiveness between spouses in dual-career remarriages. In traditional marriages, women supported men in their drive for success; they provided the environment for men to achieve in their work. Today we need to recognize that problems may occur when one spouse is more successful than the other. Therapists must recognize the often subtle competition between spouses and work to reframe it for the success of the relationship and the needs of each person.

Intimacy

Sometimes intimacy is used for power or control in the relationship. Spouses may put up barriers to closeness because they feel that they were unloved by others in the past. They believe that they have been hurt too much or were suffocated by a past relationship. The challenge for the therapist is to help the couple determine what effects this lack of closeness is having on the marriage. Partners in a remarriage may also have had affairs during their first marriages. There may be fear that this pattern will be repeated, and that a spouse will seek caring and support outside the marriage.

Sexual Happiness

In work with remarried couples, asessment of their sexual happiness is important. Partners in a remarriage may have sexual concerns left over from their past marriages. They may be vulnerable in this area but may not have the support in the new relationship to help them get past these barriers. We help couples give positive feedback about sexual behavior, discussing ideas or viewpoints that can make sexual relationships better. It is important to reserve the bedroom for intimacy, rather than discussing the day's events, arguing, or eating there. Some couples argue about lovemaking or are critical during the lovemaking

process rather than waiting for an appropriate time. This occurs because they are afraid of infidelity or are jealous and angry. The previous marriage may have lacked intimacy, and a
spouse may be repeating the pattern in order to test her or his
partner's hostility. An individual may have married because he
or she was in midlife crisis. This individual will see the marriage as a sexual conquest. Is there a desire to be youthful at
the cost of denying reality? Are the partners bored? Therapists
also need to examine whether there are components of one-
up/one-down scenarios in the relationship:

> Bonnie and Hank had a destructive sexual pattern.
> On entering therapy, each of them had been remar-
> ried twice. They were in the eighth year of this mar-
> riage, which was the longest that either of them had
> been married. Hank had engaged in several affairs
> during this marriage, and Bonnie had usually for-
> given him. Two years before, however, after another
> of Hank's affairs, she said that she could not love
> him anymore and would not have sex with him but
> also would not leave.
>
> Hank just continued his affairs and acted as
> if nothing had happened. Finally, during his latest
> affair, his lover had called Bonnie on the phone and
> described in detail what she and Hank had done.
> She told Bonnie that she wanted Hank for her man.
> This infuriated Bonnie, and she threw Hank out
> of the house, telling him to run to his new lover.
> Hank would not leave. He camped out in a tent
> behind the house, waiting for his wife's forgiveness.
> Each day he wandered in and out of the house, tak-
> ing showers, and so on. He and Bonnie would
> argue.
>
> Bonnie entered therapy at this point, to figure
> out how to divorce her husband. After several ses-
> sions, she brought Hank to counseling, and they
> began to look at the dynamics of their relationship.
> In the discussions, Hank began to reveal that he

was not satisfied with Bonnie's sexual behavior, yet he was scared to get close to her and commit himself to her in the relationship. He believed that if he were sexually committed to Bonnie, he would lose his virility. Hank's overwhelming sexual need and his inability to become intimate beyond sexual conquest led us to question whether Hank was sexually addicted or had been sexually abused in the past.

Within several sessions, Bonnie disclosed that she felt sexually inadequate and dominated by Hank. She admitted that she saw sex as one of the few mechanisms by which she could manipulate him. She thought that if she withheld sex, he would turn around and improve his behavior.

After several months of greater understanding between them, Hank admitted that he had been sexually abused as a child. He had felt tremendous remorse and self-hatred after these incidents. It was Bonnie's acceptance of Hank after this discussion, the warmth that she demonstrated toward him, that helped Hank recognize that he was acceptable. Eventually, Hank reached the point of confronting his stepfather and his mother about the incidents. He was shocked to learn that his mother had known of and gone along with the abuse. This stunning revelation left Hank alone and even more dependent on Bonnie. Through his vulnerability, Hank began to recognize what he had been searching for all these years and had not been able to attain through sexual conquest.

Direct Communication

Disagreements or differences in a relationship are normal and do not represent major problems; nevertheless, the inability to discuss them, to work out differences, signals trouble for a relationship and often brings couples into therapy. In good marriages, couples recognize what they need from each other and discuss the fears and anxieties that prohibit emotional and sexual intimacy. Spouses in healthy marriages do not withdraw or run away from their mates' aggression; rather, they learn to appreciate this as the signal of a problem.

There is a sense of hopelessness when communication styles leave individuals so angry with each other that they believe there is no possible resolution. Often these fights are characterized by yelling, screaming, or withdrawal, so that there is no discussion at all. In such disagreements, one spouse feels attacked and hurt and so berates the other, thereby setting up a counterattack. This process typically involves holding grudges. When looking at these patterns, couples are usually not aware of what sets off the process. In sessions, we deliberately try to duplicate it. During these fights, we can help determine the pattern occurring at home. We try to help couples learn to communicate instead of withdrawing or continuing their anger. Therapists must show couples how to negotiate over an issue. Empathy is the best way to get a response from a spouse and move toward resolution.

We have noticed that these cycles often end with the couple's lovemaking. This is a strong reinforcement for the continuation of conflict, and we typically intervene to eliminate lovemaking as the end of the cycle. Instead, we suggest negotiation and apology as a more acceptable method of coming to closure.

Resolving Relationship Issues

In helping remarried couples resolve conflict, we share several processes with them that we have found effective. We limit "mind reading" on the part of spouses. We tell couples that it is their responsibility to express their needs. If people can learn how to say what they want, they have a better chance of getting it or of acting in ways that will not be destructive.

We also help spouses structure time, no matter how short (say, ten to fifteen minutes each day), when they sit down and talk to each other. If partners do not set aside time exclusively for each other, they begin to believe that they are unimportant. The couple, not the therapist, should determine the preferred time. We also make it clear that spouses need to keep children out of their space during this special time, and they must set consequences for children's interference. Phones are not answered. During the discussion time, the spouses are allowed to share both positive and negative feelings and actions that have occurred that day. Sometimes it is more appropriate for certain couples to go to public places for their time together; they will usually be more polite to each other. We also suggest that one spouse not bring up major issues when he or she senses that the other is stressed or exhausted.

We teach respectful, direct communication skills. Most marital therapists find that improving communication skills is the key to helping spouses understand each other and become closer. Poor communication skills accentuate marital problems. When individuals believe that they are not being heard accurately or cannot share their feelings, they begin to make harmful decisions or to act in hurtful ways.

In teaching couples to communicate in a respectful, positive, and clear manner, we use Rogerian training exercises to show how to reflect, summarize, and paraphrase statements. Even though couples may see these exercises as contrived, they often help them speak more positively and constructively.

We also teach couples to state their goals overtly in a conversation. They may also need to learn that it is not necessary to come to resolution on an issue every time. Even if there is disagreement, people like to be heard and to believe that they are being understood.

We teach clients to observe and correctly interpret how their spouses communicate. Some individuals show their caring by buying a present, hugging, or performing other nonverbal actions; others are more open and willing to say, "I love you."

We help couples realize that conflict is an inherent part of being intimate. Katz and Stein (1983), discussing marital therapy, say that marital therapists get in a bind when they try to help couples develop peaceful relationships without conflict. Learning to be married is a balancing act between dependence and independence, love and anger, caring and withdrawal. As therapists, we help people love and yet be upset, confront each other without being volatile or violent. This is truly the "heart" of marital therapy.

Finally, we help couples recognize that when a pattern is destructive they need to end the conversation, even if the problem is not resolved. Couples need to realize that some individuals must cool off before they can understand or laugh with their spouses, especially individuals who have to win. One spouse can withdraw, saying "Let's take time out. I'm feeling pressured" or "I'm acting as if I have to win."

Remarried couples may have difficulty with communication because the sharing of feelings recalls sadness, disappointment, and failure in past relationships. Individuals in remarriages have had their trust broken, and they feel unaccepted. They need time to rebuild trust in a relationship. It is very important that these couples learn to share their needs and expectations as well as their pent-up frustrations.

Remarried couples are at risk because of the strains associated with a remarriage, including children, money, and in-laws. There are more people involved in their relationships; thus, in a sense, they need better communication skills than traditional newlyweds do. Remarried spouses must make their relationship a priority. Time alone as a couple is crucial. When children see that the marital relationship is solid, the stepfamily will be able to develop.

7

Resolving Dilemmas
with the Ex-Spouse

Members of stepfamilies need to adjust their lives once a remarriage occurs. Biological parents are no exception. Their adjustments will stem from their growth and development after the losses of divorce, as well as from life-style changes dictated by remarriage. Biological parents may have felt that they were failures when their previous marriages ended, and their self-esteem may be damaged. Some have suffered financial losses, and their life-styles may have altered significantly (Goldsmith, 1980).

For noncustodial biological parents, the loss of daily contact with their children probably outweighs all other losses (Goldsmith, 1981; Martin & Martin, 1985). In most cases, this loss involves fathers, but the number of noncustodial mothers is increasing. For noncustodial mothers, loss of contact with their children may cause more pain than it does for men, because of the stigma that society places on women who leave or lose their children. Adjusting to the loss of daily contact with children is difficult but, paradoxically, noncustodial biological parents who do have daily contact may experience even more grief. Seeing children regularly but briefly makes some parents miss them more than less frequent contact would. Harry, a building contractor, expressed typical feelings of loss:

> I used to work a lot of hours, so I didn't get to see
> our daughters much. They were young, five and
> six years old, so I thought I would have time with

them later on, after I built up my business. Instead, because I was gone so much, my relationship with my wife folded. At the time, I didn't feel close to my daughters, so I didn't think about missing them. Then my ex-wife moved about five hundred miles away and remarried. I miss my girls terribly. I know that I made a big mistake by not spending time with them and my wife. Now the girls are getting close to their new stepdad, and that bothers me. I just wanted to be a good provider for them, but I've lost everything, and someone else is being the daddy for my girls.

Moving Beyond Divorce

Many times, we see the impact of two areas from the past affecting the current remarriage and stepfamily: past family dilemmas, and unresolved issues related to the divorce. These problems from the past may be manifested in the present by such problems as infidelity, alcoholism, and abuse (Shapiro, 1984). With careful assessment, however, therapists will usually find such patterns in the previous marriage as well or will discover that they are past family-of-origin issues. Children may be the scapegoats or problem carriers of these families. Again, this pattern has usually filtered through the family for several generations and existed in the previous marriage. Partners in a remarried couple may have not worked toward the resolution of these past agendas.

Because of cultural patterns and society's reinforcement, men and women demonstrate behavior that indicates that they have not attained psychological freedom from an ex-spouse. Men present money issues and what they describe as an inability to see their children as often as they would like to see them. These men have reneged on their relationships with their children and blame their ex-wives for their losses and current sadness. Anger is an easy emotion for males, and they may display it by screaming, yelling, bickering, or belittling their ex-wives. Therapists will observe that such men expend considerable energy thinking or talking about their ex-wives. At other times, these men act like spurned lovers or gladiators who have lost an important contest. They may marry someone else to make their ex-wives jealous, and such remarriages are doomed from their inception. Other men may resort to more toxic behavior, such as chemical abuse, a pattern of relationships lacking intimacy with many women, or withdrawal into work, where career goals become an obsession. Sometimes men continue to have sexual relations with ex-wives.

For women, society's expectations dictate different behavior. They are frequently angry but may be unwilling to confront their ex-husbands. They may continue to try to change their ex-husbands into lovable people, for the sake of the children. Because women are more passive with their anger than men are, they may turn it inward. These women will berate themselves and believe that they are unlovable or undesirable, despite the affection of their new husbands. They think that they are responsible for their children's happiness, particularly when they consider the trauma of divorce. These women see themselves as the pillars of the family, and divorce means that they have failed. Many women believe that they are responsible for the success of their new stepfamilies. Rather than lash out or share their anger and hurt with other family members, women feel guilty and seek to punish themselves.

When ex-spouses continue their emotional involvement, the remarital couple fails to develop functionally (Shapiro, 1984; Berman, 1988). The question of appropriate contact between ex-spouses is a gray area, however. Most observers would say that ex-mates should strive to maintain a friendship for their own well-being and for the sake of the children. This may be true, but we have discovered that in reality it is more rare than practical. Because of cultural and developmental considerations, most beginning remarriages have difficulty incorporating exspousal friendships into the stepfamily structure. Further, as we have said, the unfinished agendas between former partners may be more powerful and therefore more threatening than the exspouses are willing to acknowledge.

If the therapist suspects the presence of an unfinished

agenda between ex-spouses, then the former mate should be included in therapy. Sometimes therapists openly discuss the intimacy between ex-spouses. At other times, they may ask about such issues as parenting the biological children, in order to observe and assess the interactions between former mates:

> Sharon came into therapy depressed and complaining that she was unsure that her remarriage was going to survive. Her first husband had been an incompetent man who could barely hold a job. The marriage had gone through considerable ups and downs; indeed, after the divorce, the couple remarried and then divorced a second time. The second marriage between Sharon and her ex-husband produced a son, who was twelve at the time of therapy.
> After the second divorce, Sharon met Randy. According to Sharon, Randy loved her dearly, but it troubled her that he was unmotivated to seek higher goals. Their relationship got off to a rocky start. The day they were to leave Ohio and move to California, where Randy had a new job waiting, Sharon abruptly announced that she would not go: her son objected to her upcoming marriage to Randy and did not want to leave his current home, and Sharon decided that she should stay in Ohio for the sake of her son. Randy was upset. He could not understand Sharon's action, but because of his new job he went to California anyway. Ten months later, Sharon moved to California and married Randy, over the continued objections of her son. She was still not sure that the marriage was a wise choice, however. She felt that she might have been able to find someone smarter, more motivated, more handsome, and so on.

In the course of therapy, two themes related to Sharon's issues came to light. First, in her family of origin, her parents were rarely satisfied with her behavior. Sharon was not bad;

she was simply never quite good enough. That led to her belief that she could never reach her potential, nor could she find anyone to satisfy her. Second, Sharon was terrified of getting close. To her, intimacy meant the parental model: the closer spouses became, the more the man robbed the woman of her individuality, until she was little more than his slave. Sharon could not comprehend how a woman could share and be vulnerable in marriage and yet maintain her integrity and individuality.

Interventions had to be carefully formulated for Sharon, because she would thwart direct attempts. We had noticed that Sharon responded well to challenges and that she would act when she had a chance to defy her parents, because she resented their efforts to control her life. Thus, our interventions were designed to reinforce for Sharon that she was not experiencing intimacy with Randy because her parents did not wish it: if Sharon achieved a close and happy marriage, her parents would be threatened because they had been unable to do so. We also told Sharon that if she tried to defy them and move toward intimacy, they would attempt to sabotage her efforts. They did, in fact, make several sabotaging maneuvers during the therapeutic process, which reinforced the approach that we had taken in planning Sharon's interventions.

We also told Sharon that she might not be able to get close to men because it would hinder her relationship with her son. Certainly, Sharon believed that she had to shelter her son and remain close to him, since she knew what it was like to grow up without that support in her childhood. As a result, however, Sharon would not be ready for mature, vulnerable relationships.

As expected, Sharon responded to the challenge; however, we recognized that she truly lacked intimacy skills. Her attempts to get closer to Randy were often misguided and self-centered. We reframed these efforts as learned behaviors from her parents, thus giving her permission to excuse her mistakes.

Sometimes her relationship with her son was utilized to help her draw nearer to Randy. For example, Sharon felt that she had to protect her son from Randy, particularly when her son had not completed tasks or had done them poorly. Randy would correct the child in front of Sharon. Before therapy, Sharon defended her son vehemently, so that his maladaptive behavior continued. Randy would escalate his objections, and ultimately he and Sharon would fight, leaving the son free to do whatever he wished. The first level of intervention was for Sharon not to participate in these encounters between Randy and her son. She soon discovered that this drew Randy closer to her, but she still fought with him over his parenting methods. The second level of intervention was to have Sharon and Randy develop a list of responses to the boy's inappropriate behavior. Randy agreed with Sharon that they would both correct her son in the same way. This prevented Sharon from raising objections to Randy's attempts to discipline. Next, they agreed to support each other on parenting issues whether they actually agreed or not. Differences could be discussed only between the two of them in private.

In one session, Sharon told Randy that she was afraid that he would slip into her life as he got closer and closer to her son. Her fear was that Randy would take advantage of her as her parents had. She was scared to trust him. Through the interventions on parenting issues, Sharon learned about the source of her anger toward Randy when he corrected her son. She used the anger to cover her fear of commitment.

Without an emotional as well as a legal divorce, the biological parent in a stepfamily will become stagnant. In examining biological parents, the therapist may see grief behind overt anger and depression. Sometimes children demonstrate these emotions by imitating their parents or through a unique transference between parent and child:

> Jamie was nine years old when, without warning, his father left his mother for another woman. Jamie's mother fluctuated between anger and depression, often yelling about his father. After a while, Jamie modeled his mother's behavior when he visited his father. Jamie treated his father rudely, bombarding him with inappropriate questions. He also displayed aggression at school and eventually was referred for therapy by his school counselor.

During an initial session, Jamie's mother was calm and distant. At eleven years old, Jamie was tormenting his father so that his mother would appear "detached." When we questioned Jamie's mother about her relationship with his dad and her life since the divorce, she began to show some signs of emotion. Jamie's mother was reluctant to allow us to speak to the father about Jamie's behavior. We persisted despite her reluctance, saying that we needed to talk to the father in order to have a better understanding of Jamie's problems.

In the first session that the father attended, he discussed his ex-wife's emotions. From his perspective, she had never recovered from the ending of their marriage. He saw her as still angry, curt in her communications with him, and poisoning Jamie's mind against him. We also noticed, however, that Jamie's father reacted to Jamie's dysfunctional behavior by distancing himself from both Jamie and his ex-wife. He saw Jamie infreqently and became more involved with his remarriage, his wife's young children by her first marriage, and their new baby.

In planning our interventions, we noted that Jamie's mother had never expressed her grief over the end of her marriage. Instead, she hid her sadness in anger and used her son to get back at her ex-spouse. To bridge the gap between her emotions and her experience, we revealed our own feelings and reactions to the end of a relationship, discussing the sadness involved in looking at a relationship that is forever changed. We also observed her confused perceptions: that she had little worth because the relationship had failed, that her ex-husband was happier without her, that Jamie's father had planned for the marriage to end from the beginning, that she would be unable to enter another serious relationship because she could not understand men, that she preferred to be alone rather than in a relationship because all relationships are painful, and that she was physically unattractive and undesirable and so men would not be interested in her. As Jamie's mother began to understand her thoughts, she realized that her hurt was pulling her back into a past that she could not change. Gradually, she faced her future and knew that she could go forward.

We also helped Jamie and his father negotiate a contract to accomplish changes in their relationship. We said that Jamie's inappropriate behavior was pushing his father away. We also said that his father had a low level of commitment because he was unwilling to work through problems with his son, retreating instead. In one session, we encouraged Jamie's father to express his sadness about the ending of his first marriage, as well as his reasons for leaving. That was difficult for Jamie to hear. We also helped Jamie's father tell Jamie that not all relationships last, that his father had good reasons for leaving, and that he saw the divorce as a choice he had needed to make for himself. From that discussion, we helped Jamie see that he too would have challenging decisions to make in the future, decisions that might involve unhappiness for those around him. In their contract, Jamie and his father determined consequences for Jamie's maladaptive behavior. When Jamie's behavior was acceptable, they would spend more time together and engage in fun activities. Jamie's father began to become more involved in Jamie's schoolwork than he had been previously. He would call Jamie's teacher and check Jamie's homework.

Jamie's mom and dad remained argumentative, and so we encouraged them to stop talking to each other as much as possible. Instead, we instructed Jamie and his father to make their own arrangements, and then Jamie could transmit the information to his mother.

Through his discussions with both parents, Jamie also realized that he could control his behavior. He understood that he needed to respond and act from his own feelings rather than mimicking either of his parents. We reframed Jamie's anger and criticism of his father to indicate that he was disappointed in his father's lack of involvement with him. Jamie wanted more closeness with his father, but we explained that Jamie's behavior distances people, forcing them to set rules and consequences for him. Early in therapy, he insisted on testing this hypothesis, and the parents did set consequences. Jamie was surprised by the change in their response, and he quickly improved his behavior. Jamie also learned to see his mother as an adult who could control her own life herself instead of as an inept adult whom he had to care for. Removing Jamie from the rescuer role enabled him to have better peer relationships, and he began to reach out to peers and others for support. Finally, we taught Jamie to stop carrying messages between his parents and to relate to them in a one-to-one fashion. His parents were instructed to work out their own issues between themselves, without involving Jamie.

In Jamie's case, what had begun as a referral for his aggressive behavior in school was actually a case of grief and an emotionally incomplete divorce. Jamie's parents are not atypical. People are afraid of their feelings and seek to avoid them. Avoidance of the past often leads to a hasty remarriage. Such a remarriage is highly unstable, and the partners often end up seeking therapy. Determining the goals of therapy while working with a remarriage in which one or both of the partners may be rebounding from a divorce places the therapist in a difficult position. Once the grief work begins, the partners either will be forced to recognize that they do not belong together or will become even more entrenched in their essentially unhealthy relationship and continue their avoidance of pain.

It is interesting to note that therapists may mimic their clients' avoidances when working with a remarriage on the rebound. Therapists may use the excuse that a remarriage was too hasty in order to rationalize their own failure to do adequate work. As therapists help individuals and couples explore their past relationships and unresolved issues, they need to ascertain what the grief process means to them on a personal level. Questions to consider include the following:

- What reactions do the messages received from the grief process engage in the therapist? Does he or she have issues to resolve?
- If grief work is starting to push the marriage apart, how does the therapist handle this dilemma? Does she or he help the spouses separate or help them get closer?
- Does the therapist rationalize to avoid pain in the therapeutic

relationship? If counseling is not helping the couple stay
together, is it because the therapist is mimicking the failure
of his or her own past spousal relationship?
• Is the therapist comfortable sharing with the couple during
grief work? Can he or she move toward a closer bond with
the couple, to help the partners understand and break their
ties with the past?

We believe that grief work is one key to freeing couples
to be more intimate, but it requires considerable energy and
personal investment from therapists. They must have a true understanding of themselves, as well as a willingness to experience pain with their clients. In our supervision and training of
therapists, this is one of the most difficult concepts to teach effectively. The capacity to engage successfully in the grief process
often separates therapists who can help stepfamilies from those
who cannot.

The Biological Parent and the Ex-Spouse

The ex-spouse may be a hindrance to the healthy development
of a stepfamily. Triangulation can cause deep resentment on
the part of the new mate. It can also cause children to remain
maladaptive in the development of the new family. The therapist needs to assess several factors concerning the biological
parent and the ex-mate when developing interventions. First,
the therapist needs to know the involvement level of the ex-
spouse and the amount of time the ex-spouses have spent together
since the divorce. When a rebound is involved, it is likely that
the ex-spouse will be an active influence in the remarriage, and
that little processing of divorce issues and grief will have taken
place. A second factor to explore is whether the biological parent ever sought counseling for the original marriage. If so, what
was the outcome? What is the biological parent's understanding of the divorce? Third, the therapist must assess how the biological parent is functioning in the remarriage.

Some ex-spouses communicate reasonably well, and others
actually have good relationships that are truly friendships. Still

others have been able to settle disagreements, and at least communicate effectively about their children, but it is rare for therapists to see any of these individuals. In a random sample of cases taken from an outpatient psychiatric facility, an inpatient hospital, and a school–family–children's counseling center focusing on families with adolescents, nearly 52 percent of the stepfamilies we examined had severe difficulties with ex-spousal relationships, and 37 percent had moderate to severe impairment because of such relationships. Relatively few had only minor problems related to an ex-spouse's involvement in a stepfamily. In looking at the relationship between biological parents and their ex-mates, we have found several types of ex-spouses who are likely to seek triangulation with a former mate who has remarried (Martin and Martin, 1992).

The Angry Ex-Spouse

When this type of person is involved, the therapist must assess both the anger and the hurt of this person. Was anger part of a regular life-style for the ex-spouse before the divorce, or has it appeared only since them? Has this person said that he or she got a lousy deal in the settlement? Obviously, angry ex-spouses may demonstrate a variety of behaviors, but we have found several common ones:

- Refusing to pay child support in a regular and timely fashion
- Yelling and screaming during phone conversations
- Physically and emotionally hurting children by neglecting their needs
- Embarrassing the remarried ex-spouse in social situations
- Frequently harassing the remarried ex-spouse by threatening legal action or by taking him or her to court for an endless variety of adjustments to visitation rights and support payments
- Fighting over bills, especially those pertaining to the children
- Hassling about parenting issues

The angry ex-spouse engages the client in endless turmoil and frequent battles. To the client, some of the battles may seem worth fighting, but that response enables the angry ex-spouse to continue his or her involvement and triangulation. Therapists have the task of helping clients determine which battles are worth fighting and which they should remove themselves from. As with any other kind of maladaptive ex-spouse, clear boundaries are important; in fact, a maladaptive ex-spouse pushes the therapist to help the healthy client set such limits. Because an angry ex-spouse can hurt the children, the therapist may also need to help the custodial parent make difficult decisions affecting the amount of time the children spend with this individual. The custodial parent certainly has the right and duty to protect the children, but emotionally she or he believes that "removal" of the children deprives them of the other parent:

> Terri and her new husband, Daniel, came to counseling because they thought that her adolescent son, Oliver, was not receiving sufficient attention from his biological father, Bob. Oliver's behavior in school was worsening, and Terri thought there might be a connection between it and her problems with her ex-spouse.
>
> Oliver had been born in Miami. Bob drank a lot and drifted from one job to another, telling Terri that this was simply the Miami way of life. Since their divorce, Bob had also remarried, and he and his wife now had a baby. The birth of this child had seemed to diminish Bob's interest in Oliver even more, according to Terri.
>
> Shortly before the therapy began, Bob had failed to acknowledge Oliver's birthday with either a call or a present. Terri and Daniel noticed that at that point Oliver's behavior became more maladaptive in school. His grades went down. He did not want to go to school. He was angry at home and misbehaved by not listening to directions and by disobeying instructions.
>
> Terri had tried to involve Bob with Oliver throughout the separation and divorce and her

single-parent days, and she had continued her efforts since her remarriage. She wrote to him about upcoming events and called him to encourage him to contact Oliver. When the new family traveled back to Miami to see her parents, she made sure that Oliver had time to spend with Bob. When she could, she sent Oliver to Miami by himself to visit his grandparents. During those visits, she arranged for her parents to take Oliver to see Bob.

Terri and Daniel had been married less than one year. Their marriage was healthy. Daniel had been integrating well with Oliver before the birthday incident, although he said that sooner or later Oliver's poor relationship with Bob would cause problems for him as the stepfather. Besides Oliver's overt problems at school, both Terri and Daniel wanted help because they did not want Oliver's problems to hurt their new stepfamily.

The first area we focused on was Terri's guilt. She felt guilty about leaving Bob because he was so helpless. She had grown tired of his staggering in late and drunk or not coming home at all because he was with other women. Despite Bob's obvious abuse of their marital relationship, Terri still felt that perhaps she should not have abandoned him. She was sad that he had not pulled his life together and that she had been unable to solve his problems for him. In therapy, Terri realized that she had a right to a better life, and she saw how her continued caretaking of Bob could threaten her marriage to Daniel. In looking at her family-of-origin patterns, Terri discerned how she had been taught that taking care of a man meant that she was all right as a woman. Working with Terri and Daniel, we helped Terri understand that she had true strengths and did not have to feel incomplete without a man in her life. Daniel had recognized those strengths during their courtship and worked to nurture and support Terri's development.

Together, they began to see that protecting Oliver from his father was not the proper course of action. It was painful for Terri to see Oliver hurt, but she began to remove herself from situations and dialogues with Bob. She and Oliver talked about who his father was and what he had been like when they had lived together in Miami. Terri helped Oliver realize what he could realistically expect in a relationship with his father. After Terri stopped intervening, Oliver acted out some of his anger with his father against Daniel, but he admitted eventually that Bob was not very interested in him as a person.

> During therapy, Oliver made a trip to Miami to see his grandparents and to visit his father. Bob was off drinking and playing pool at the local tavern almost the entire time; Oliver was left with his stepmother, who gave most of her attention to her new baby. It was an awful trip, according to Oliver, but a freeing experience. Shortly after his return, Oliver's behavior at home and at school improved dramatically.
>
> Bob, however, began to display intense anger when he realized that both Terri and Oliver were decreasing their efforts to stay connected with him. While Oliver had been in Miami, his father's brief contacts included yelling and threats. Bob accused Oliver of failing him as a son because he liked Daniel. After the Miami trip, Bob made numerous angry phone calls. Initially, Terri would take the calls and tell Bob that his behavior was inappropriate. She would say that he was welcome to call back when he could behave appropriately, and then she would hang up. The result was that although Bob did not call frequently, he was at least sober and conversational when he did.
>
> When his phone calls were thwarted, Bob turned to angry letters. With Oliver's permission, we suggested that Terri screen Bob's letters because they were upsetting to Oliver. Terri felt bad to be reading the letters, but she knew that it was better for Oliver to see only the appropriate parts. Letters

that were vindictive and angry were returned with a note explaining that only communications of a positive nature would be given to Oliver. Bob stopped writing.

Daniel was encouraged to be supportive of Terri's actions and to continue the level of parenting he had already initiated before therapy. We instructed Daniel to let Oliver sort out his conflicting feelings of loyalty and disloyalty to his biological father before attempting to advance the stepfather-stepson relationship. At first, Oliver dismissed much of his relationship with Daniel. After his visit to his father, however, he initiated a closer bond with his stepfather. At that point, both Terri and Daniel were advised to set boundaries as united parents for Oliver. Oliver's maladaptive behavior was reframed as indicating a need for firm, consistent boundaries. When Terri and Daniel did not set boundaries, Oliver thought that they did not care about him. Sadly, Bob wrote approximately a year later that he did not wish to continue child support and asked whether Daniel would adopt Oliver. Daniel, Oliver, and Terry agreed, and this decision has appeared to benefit them.

The Helpless Ex-Spouse

Helpless ex-spouses do not make decisions. They give the appearance of being confused and incompetent. They act as if they require the assistance of a parent for the rest of their lives. These individuals may be passive-aggressive. If they are, however, they have usually mastered the subtleties of that pattern. Helpless ex-spouses may exhibit an underlying sadness because they miss the direction and assistance they had in the marriage. Other kinds of behavior may include the following:

- Missing appointments with children
- Being unable to solve minor household problems concerning plumbing, painting, and so on

- Forgetting to take needed medications
- Losing things
- Being fired from a job particularly because of irresponsible behavior
- Eating poorly, with associated ill health
- Neglecting physical needs, so that appearance suffers
- Abusing substances

Helpless ex-spouses stay connected with their former mates by pushing for assistance with problem solving and care-taking. As a client withdraws from an unhealthy relationship with a helpless ex-spouse, the latter's condition worsens. This may increase difficulties in a newly formed stepfamily. Helpless ex-spouses may go to extremes to reconnect with their former mates. The goals of therapy in such cases must include helping clients achieve awareness and understanding of manipulative behavior, particularly its damaging effects on children. Therapists should also work to help clients recognize that their ex-spouses can choose whether to remain helpless or to become productive.

The Uninvolved or Nonchalant Ex-Spouse

Some individuals pretend that the divorce was of little concern to them. They pay scant attention to their children, sometimes using their careers as an excuse. The uninvolved ex-spouse is good at avoiding both conflict and intimacy. As a result, the custodial parent gets cast in the role of trying to protect the children from disappointment by setting up visits and other contacts with the noncustodial parent. These ex-spouses are erratic. Sometimes they keep appointments arranged for them by their former mates and are delightful with their children. At other times, they do not keep appointments or, if they do, are uninterested or disgusted at having to be present. In actuality, these individuals are immature and narcissistic and have genuine difficulty with intimacy.

What frequently complicates matters for stepfamilies affected by the actions of uninvolved ex-spouses is that these individuals may have stature in the community through their commitment to their careers. If an uninvolved ex-spouse is affluent, she or he may receive praise from associates, and that prestige is confusing to children struggling with lack of attention and affection. Although these individuals may be able to provide adequate financial support, they often refuse to acknowledge the emotional needs of their children.

The Sad or Depressed Ex-Spouse

Some individuals are devastated by a divorce and do not recover. Whenever children come to visit, these ex-spouses are crying. By the time the children return to the custodial parent, everyone is sad. It is difficult for younger children to confront this situation. Older children, however, can see how manipulative this parent is. The sad ex-spouse needs intensive therapy but refuses to seek help. When this person's needs are not met, anger may surface, and behavior typical of angry ex-spouses will begin. Sad ex-spouses can also be manipulative enough to threaten suicide or other overtly destructive acts. When clients are involved with sad ex-spouses, they experience guilt, as if they have destroyed these people's lives. Obviously, continued involvement coupled with such guilt creates an unhealthy dynamic in a remarriage.

These four types of ex-spouses may display behavior from more than one category, thereby complicating an already difficult situation. What keeps clients who have attempted to go forward with their lives connected to ex-mates such as these? We have found three major "hooks" that catch clients seeking to establish healthy relationships with their ex-spouses (Martin & Martin, 1985).

First, if one admits the ex-spouse's faults, one has to admit one's own, too. Admitting one's faults is not a favorite adult activity. At certain stages in a divorce, each spouse will criticize the other. Once the divorce is final and a remarriage has taken place, an honest evaluation of an ex-mate demands an equally honest evaluation of oneself. Clients need to recognize that the reasons why they were attracted to their former spouses often had to do with those people's worst traits. In other words, they were codependent and their own faults complemented those of their mates.

Second, feeling good about the past is a way of avoiding commitment in the present. Commitment scares individuals in stepfamilies, and spouses may avoid it by maintaining connections with former mates. To do that, however, individuals must pretend that the past was much more lovely than it actually was. Ex-spouses can provide multitudes of excuses. Keeping an ex-spouse active in a new stepfamily unit enables the clients to withhold intimacy in the new remarriage.

Third, refusing to face the reality of the previous relationship is a way of avoiding change or happiness in the present relationship. Sometimes it is easier to blame the current spouse or the children for dilemmas than to recognize dysfunctional patterns from a previous relationship. Therapists can help clients understand the true nature of the failure of former marriages. Understanding the problems of the past means being able to see unhealthy patterns that have been carried forward into the present. Because individuals want to avoid that discomfort and that reponsibility, many remarried couples do not truly discuss the behavioral patterns of their previous relationships. In our assessment of couples, we question them about their former marriages, to enable them and their new mates to acquire a reasonable image of the past.

Helping Clients Set Rules for Ex-Spousal Relationships

In our research, we have found that clients and their ex-spouses disagree the most about their children, who often get put in the middle and may be used as spies or confidants. Children may feel guilt because they do not spend much time with one of their parents, or they may be interrogated after a visit. Our position is that a relationship with an ex-spouse must be defined for the benefit of the children, not for the preferences or convenience of former mates. To that end, we have several rules that we share with clients for setting boundaries with their ex-spouses.

1. *Remind clients that they are no longer married to their ex-spouses.*

Efforts to remain connected in ways not involving the children are inappropriate. There is no further obligation between the adults, other than that associated with the mutual raising of the children. Clients need to keep a proper perspective on the relationship with a former mate so that it does not interfere with the remarriage.

2. *Ex-spouses are responsible for their own behavior and in charge of building and maintaining their own relationships with the children.* One parent may seek to protect the children from disappointment by trying to keep an ex-mate involved. We believe that children realize, although they may wish to pretend otherwise, when one parent is not emotionally interested in them. No matter how hard clients try to keep their ex-mates actively involved with the children, if the effort does not come from these ex-spouses themselves, the children will eventually be disappointed. If an ex-spouse is unwilling to make an effort to keep a relationship going, it will die. This is particularly true when a custodial parent enables and tries to keep the noncustodial parent involved with the children, despite a continual demonstration of noninvolvement through uncaring behavior. The therapist must help establish direct communication between children and their biological parents, without the influence of an ex-spouse, when that is age-appropriate and feasible.

3. *Clients need to establish a sense of finality with their former relationships.* Sometimes custody and other legal agreements between ex-spouses are deliberately written in a vague fashion, to perpetuate fighting. For example, one spouse may be financially hurt by an agreement and could go to court and settle the matter but refuses to do so. Instead, this person complains bitterly about the unfairness of the system and the poor deal received at the hands of the ex-mate. Therapeutic interventions may be thwarted as individuals remain in continual turmoil and conflict. The remarried couple can endlessly bring up issues around the unsatisfactory settlement instead of confronting their own dysfunction. We choose not to reinforce the unhealthy behavior of ex-spouses and we help clients set clear boundaries. We teach couples how to define their relationships with an ex-spouse through determining what they want in the relationship

and what behavior they will accept. Sometimes clients are shocked that they can tell people what they want in a relationship. Jack, who was continually attempting to please people at work and at home, fit this description. His marriage ended because his wife "found another man," but she kept demanding things of Jack, and he would not say no. Even his fifteen-year old son said, "Dad is just too nice. My mom takes advantage of him." In therapy, Jack admitted that he still loved his ex-wife, and that this love kept him from finding other relationships. As he experienced his grief, he began to realize the emptiness of his life and the manipulativeness of his ex-wife. With the support of his son, Jack began to stop doing tasks for his wife and listening to her on the phone. Although she became angry, Jack became aware of her manipulativeness, primarily because of his son's openness. Jack and his son became closer, and eventually Jack began dating another woman.

4. *Clients cannot change their ex-mates.* In therapy, we work to help individuals learn that people are responsible for their own choices. No one controls the life of another. For success in stepfamilies, ex-spousal relationships need to be assessed for what they are: relationships with former mates for the sake of biological children. They are relationships outside the new stepfamily. Therapists must work to create an environment where the biological parent and the new stepparent focus on their own marital relationship. Individuals in remarried couples need to choose their new spouses over ex-spouses. That choice must be affirmed daily. The single greatest cause of chaos and destruction in stepfamilies is ex-spouses' choice of each other instead of their new partners.

8

Supporting
Stepmothers and Stepfathers

More communication problems, negative family processes, distancing between family members, and tendencies to form coalitions have been found in stepfamilies than in traditional families (Bray, 1988; Hetherington, 1987). When parental structure is lacking in a stepfamily, the therapist may intervene to engage a stepparent as a stabilizing element. The hope is that this person will assume parental duties, thereby helping the marital couple to function in an executive capacity in the family. It is important to realize, however, that the poorly defined role of the stepparent may actually contribute to the extent of dysfunction (Giles-Sims, 1984).

One area where this is noticeable is the stepparent-stepchild relationship (Sauer & Fine, 1988). The emotional connection between these individuals is usually lacking, and this causes a natural distancing. Stepparents may not be as understanding as necessary with their stepchildren, and stepchildren may not give stepparents the freedom to make mistakes (Jolin, 1981). Both may have unrealistic expectations. At other times, they may care for each other but not know how to show their affection. Stepchildren may want to be close to their stepparents but be afraid of being disloyal to their biological parents, and so they react with anger, to mask their true feelings and confusion. Stepparents can perceive those actions as rejection and pull even farther away.

For individuals in a single-parent family, a future stepparent may initially seem to be a savior who can help the families return to an anticipated level of normality. Just as the stepparent-stepchild relationship often presents unexpected difficulties, however, the parenting relationship between the adults may also be challenging. Again, the poorly defined role of the stepparent contributes to the confusion. Initially, biological parents may want help from their new mates, particularly in disciplining children. Soon, however, the biological parents may discover that the relationships with their children will have to change if their spouses are going to parent. Instead of being supportive of their partners' roles, they may begin to sabotage stepparents' efforts as a way of avoiding changes in the cross-generational relationships they have with their biological children.

In general, then, parenting stepchildren is a major task and stressor in new stepfamilies. Bray and Berger (1990) have determined that it may take two to four years for stepparents to be accepted as parental figures by children in stepfamilies. That this adjustment process is complex is further demonstrated by Bray's research (1988), indicating that stepchildren between the ages of six and nine have more behavioral problems after six months of remarriage than comparable children in intact families. This study also reflects that after two and a half years of remarriage there are no differences in the behavioral adjustment of stepchildren between eight and a half and eleven and a half and that of children in intact families. After five years of remarriage, however, stepchildren between eleven and fourteen again have more behavioral problems than children entering adolescence in intact families (Bray & Berger, 1990). While some difficulties persist, the most problematic period for stepfamilies appears to be the first two years of transition from the postdivorce family — the same period during which stepparents are seeking to define their roles. In later remarriage, as stepfamilies become more stabilized, workable patterns of family relationships and processes emerge. Nevertheless, therapists must remain aware that many of these patterns continue to distinguish stepfamilies from intact families even five to seven years after remarriage (Bray, 1988).

Transactions Toward a Healthy Environment

To help families progress toward a more caring and open environment, we incorporate several guidelines into therapy (Martin & Martin, 1985). These become part of our transactions with the family unit.

Treating Others with Respect

We try to stop behavior that demonstrates lack of courtesy and civility (such as screaming, yelling, and criticizing). The term *respect* changes definition over the course of therapy. At first, we use it as an antonym of overtly offensive behavior. Later, the definition becomes more subtle. For example, while dysfunctional stepfamilies are out of control in one sense, in another they have stricter boundaries and are less tolerant of members' mistakes. Biologically related individuals can readily borrow one another's property. If they treat it disrespectfully, they will be annoyed with one another. If steprelated individuals borrow property and treat it carelessly, an escalated encounter will ensue.

Criticism is another arena where respect is important. The individual in a stepfamily is often insecure, struggling with guilt, and living with a fragile ego because of past hurts and loss. Biologically related individuals may be able to criticize each other or reflect a sarcastic attitude with each other and the message is understood. Steprelated individuals have a less secure footing with each other. Messages can easily be misunderstood. In therapy, teaching appropriate communication skills is essential.

Limiting Comparisons

Too often, stepfamilies create myths around biological parents. Members try to push stepparents to be like one of the biological parents, yet stepparents' attempts to prematurely replicate the closeness between a biological parent and a child during early remarriage are associated with poorer outcomes for children and more problems in the stepparent-stepchild relationship (Bray

& Berger, 1990). Children cannot be pushed to care for a step-parent in the same way they care for a significant biological relative. Instead, family members need to learn to see each other as individuals and give their relationships a chance to develop.

Establishing Places Where Members Can Have Their Own Identity

All members of a stepfamily need to have a place, even a small space in a shared room, to be separate from the rest of the family and be by themselves. Setting aside space for each member sends the message that all are valued and accepted. In fact, stepfamilies need to consider the environment and its impact more than traditional families do. We suggest to stepfamilies that they relocate to a neutral home if possible and, if not, that they at least paint and redecorate as much as they can. They also need to reduce furniture and mementos from the past.

New rules about personal property and family operations need to be made. Biological members tend to assume that life will continue as in the past. Those assumptions may bring them into direct conflict with stepparents or stepsiblings taking the same approach, but on a different path. We help stepfamilies discuss rules for the living environment. The workability of these rules and final arrangements will be decided by the parents. Topics include chores, neatness, borrowing items from one another, eating food from the refrigerator, table manners, greetings to one another, routine expenses, and the use of tools, stereos, electricity, hot water, cars, and so on.

Communicating Openly

When training therapists, we present the analogy that a stepfamily is somewhat similar to a group in a therapeutic environment. In the initial stages of its formation, the group is frequently conflictual as the members try to express their feelings. They may attack the leader. At this time, the leader's job is to step back, listen to feedback, and integrate it without being defensive. In this way, the leader helps the members realize that they are part of the problem and part of the solution. In a stepfamily, either the biological parent or the stepparent may be the leader and may be under attack. The therapist must assess which individual is capable of filling this role. Once the leader is identified, the therapist can help this adult learn to foster the sharing of feelings in the family. As in any other effective group process, adults should be respected. Yelling, abusive language, and dumping too many problems at one time are ineffective ways to communicate.

Lois, her new husband, Bill, and her teenage son, John, show how the leader role works in a stepfamily. Lois related the following events:

> Bill told my son, John, that he could not use the car for a couple of days because he came in two hours past his curfew. John had a fairly good reason for being late, but he could have avoided it. I was out of town at the time. When I got home, John complained bitterly about how unfair Bill was. He felt that Bill had no right to set rules for him. We'd been married only a few months — and, actually, I had been afraid to go out of town, because I knew Bill and John would probably fight. At this point, I figured I should try what we talked about in our last session: I mean feedback. So I asked John to sit down, and I sat down and let him talk. I didn't interrupt him. I could tell he was angry, and he went on and on. Sometimes I would say, "I know you are angry," or "I hear what you are saying," but I didn't lecture him or contradict him. It's not that I didn't want to. Part of the time I wanted to yell at him and tell him what a jerk he was being. But in another way, I wanted him to defend himself; I wanted him to believe he had a worthwhile viewpoint.
>
> After he finished, he calmed down. I told him I would repeat back to him what I had heard, so I could check to make sure I had gotten it. We got

through that step, and then I told him that I felt his concerns were a family matter, which we needed to discuss that evening. During the afternoon, I found Bill, and we chatted about his view of what had happened. I knew it was important for me to support him. As Bill talked about what he saw happening in the family, it made sense to me, and I knew that he had been right to ground John for a few days. John had broken a rule, set beforehand, and the consequence was grounding. We all knew that.

Later that evening, we sat down for a family discussion. I stayed out of it and let John and Bill talk. John even shared his anger, although he was calmer with Bill than he had been with me. Both of them tried to pull me in, but I was determined to stay out of it. I told them I was there to listen. In the end, I said that I supported Bill because we had family rules and he had fairly applied one of them. I also gave John a few alternatives he could have taken to avoid the problem. Bill suggested some ideas to John, too, like calling to let us know what was going on. John was upset, of course, but he did realize that if he broke a rule, he needed a strong reason, and he needed to let us know in advance, not after the fact.

Communication in Lois's family was typical of that in many stepfamilies—there was an overabundance of an emotional, conflictual tone. In sessions with the family, we had been working on conflict communication. Many therapists simply assume that it is possible to have members of stepfamilies calmly share with each other. Our clinical experience demonstrates that this is unrealistic. Stepfamily communications tend to be either highly conflictual or extremely avoidant of conflict. Thus, the therapist must assess the structure of the family and teach members how to overcome their dysfunctional pattern.

Understanding Effective Communication

In stepfamilies that are conflictual, there is heightened emotion. Conversations are loud, sarcastic, attacking, and hurtful and contain metamessages. The aim for therapists is to reduce the volume of the conversation without denying or discarding the message, particularly the feelings behind the message. Family members can be taught such responses as "I would like to hear what you are saying, but I can't hear you through that volume." Another example would be "Let's sit down, and let me hear what you have to say." Therapists also need to teach members that when they recognize abusive language or attacking, hurtful messages, they can respond with something like "I recognize that you are angry. I would like to hear what you are saying, but if you continue to say abusive things to me, I'll have to leave the room or end the conversation." The goal is to reduce the intensity and yet demonstrate a desire to hear the message.

When the family is avoidant of conflict, the therapist's initial goal is to push family members toward sharing with one another. Conflict-avoidant stepfamilies are controlling. They have rules inhibiting self-expression. As family members begin to realize that they have no say in their lives, self-concept disintegrates. These are families with manipulative adults. In dealing with such families, therapists need to assess family-of-origin issues. Conflict-avoidant parents usually grew up in families that were either highly conflictual or verbally and physically abusive. In adulthood, they react to their childhood experiences by polarizing to the opposite extreme. Occasionally therapists find parents who grew up in conflict-avoidant families and are simply living out what they learned in their youth.

For conflict-avoidant stepfamilies, the therapeutic process involves identifying feelings and learning to share in a systematic way. Individuals in a conflict-avoidant stepfamily are afraid that sharing their true feelings will result in the dissolution of the family. It takes time for them to learn that with directness and openness the family actually will grow closer. Fortunately for the therapist, no matter what the presenting problem is, such a family usually realizes that something is not working. It is important not to blame parents for their reactions to what they learned in their families of origin. Instead, their behaviors can be explained as mechanisms that they believe will help them survive.

Conflict-avoidant stepfamilies can exhibit many variations. For example, the children may be conflict-intensive instead of conflict-avoidant. In such a case, the children push the parents toward increased involvement. Therapists can reframe the children's behavior as seeking intimacy. Therapists will also see this in couples where one spouse is conflict-avoidant and the other is conflict-intensive; then the aim is to work toward a balance. This is a particularly difficult combination, because for each partner the reaction of the spouse solidifies this initial position. For the conflict-intensive person, dealing with a spouse who completely withdraws indicates that a conflictual approach is working, at least on some level. The conflict-avoidant spouse runs away, thinking it is crazy and impossible to fight. Therefore, this spouse stays entrenched in withdrawal.

A good starting point in working with a conflict-avoidant stepfamily is to have members stop reading one another's minds. In therapy, they are permitted to act only on what they know — on messages that they actually receive. This creates a crisis in the family because individuals must face one another's behavior openly and directly. Instead of sneaking around and guessing feelings and meanings, members will have conflicts. As the family members learn to discuss and resolve conflicts, they will also learn that they are a part of relationships that are worth working through.

Setting Rules and Developing Traditions for the New Family Unit

Stepfamilies must create an environment for themselves that is truly theirs. This includes accommodating the presence of children who move in and out of a family's surroundings and who may be put in the position of bringing back old family messages. It involves the new family in developing family traditions and celebrations for holidays and other special occasions. Having a way to celebrate birthdays, for instance, gives the family identity. Children begin to see the stepfamily as a unit when they can say, "This is how we do it in my family."

Discussing Sexuality

When stepfamilies are formed, it is not uncommon for adolescents and adults to experience sexual attraction toward one another. In fact, these feelings are normal in the early stages of remarriage, before bonding and traditional boundaries have formed. If they are left unaddressed, they can have detrimental effects on the family (Martin & Martin, 1992). Members with such feelings may shift from simple, normal attraction to unhealthy fantasizing about a relationship. Rationalizations, such as "It's not like she was my real child" or "He's not my real brother" can lead people to act on the feelings. The destructive power of incest is obvious.

Unaddressed sexuality can hinder stepfamily development in another, more subtle way. Initially, a stepparent may be friendly and appropriately affectionate with a stepchild. Once sexual feelings occur, however, the same parent may presume that he or she is guilty of breaking a powerful taboo. In healthy stepfamilies, these experiences can be discussed and dealt with constructively. In dysfunctional stepfamilies, such conversations will not take place. Instead, the guilt-ridden stepparent will probably withdraw (Visher & Visher, 1988). One such withdrawal mechanism is increased criticism of the stepchild, which serves to distance the stepparent from this child. Withdrawal and distancing are harmful to the bonding that should be taking place. Furthermore, if the stepchild involved is an adolescent already confronting insecurity in the struggle for independence, the stepparent's distancing may be interpreted as rejection. The adolescent stepchild is probably beginning to enjoy the attention of this stepparent, and without warning or explanation that attention is replaced with criticism.

Therapists need to help stepfamilies confront the sexuality of older members and define appropriate family behaviors. The therapeutic environment is a good place to begin such discussions.

One way to approach the subject is to treat it as something that "might" occur, rather than something that actually has occurred. Then family members can voice their opinions in relative safety, and the therapist can guide them to see the normality of the situation. Once the subject has been introduced, the stepfamily can set dress codes, bathroom and bedroom etiquette, and rules designed to circumvent situations where inappropriate behavior could develop. For example, scanty dress may be deemed unacceptable outside an individual's room, and everyone could be required to knock before entering a room. The therapist can also help the marital couple set limits on the amount of time that teenage stepsiblings of the opposite sex spend alone together.

While respect, communication rules, and sexuality are certainly generic issues for stepparents and the stepfamily, there are also issues that are specific to either the stepmother or the stepfather. Some of these are role-related issues, primarily influenced by our culture; others are unique to stepfamilies.

Stepmothers' Dilemmas

Think of a stepmother, and what comes to mind? Obviously, a Cinderella-type stepmother, who is self-centered and cruel to her stepchildren. In our experience, we have found that certain stepfamily structures actually push for this type of stepmother relationship. Her role is so confused, and others place such unrealistic and contradictory expectations on her, that she may easily withdraw in anger and hurt (McGoldrick, Anderson, & Walsh, 1989).

Conflictual Nurturing

The difficulty begins with the societal norms that mothers, biological or otherwise, have responsibility for nurturing in the family. This does not change whether women work in the home, outside the home, or in both places. The caring aspect of motherhood may conflict with the desire for a mother who is an assertive family organizer. Stepfamilies also expect stepmothers to handle inherent communication problems in the family (Skeen,

Robinson, & Flake-Hobson, 1984). Thus, stepmothers need to model good communication skills, but doing that can trigger additional problems. Good communication will increase conflict and conflict resolution, with the result of greater intimacy, and intimacy is scary for newly formed stepfamilies.

Communicating

Stepmothers are supposed to be assertive and hold their families together. At the same time, men do not want "their" power questioned. When threatened, they may sabotage their wives' efforts, whether nurturing or assertive. A stepmother may also find herself torn between two men: her current spouse and her ex-spouse. The societal norm for women, in their nurturing capacity, is that they are caretakers of men; thus, a woman may try to please both men and bounce like a ball between them. An additional burden is placed on stepmothers when they are taught how to be expressive to their children and husbands. When others are upset with them, these women can be left with a sense of guilt. Rather than face negative feelings or rejection from stepchildren, stepmothers may rationalize that the children's behavior is worse than it truly is. This allows stepmothers to distance.

Husbands' Support

It is vitally important for men to support their wives in the role of stepmother, but men typically shy away from this, often because they are the noncustodial parents and see their children part-time. When a visit occurs, they want no conflict. These men also believe that their wives should work out the relationships on their own: that is part of a wife's duties as the family caretaker.

When men withhold support from their wives, their families will not work. The reason stems from the children's image of their stepmother as a depriver when she sets rules and limits. One way to make certain that rules will not work is for parents to disagree about them or not be equally committed to them.

Another way to guarantee failure is to avoid setting and explaining rules beforehand. The result is chaos. Children continually push for limits but do not care for the stepmother when she sets them without her husband's support. She feels rejected and withdraws, thereby signaling to the children that she is not interested in a relationship with them.

Distancing

With these confusing, contradictory signals swirling in a new stepfamily, it is not surprising that stepmothers find the experience defeating and that they struggle for their survival. Bonding between adults and children is not instantaneous. Children may remind a stepmother of her husband's ex-wife. They were raised by her, may look like her, and may have mannerisms similar to hers. Without the full support of her husband, a new stepmother feels that she is disliked and not respected and in a house full of foreigners. She may also resent that a child with past behavioral problems has now been dumped on her. She may be confused about what level of involvement is appropriate, particularly if she has not had children of her own and if her stepchildren are close to her in age.

Expressing Anger

Another complexity in the stepmother-stepchild relationship is that women are traditionally criticized for expressing anger, yet as this relationship begins to grow there will be conflict. Often the children and the husband in a stepfamily view the wife and stepmother as explosive. In reality, they are unwilling to listen to her, and they dismiss her feelings. Competition for love is common in stepfamilies. Some of a stepmother's anger may involve her feelings that the children are closer to her husband than she is. When the father is not supporting the stepmother, her jealousy will grow.

Fear of Children's Affection

Stepmothers can easily develop something like an inferiority complex with respect to stepchildren. These women know their societal image, and they are quite sensitive about what the children are thinking (McGoldrick, Anderson, & Walsh, 1989). Thus, the stepchildren may be treated with a distant, kid-gloves approach. In one session with a stepfamily in which both adults had children in the house, one of the stepchildren said to her new stepmother, "You yell at Johnny [a biological child], but you don't yell at me. It's okay to yell at me, too." Laughter followed, but it was evident that the child wanted the same rules and boundaries, as a sign of caring. Yelling may not be appropriate or ideal, but the child understood that her stepmother loved Johnny.

In looking at issues for stepmothers in the family structure, responsibility is a primary focus. Responsibility takes many forms. Children, for instance, may become resentful if they believe their stepmother has taken over the family and their biological father has little say in matters. The biological father may actually be fostering this role for the stepmother, rather than accepting responsibility himself in certain areas. Another possibility is that a stepmother may make unflattering comparisons between her biological children and her stepchildren in such areas of responsibility as homework and family chores. Stepfamilies often promote an organizing, assertive role for stepmothers, and a stepmother may become angry when children push her in a family matter that she feels responsible for. Confronting issues of responsibility usually provides a vehicle for therapists to teach stepfamilies how to negotiate.

Defining Affection

Another key issue involving stepmothers is the level of affection in the stepfamily. Determining that level is often a responsibility of stepmothers. How affectionate a parent is may depend on several factors: how affectionate the parent is by nature and experience; how receptive the children are to affection; and the children's background concerning the level of affection in their family of origin. Were they abused or in a situation where they did not receive affection? If so, it may feel awkward and uncomfortable to them.

If older children are close in age to a stepparent of the

opposite gender, the therapist also needs to discuss openly any sexual issues that may arise. For example, Roger said in one session that he had noticed his teenage son, Eric, behaving oddly around the house since breaking up with his girlfriend. Roger's new wife, Charlene, was only eight years older than Eric. Roger noted that Eric appeared uncomfortable if Charlene was only partially dressed, particularly when going to or from the bathroom. The therapist brought up the idea of sexuality. He confronted the couple with the possibility that Eric, without the companionship of his girlfriend, had become attracted to Charlene. She laughed at the idea and did not believe it could be true. At the therapist's direction, Roger asked Eric about his feelings. Eric replied that it would be easier for him if Charlene covered herself and kept the door closed.

Stepmothers need some basic support mechanisms if they are to survive in their new stepfamilies. We use these guidelines in our clinical work to help family structure develop functionally (Martin & Martin, 1983, 1992).

1. If stepmothers spend the majority of their time with children, they need to have a parental role with the authority to exercise parental rights.
2. The father needs to remain involved and must not be allowed to create personal distance through work or other pursuits.
3. The stepfamily needs to create a structure for discussion. Stepmothers can be helpful by pursuing their nurturing role and promoting open sharing of feelings and concerns.
4. Therapists must realize that if a stepmother becomes disheartened, the family unit will disintegrate. It is critical that the stepmother be encouraged and supported to take an active, involved role in the family.

Stepfathers' Dilemmas

Research findings are beginning to indicate that stepfathers have a more important role in stepfamilies than was previously recognized, partly because there are more stepfathers than stepmothers.

In our society, women usually retain custody of their children in the divorce process. Therefore, their husbands face the likelihood of parenting another man's children after they remarry. Stepfathers are used to the traditional role of the distant, disciplinarian parent (Stern, 1984). Our clinical experience has shown us that few are willing to make the commitment needed to be a strong, positive influence in the stepfamily structure. Stepfathers' early expressions of emotional closeness and affection may meet with sullen, rejecting responses from children. This often results in unfortunate, hostile withdrawal by stepfathers. Hetherington's findings (1987) illustrate this dynamic, revealing that most stepfathers during early remarriage were disengaged, adult-oriented parents who were easily angered by the demands of their stepchildren.

Discipline

With young children, a stepfather's job is not as difficult as when teenagers are involved. Younger children are more willing to get close to a caring, interested adult. They have fewer feelings of disloyalty and other emotional baggage. The problems between stepfathers and younger children are related more to such parenting issues as discipline. Another source of difficulty is biological mothers' unwillingness to permit their new husbands and their children to get close. With open discussion, these issues can usually be resolved.

With adolescents, however, the stepfather-stepchild relationship is far more complex. Adolescents are seeking independence and are often rebellious and troublesome to biological parents. Their conflicts with their stepfathers typically involve territory and discipline. Stepfathers who expect to be able to develop a relationship with teenagers without conflict are naïve. On the contrary, the relationship between a stepfather and an adolescent stepchild can bring about the failure of the stepfamily and the remarriage. Many men enter remarriage with the fantasy that this time the marriage will be happy and problems with the children will be negligible. They believe that they have learned from the past and that this time they are wise enough to avoid previous mistakes. Such optimism will fade rapidly. Vito, for example, had not anticipated conflicts with his two stepsons. He said, "When I came into my wife's family, I wasn't ready for the fighting. I had young girls myself and they had never given me trouble. These boys were one problem after another." Vito did not understand why his stepsons were so rejecting. "Heck, I was the only father in the neighborhood. Their real dad couldn't have cared less. He never came around, never gave them money or anything. I worked my hide off to help them get a decent life, and all I ever got were gripes and complaints. My wife wasn't any better. She never supported me, and now I'm fed up with it."

Disengagement

Stepfathers' disengagement is a major consideration in therapy. By the time stepfamilies enter therapy, children and stepfathers alike are angry and hurt, and both have learned to distance from their feelings. Neither pushes to achieve closeness in the face of conflict and rejection. In fact, each has hiding places in the family unit to avoid connection. In assessing these families, therapists often discover that the children are virtually absent from the family. They spend hours watching TV, oblivious to other family members, or they hide in their rooms. They go to friends' homes or have endless lists of activities (music lessons, athletics, school projects, church youth groups, and so on).

Stepfathers who have been surprised by their stepchildren's hostility will seek refuge in their work. Since they are frequently seen as financial saviors, they can capitalize on this role to avoid connection with their stepchildren. As adults, they also have a variety of other options for escape, including civic groups, "nights out with the boys," athletics, church obligations, and so on. Stepfathers are adroit at arranging their schedules so that they simply are not present when the stepchildren are interacting with their biological mother.

Researchers have demonstrated that children with involved fathers do better in school, have higher levels of self-esteem, and are less likely to develop maladaptive behaviors. Thus, for therapists, resolving stepfathers' dilemmas is another key objective (Martin & Martin, 1985). In our clinical work, we have found the following ideas helpful in aiding stepfathers to become more integrated with their stepfamily units:

1. Finding a balance between stepfathers' disengagement and the perception of stepfathers' overinvolvement is a difficult task for therapists. In most stepfamilies, it is easy for the biological mother and the children to bond against the stepfather. Therapy needs to support him and reframe his efforts at involvement, to indicate that he has something substantial to contribute to the family. Men who believe that they have minimal input and support will quickly terminate therapy.

2. Stepfamilies need to make the marital relationship the highest priority. This includes working with the biological mother and the stepfather to define the family's structure and present a united approach to parenting.

3. Therapists need to recognize the competitive feelings of many stepfathers. It is natural for them to feel "one-down" when compared with biological fathers. At the same time, these men may not admit their feelings, because they may believe that they should not feel that way. Men in this position often try to put biological fathers down, but this makes the children uncomfortable and is not a successful tactic.

4. Parents need to recognize, within themselves and within their partners, the gifts each one brings to the stepfamily. Therapists need to help them create an environment where the gifts can be used and shared.

Clinical Rules for Increasing Parental Involvement

Many stepfamilies enter therapy in chaos, looking to therapists to create order. It is our contention that stepparents and biological parents alike need to exercise their influence as adults in the family. They need to establish guidelines for children. We have found that if adults in stepfamilies refuse to take responsibility for what occurs, significant, healthy change is unlikely.

Some therapists try to insert a free-flowing, democratic model into the chaos of the stepfamily; we believe that, once structural boundaries are in place, parents and children can begin to negotiate loosening them when that feels comfortable and appropriate.

We also believe that stepparents have to take an active adult or parental role in the family. It is impossible for an interested adult living every day in a family unit with children not to feel a need to participate and discipline. When we say this to families, we discuss the concept that adults need to care for children. Thus, stepparents must exhibit behavior that communicates caring. If the goal is clearly what is best for the children, rather than concerns about love or rejection, then stepparents can more easily assume an active role in the stepfamily. Larry, a new stepfather at the age of forty, gave us his story:

> You know, I had read all these books, and they acted as if everyone is wonderful friends and everything after the divorce. I thought we were just a weird family. Here I was, newly remarried with two adolescent boys, and I was going crazy. Their dad wasn't involved with them, and they had pushed their mother around for years. I came into the house and couldn't stand by while they kept pushing my wife around. They did things I thought would get them into trouble, but no one took action. I thought I wasn't supposed to say anything. I mean, that's what I'd read. I was supposed to spend time building a relationship, they'd get to understand me, and we'd do stuff together. Real gradual. Well, that's just bull. I mean, these kids were pushing me from day one. Screaming, yelling, fighting. I looked at all this stuff going on, and I knew I could not live in this house that way. I had to get involved, and it was the only choice.

The appropriate level of a stepparent's involvement in a stepfamily will be determined by the therapist's assessment of the family structure. If the family is functioning fairly well and there is already good parenting, then our approach would be to allow the stepparent relationship to develop slowly. In our clinical practice and in our at-risk counseling center, however, most of the stepfamilies we see are multiproblematic. The stepparent is frequently the adult with the lesser amount of baggage. From an intervention standpoint, utilizing the stepparent in the parental role can be effective, provided that the therapist supports the stepparent. To infuse stepfamilies with structure, we have developed a series of approaches that we turn into behavioral objectives. Interventions are created around them.

Supporting the Parents

If we cannot support the parents quickly, we will lose the family to therapy. This is not to say that we do not listen to the children, but in most situations we are initially concerned with creating parental structure in the family unit. This goal also helps us bypass the "identified patient" (typically one of the children) and the presenting belief of the parents that we will "fix" the child. Instead, we support the parents so that they can help their child. We teach parents to move away from yelling and screaming at their children to obey. We also discourage pleading with children, begging them, or in some other way wishing for obedience. Parents learn to determine responsible behavior and appropriate consequences for misdeeds.

In those rare instances when parents are extremely inept, we may support an older child so that younger siblings can function more effectively. We may also give support to an older child when the parents have crossed acceptable boundaries, as in cases involving physical or emotional abuse.

Helping the Family Create an Environment Where Members Can Determine Their Roles

Initially, this means attempting to hear each family member's point of view about what is occurring in the family, as well as recommended solutions. We try to help people learn to talk to one another respectfully and calmly, with everyone getting a turn to speak. "Mind reading" is common in stepfamilies, and we discourage it.

In these initial discussions, we reframe the family's problems in a more positive light by giving interpretations other than those the family has presented. This puts members off their guard a bit and allows us to suggest that they do care for one another and want what is in the family's best interests.

When the children's roles are being discussed, we limit their participation in the determination of responsibilities and consequences. In fact, our general rule is that children should be told the reason behind a decision only if they are capable of understanding it and are willing to listen. That willingness to listen is an important component of teaching families to discuss matters. The high emotional charge in stepfamilies usually means that healthy discussions seldom occur; in fact, family members may not know how to discuss a potentially conflictual matter. If children are willing to talk calmly and respectfully about a decision, then we encourage parents to work with them. Conversely, if children are argumentative, we insist that parents not discuss the matter or offer rationalizations about it. Instead, they are to set and carry out consequences for maladaptive behavior. The message to the children is clear: discussion works better than arguing.

Helping Parents Create an
Authoritative (Not Authoritarian) Family

Our objective is that the parents set the rules, but they must be reasonable rules and enforced with kindness. Parents are responsible for family decisions, especially when children are young. As children grow older, however, they should receive more responsibility and benefits commensurate with their level of responsibility. In many stepfamilies, children receive independence without earning it. It is easy for parents, struggling with a lack of structure in the family and in their personal responsibilities, to minimize their involvement with the children. As long as there is no overt trouble, children go on their merry way.

Unfortunately, however, receiving independence in this fashion does not teach responsibility. Therapists must help parents balance discipline and love. We are not saying that parents should create fear in their children, or that they should dominate their lives. Parents must have expectations for their children, and it is appropriate for parents to require compliance.

Parents' Consistency with Discipline

This is a commonly heard theme, but it is especially important to integrate it into stepfamilies. The stepfamily in the therapeutic environment is likely to be chaotic, with confused roles, few boundaries, shifting expectations, loyalty conflicts, and so on. Parental consistency is a necessity for children in these families. Furthermore, if parents are inconsistent disciplinarians, they send a message that their own lives are undisciplined. We believe that it is the children's job in families to test the rules. Unless there are consequences for breaking the rules, children will learn that the rules are not really there. That is the concrete nature of children's thinking. Thus, as we have mentioned earlier, we tell parents that consequences, proving the existence and reality of rules, are far more effective than yelling, screaming, debating, and physical abuse.

We also say that children will become responsible and feel secure in a consistent environment. When rules shift, children are unsure of what is demanded of them and their insecurity increases. These children do not feel in control of their world, and so they act to acquire more control. Instead of being helpful, however, their actions frequently make children more demanding, disrespectful, and out of control. As their behavior worsens, their stepfamilies do not know how to respond, and parental discipline usually becomes even more inconsistent. This causes the children to escalate their maladaptive responses, and soon a destructive cycle takes hold.

Therapists in initial sessions with stepfamilies must break that cycle. A colleague of ours has shared an image with us that she has successfully employed for that purpose. Most families are aware of the role of a referee in sports. Inconsistent parents are like an inept referee who merely reviews the rules of the game, but there are no penalties for infractions. If a player breaks a rule, this referee reacts angrily and threatens the player but does not really do anything. At other times when a player breaks a rule, the referee says, "Well, did you mean to do that?" The referee may also say, "How many times have I told you not to do that?" or "Why did you do that?" There are still no actual consequences. This referee also calls players for rule violations when no one knows that the rule exists. Obviously, a game like football or basketball would soon disintegrate under such conditions, and that is exactly what happens in many stepfamilies.

Establishing Good Parental Communication

When we see a family for the first time, we help the parents talk briefly about their issues. Many parents are too talkative, and the flow of issues becomes confusing if the therapist does not exercise some control. Throughout therapy, we work with parents to attain clarity about their expectations for family members' behavior and the consequences for disobedience. There are several ineffective communication patterns common in stepfamilies, which we work to overcome. For example, parents in stepfamilies often give multiple instructions to children instead of giving one directive at a time. These parents feel that they must justify every decision they make, but we teach them that they do not need to give reasons, nor do they need to try to convince their children to behave. Some parents phrase instructions as if they were questions and indicate that they hope their children will comply. We teach them that compliance is not optional; disobedience brings consequences. Our approach is to work with parents to improve structure in the stepfamily. This includes stating children's responsibilities and limits in concrete, behavioral terms.

Many therapists create complicated plans for stepfamilies, which are really reactive. Our goal in therapy is to help the family, particularly the parents, get organized and simplify their approach to life. In this way, the family can anticipate what will occur and be prepared for unexpected events. In other words, we believe in helping the family find a structure that will be proactive. From a clinical standpoint, it is important to help parents trust themselves. They usually have good, common sense about their difficulties, but often parents in a stepfamily have lost trust in themselves, and then the family suffers. We work to help mothers and fathers unite in caring, disciplining, and making decisions. This is particularly important in stepfamilies, where stepparents and biological parents may be opponents rather than partners. As a unit, these parents need to focus on the behavior of their children. Parents need to provide an environment where children can be successful. Helping parents and their families determine structure, improve communication skills, set chores, and assign responsibilities will enable them to reduce chaos.

9

Helping Stepchildren
and Their Families

Most stepfamilies enter therapy with one of the children as the "identified patient." These children may have exhibited maladaptive behaviors in their traditional family units and continued those behaviors in their new stepfamilies. They may also escalate their harmful actions (Guidubaldi & Perry, 1985). Further, as a result of the divorce and issues related to it, these children may develop new problems. They confront loss and mourning. Relationships are scarred and confused. Therapists may not see children during the first year or two of stepfamily development. Thus, by the time the family seeks therapy, patterns are fairly fixed. It is a time of chaos, instability, and high anxiety. The objective of therapy is to reduce this anxiety and to rebuild trust and stability in the stepfamily unit. Understanding the rationale behind children's actions and parents' reactions in basic stepfamily dilemmas helps the development of appropriate interventions and brings this objective closer to reality.

Understanding the Past and the Present

In meeting with children, therapists must determine where issues are related to the stepfamily as it is now or to divorce and previous relationships. With remarriage, old anxieties resurface because there is a sense of uncertainty about the future. Also, most families do not adequately mourn past relationships. It has not been atypical for us to have children give inadequate explanations or share uncertainties and misassumptions concerning their parents' divorce. This is often because parents do not inform their children fully enough for them to comprehend what is taking place as the family changes. When a new family is developing, structure is needed to help deal with confusion and anxiety. Children need to know their boundaries. While acceptance and reassurance are important, many families forget to address the uncertainties surrounding stepfamily formation. Furthermore, they do not confront misbehavior; they simply provide excuses. These stepfamilies, as well as their therapists, must understand that change takes time and is difficult, and yet people in a family need to learn immediately how to treat one another with respect and caring.

In our research with stepfamilies, we have discovered that there are certain issues, specific to working with children, in which therapists need to help families define effective behaviors.

First, therapists need to help children define the relationships with both their biological parents and stepparents. They also need to assist with identifying and dispelling stepfamily myths, such as the myth that a stepparent can take the place of a biological parent, and the myth that stepfamily members will love one another instantly (Baptiste, 1983; Prosen & Farmer, 1982; Visher & Visher, 1982). The therapist's task is made easier when all the parents can agree and get along with one another. Then it is good to have them interact as much as possible around the children and let the children have access to those who can provide them the most help with particular encounters. An effective method in therapy sessions is to have family members share their perceptions of their roles and the roles of others in the stepfamily, along with their thoughts on how those roles have changed (Baptiste, 1983; Prosen & Farmer, 1982; Visher & Visher, 1982). This activity provides therapists with the opportunity to emphasize that stepfamily roles may not parallel roles in traditional families and to stress the benefits of being able to interact with so many caring adults.

Unfortunately, the stepfamilies entering therapy are often in conflict. Much emotional baggage still exists from past marriages, and war breaks out when biological parents get together. In these situations, the better choice may be to limit interactions between parents. Therapists can direct these adults to structure environments where the children see each parent alone. At the same time, therapists must try to clarify for the parents how damaging their behavior is to their children. This can often be done in the guise of discussing how a child's drug addiction, promiscuity, truancy, and so on, may be related to the anger and unfinished business of the parents. At the very least, therapists should intervene to stop parents from making their children act as messengers and from talking negatively about their ex-spouses in conversations with their children.

Therapists also see cases in which one parent has literally abandoned the family. The children are left wondering why they cannot continue sustained contact with that parent. In such a case, the therapist should encourage the family to stop making excuses for the absent parent. Interventions should also be constructed to stop the custodial parent from attempting to convince the absent parent to become involved with the child. These losses must be faced before the family can change.

Second, therapists need to help the family create a world where children feel they are wanted and needed. This includes providing them with living spaces, talking to them about new family rituals, establishing sibling subsystems, and helping them learn how to communicate with one another more effectively than in their original families because of the complexity of their new relationships. They also need to understand that their world, while different from the domain of traditional families, is still a world shared by others. Stepfamilies need to realize that they are not alone in the difficulties they face (Baptiste, 1983; Prosen & Farmer, 1982; Visher & Visher, 1982).

Third, therapists need to help children resolve their dilemmas about caring for all these parents. Children do not have only a limited amount of love; the problems they perceive are usually the result of parents' being jealous of one another. Of all these relationships, the newly remarried couple most portrays stability for the children. If this couple does not do that, the children will experience disabling fears of being alone. If the remarried couple begins to conflict in a way similar to what the children have seen in the past, they will think the marriage is ending. Thus children need stability, whether they are in the family on a part-time or full-time basis. Continuity and consistency are two goals for stepfamilies, which therapists should work toward effectively.

Fourth, therapists have to be aware of their language when working with stepfamilies. Careful use of such terms as *natural*, *failed relationship*, and *broken home* is indicated. Terms that connote something that cannot be fixed can have a negative impact on the stepfamily, particularly when they come from the person in the trusted position of therapist.

Fifth, sibling rivalry is an issue in most families, but stepsiblings are often fighting over the need to be loved and accepted. Children fear that they will lose their biological parent if they share. Children may be jealous of a stepsibling's relationship with their parent and because the hierarchy among children changes when older and younger siblings move into the house together. Basic parenting techniques and processes can work quite well with stepfamilies. Neither parent should provide excuses when children treat each other badly.

In work with stepsiblings who are in conflict, it is our approach to discourage other family members from entering the conflict. If they do become involved, triangulation is a potential danger. We believe that the better choice is to see whether the stepsiblings can resolve their issues effectively by themselves. In fact, we have discovered that stepsiblings resolve conflict effectively most of the time when parental rules and consequences are understood. When stepsiblings are in continual turmoil, the therapist will probably discover that there is a hidden agenda much deeper than routine conflict. It is our impression that children learn from one another as they work together to resolve their conflicts. Through the resolution of conflicts, they can begin to develop close ties.

While the journey for children in stepfamilies can be difficult, we have discovered through our research that it is the parental relationships — between the biological parents, and between the biological parent and the stepparent — that often predict and actively influence the adjustment of the children. Therapeutic caseloads typically involve conflictual families where parenting is chaotic. It is the responsibility of the therapist to help the family develop effective parental coalitions, so that the children can have consistency and continuity. If conflicting parents are unable to see the impact of their destructive behavior on their children, then the therapist is confronted with the more difficult task of helping the children separate from the family's emotional traumas. The children need help to find support elsewhere, from coaches, counselors, teachers, probation officers, or other individuals willing to provide some semblance of structure for the children. When children have left home and are without parental involvement, it is much more difficult to help them find support, and the likelihood of success is greatly diminished. In such circumstances, the most important things are developing a strong therapeutic relationship and giving children access to interaction with others who are willing to assume some parental roles.

Treatment with the Family Unit

In our work with at-risk stepfamilies, we have found that interpersonal communications in these families are distorted and often hostile (Martin & Martin, 1992). Misunderstandings are common, and parental discipline is inconsistent. These families are not adaptive or cohesive. Thus, in our initial sessions with a family, we attempt to align with the parents, because one goal is to have them function effectively as the executive unit. In addition, if we do not establish a cooperative, caring relationship with them, they often lose interest in treatment. For example, we recognize the influence of peers and culture on adolescents, and we try to remove the parents from a "blamed" position. Parents experience various systems, especially school systems, as unapproachable and always negative to them about their children. They may even be in therapy because the school system has threatened them. Unless we overtly reinforce their abilities as parents, therapy will not have a chance to work. Our approach is to redefine children's misbehavior (and any subsequent mandate for therapy) as a cry for help. We present ourselves as being ready and open to listening in response to that cry.

At first, we attempt to initiate small changes. Setting small, readily achievable goals keeps parents excited about returning to counseling. These adults feel defeated. They need to learn that major change takes time and is the sum of multiple, smaller adjustments. Our interventions are family-based and require that specific guidelines be set for school performance, chores, relationships with peers, and relationships within the family. Parents set consequences before behavior occurs or recurs, and they are taught to increase the severity of the consequences in accordance with the behavior.

In dysfunctional families, marital difficulties are prevalent but may not be the primary focus of therapy. Some of these problems can be overcome as the parents learn to be successful parents. For example, discipline can be reframed as a sign of caring for children. Gradually, spouses learn that they can provide emotional support for one another and for their children by doing something for one another and by listening.

One main objective of our therapy is to provide a system of interventions that can build on and support family strengths, rather than focus on weaknesses. We believe that the parents are the mainstay of the family, and we seek to reinforce that unit. To that end, we identify what is getting in the way of solving a problem, and we determine logical interventions to help parents gain the belief that they can handle the situation. Our therapy is systemic in orientation — that is, it not only deals with the family system but also recognizes the impact of other systems (social services, the schools, peers, extended family, friends, and co-workers). Interventions are designed to target problems directly and influence the various subsystems that can help the change take place.

Major Issues in Treatment

We have noted that children in stepfamilies, in particular, experience a spectrum of emotions that they may not be prepared to handle by themselves. Misbehavior is often the result. One such emotion is anger. These children feel out of control of their lives. Their known world has been replaced with a greatly altered one. In some custody arrangements, children are continually moving between two households. Their biological parents may be in conflict, and stepparents are probably confused and inconsistent. In their anger, these children blame one or both of their biological parents for the upheaval in their lives.

Another common emotion is confusion. Trust has been shattered. The adults who used to be the mainstay in the lives of these children have changed. From the children's perspective, their parents have abandoned them. Children may also see their parents exhibiting angry, destructive behavior, including aggression, substance abuse, and sexual promiscuity. Most children do not have the maturity to process the confusing signals they receive from their dysfunctional parents.

Simply becoming part of a stepfamily does not provide a solution for these children. Beyond being resentful about the remarriage, they are not sure of the structure. Fear is another emotion that children contend with. Small children withdraw or cling. Adolescents demonstrate their need for help through declining performance in school, truancy, and involvement with peers who exhibit unhealthy behavior. One ideal, of course, is for biological parents to agree about parenting and have a good relationship with each other and with any stepparents. Many stepfamilies seen in clinical settings are far from this ideal, however. They are families in upheaval. Several structural issues stem from this estrangement. Therapists confront them in seeking to improve the functionality of stepfamilies in crisis.

Visitation

Joint custody has become a popular arrangement in divorce settlements today. Generally, we agree with that choice. Both parties must recognize, however, that as children grow older, one parent will probably spend more time with them and be more responsible for them. Obviously, this is accentuated when geographical distance becomes a factor. Often problems surrounding visitation motivate stepfamilies to enter therapy.

For children, the sporadic and ill-defined nature of visitation triggers maladaptive behavior, ranging from mild to severe.

The word *visitation* implies what most children feel: when they see a parent for relatively brief periods, they are more like visitors than like intimate family members. These children are expected to behave within the social conventions of visitation. In some families, that means they receive special attention and gifts, and special activities are planned for them. In other families, it means limits on what is shared about everyday life. These children feel as if they are outsiders. Their families expect them to get along well with everyone without creating any impact. Problematic parental visits may range from those occurring only once every three or four years to those in which the noncustodial parent drops in whenever he or she wishes. In some cases, children may live with grandparents, seeing their biological parents whenever they visit. This arrangement represents a type of pseudostepfamily.

Roy, a recent client, shared some typical feelings:

> I went to my dad's house. He had just gotten remarried, and it seemed like he was paying attention to Molly and Jo, my stepsisters, rather than to me. I know he was real busy at work, and I think that's one of the reasons Mom divorced him. He was always gone and didn't seem to have much time for her or me. When I visited, I ended up spending most of my time with Sally, his new wife. I didn't have much fun. When I got home, I told my mom about it, and she called Dad. He told her he'd change things and spend time with me, but he hasn't done it. I guess he just doesn't want me.

Our belief is that therapists need to help and protect children, particularly when the adults in the situation are not rightfully concerned about them. Adults are capable of doing that for themselves; children are more vulnerable, and that means working with stepfamilies to help them create situations where children feel comfortable when visiting. Children need a space to identify with, a space to call their own. Stepsiblings need time to get to know one another. Children need time alone with the biological parent, to receive the reassurance that they are loved. Therapists need to assess these areas in the stepfamily environment so that adjustment can proceed effectively.

A dialogue among all the concerned parties helps determine the most functional adults and the appropriate interventions. In Roy's case, we brought his father into a session with Roy's mother and Roy, to have some discussion about how visits could be arranged in Roy's best interests. It seemed that Roy's mother, Wanda, wanted Roy to have an ongoing relationship with his father, Hal. Hal appeared to be somewhat resistant, however. He was very busy, as Roy had reported. Hal said that he felt overwhelmed with the number of children he was responsible for now—his two stepdaughters and Roy—and so he felt obligated to work more hours. He was angry with Wanda because of what he perceived as excessively large support payments. Hal felt stuck. Wanda said that she needed the money to live on, and the animosity between these adults quickly became apparent. Conflict between divorced biological parents is common, and therapists need to refocus sessions such as these so that the primary concern—the well-being of the children—is the issue discussed.

We shared our viewpoint as therapists that if Roy was seeing his father only sporadically, then the visits had to be structured in the way that would be best for Roy. Whenever Roy visited, he had a right to expect his father to spend some time with him and make a commitment to their relationship. The parents had to work together to make the visits reflect the true nature of the relationship and be more reasonably organized. If Hal could realistically see Roy only once every six weeks or three months, then that would be a better arrangement than pretending to want him every weekend or every other weekend while spending no time with him. At this point, Hal indicated his desire to be involved in Roy's life. He felt that they had spent some good times together, and he was hesitant about an arrangement reducing the number of visits. Hal expressed the desire to try again, so that he could spend more time with Roy. We left it open for the family to continue the discussion and see how things went during the next six weeks. If changes were needed in the visitation structure, they could be made later.

We told Wanda that it was appropriate during this time for her, as a parent, to assess the progress of Roy's relationship with his father and determine what was in Roy's best interests. When he arrived home after a weekend visit, she was to observe whether he seemed sad or depressed. If she detected that the visit was unsatisfactory, she was to ask Roy about his feelings and help him make decisions about the visitation that were comfortable for him.

Meanwhile, we used these sessions to help Roy define what he wanted from the relationship with his father. To that end, we removed Wanda as an intermediary between Roy and Hal, so that direct communication could take place between them. At that point, Roy began to talk about his father's apparent reluctance to have him visit. Roy said that perhaps he should decrease his visits, because he felt sad and rejected when he did go and his father avoided him.

During the six-week assessment period, Hal's relationship with Roy did not change. Hal stayed very busy and spent little time with Roy during the weekend visits. In the next session, Roy told his father that he wanted to rearrange his visits, and Hal reluctantly agreed. In subsequent weeks, Roy's depression began to lift, and he spent more time with his local friends. Roy was relieved by gaining a clearer definition of his relationship with his father. Hal honored Roy's feelings. When they did get together, the visits were more enjoyable, and they continued to talk openly.

In this family system, the choice to limit visits was a positive change in structure, which increased the child's comfort. In other instances, nearly the opposite is true. When one parent is angry and attempting to continue involvement with the ex-spouse through harassment, he or she may restrict or prohibit visitation. Obviously, the child is the one hurt in these cases. Such was the case of Dan, who was having a constant battle with his ex-wife, Linda, over their daughter, Kris. He had custody of Kris and felt that Linda was not paying enough child support, given her excellent position as a lawyer for the federal government. Dan agreed to come to therapy with Linda after she threatened to take him back to court.

In the first session, Linda shared her anger and her belief

that Dan was deliberately preventing her from seeing Kris. She said that he had an excuse every time she was scheduled to see Kris: he was busy and could not arrange it, or some activity for Kris had come up and she would not be free. Linda felt that the situation was much more complicated than necessary, especially since Kris was only three years old. Our impression was that Dan was in denial. As the session continued, however, he began to share some of his anger and hurt. This couple had not yet divorced psychologically. Dan was still in love with Linda and used Kris as a way of involving her, even if it was through anger and threats.

At the end of the session, we said that we wanted to talk to them some more, to gain a better understanding of their relationship and what they could structure for their daughter. We also arranged to see Linda alone. During our session with her, we learned that Dan had been in therapy but they had never discussed their feelings about their divorce. Linda, who was dating by this time, did not think this was necessary for her. In fact, she did not want to deal with Dan's pain, nor did she wish to share her feelings with Dan. We explained that if she did not resolve her relationship with Dan, the custody and visitation hassles with Kris would probably continue for years.

We spent the next four sessions with Dan and Linda discussing the end of their relationship. Eventually, Dan admitted that he had not wanted to use Kris but had discovered that it was a way for him to continue talking with Linda. He began to let Linda see Kris without restraint, and this opened the way for her to show she cared for him without implying any romantic involvement. In follow-up a year later, we learned that Linda was contemplating marriage, Dan was dating, and the relationship between Linda and Kris was healthy.

In other families, behavior associated with visitation problems may last much longer. Children mourning the loss of a biological parent may return from visits and be sad, crying for several days. In some cases, children hold on to these symptoms for years. Occasionally, children use their depression to get attention, or they try to get their parents reunited. More often, however, depression is a true indication of loss and grief.

In these cases, therapy seeks to engage the biological parents in communication. It is particularly important to involve the noncustodial parent, who may be able to help the children by modeling healthier affect. In these families, we often find that the children are depressed because the noncustodial parent is.

When children return home after a visit, custodial parents need to connect with them about the experience. If inappropriate, unhealthy behavior, such as crying, persists, then custodial parents need to provide other options for their children, which may include restructuring visits and entering therapy with the ex-spouse. Adolescents in particular find moving back and forth between parents upsetting. At their stage in life, issues with their friends and social life are important to them, and they may wish to remain in one home and visit less frequently. Therapy can ease the necessary conversations about such changes.

Cases involving parents who have abandoned their children and ex-spouses are especially difficult. These adults pay no support and often have moved away, leaving their children feeling rejected and unloved. Such children may display both anger and mourning. They also internalize their feelings and believe that something is wrong with them and that is why their parent has left. To help abandoned children, we tell them what we have learned from clinical experience about why parents do not visit:

1. For some parents, visiting is too painful, and so it is avoided. These parents believe that they cannot handle seeing the ex-spouse, and that they are too vulnerable to put themselves in this position.

2. In other cases, seeing the children reminds parents of ex-spouses, because of similarities in appearance, mannerisms, and so on. For some adults, this is too difficult to bear.

3. Other parents feel that their children have rejected them, and so they do not visit. Angry ex-spouses may work to turn children against their noncustodial biological parents. Then, when visits take place, those parents are subjected to the same harassment and hostility the children learned from their custodial parents. After a while, the noncustodial parents, finding no pleasure in repeated rejection, stop visiting.

4. Some parents deliberately step out of the picture so that their children can grow up in a stepfamily without confusion. These children may still miss the absent parent and may not understand what has occurred.

Children may idolize an absent parent, making excuses and rationalizations for her or him while blaming the custodial parent for the lack of visits and contacts. Therapy sessions with these children are difficult because the therapist must first break through these defenses. One thing that complicates therapy is the reality that these parents may show up once in a while, with various excuses, and often with gifts and money. Such behavior confuses children, who want to believe the best about their parents.

Parents who abandon their children may have problems with substance abuse. A few such parents can receive treatment, return, and be a better force in their children's lives; but most do not. An adult who does undergo treatment and begin to live appropriately should be gradually reintroduced into the children's environment, provided that the children desire to renew the relationship.

In certain stepfamilies, children may experience similar losses because of separation from beloved grandparents or siblings. Therapists must attend to these feelings as well. Again, the focus should be the well-being and best interests of the children, and the parents need to work toward those ends.

Death of a Parent

A small percentage of stepfamilies are formed because of this type of loss. Children who have lost a parent in this way usually experience tremendous grief and sadness. The older the child, the greater the loss. In one sense, it is easier for these stepfamilies to form. They do not face competition between two families, intefering ex-spouses, and problems with noncustodial biological parents. Nevertheless, children in these stepfamilies may feel that they are betraying the deceased parent if they love a stepparent. This loyalty conflict may be heightened by the tendency to idolize dead parents, until they are remembered as nearly perfect human beings. In therapy, we have the surviving spouse explain to the children in detail what the deceased parent was like, with an effort to be objective.

Stepsiblings

Children may resent sharing a biological parent, and competition for affection may arise. Parents can reduce jealousy by spending time alone with their biological children, openly sharing their feelings about the remarriage and the new family, and nurturing the siblings to participate in activities together.

A more difficult issue with stepsiblings may be the shifting of roles in the stepfamily. A child who was the oldest may suddenly become a middle child. The picture may be confused still more if the parent and the stepparent have a child together. In these cases, children feel misunderstood, overlooked, and unsure of their position. Depending on their ages, some may want to invest the energy to form strong family relationships; others may be ready to go their own way. Our clinical experience has shown us that while children are flexible, they are also egocentric. Resolving these role issues will require structure, set by the parents, that encourages the formation of relationships. Other considerations in these new families include the following:

- Biological siblings may care more for each other than they care for their stepsiblings. Stepsiblings may feel that they are intruding on those relationships, and that they are not part of the family, particularly if there are more biological siblings.
- There may be issues with friends. It may be uncomfortable or even threatening for children to feel that they have to share their friends with a new family member. Adolescents, believing that their stepsiblings will be more popular or are better looking, may be reluctant to include them in their social life.
- Children may get upset if a biological brother or sister is paying attention to a stepsibling.

In most cases, we have found that it is helpful for siblings to work these issues out themselves, without parental involvement. We recommend parental intervention when siblings are unable to arrive at equitable solutions. Some stepsiblings' arguments may be influenced by sexual attraction when adolescents in a new family are close in age. Their attraction to each other is normal for their age but it needs to be discussed. In such cases, parental involvement is highly recommended. The parents need to create distance between the teenagers until they can get used to their feelings. At first, for example, parents may not allow them to be alone together for extended periods.

Stepparents and Stepchildren

Therapists agree that stepparent-stepchild relationships are the most frequent problem area in remarried families seen in clinical settings. When couples enter therapy with the marital relationship as the presenting problem, rather than having a child as an "identified patient," it is usually because problems in the stepparent-stepchild relationship have escalated to the point of marital disintegration. Mills (1984) argues that the stepparent-stepchild relationship is best helped from the clinical perspective if it is not based on the biological parent model or on traditional roles associated with parent-child relationships. He points out that if a family in treatment has a presenting teenager as a problem, the adolescent's push for freedom and independence is in direct opposition to the stepparent's goal of achieving an adequate relationship with that child. We agree with Mills's viewpoint. It is difficult for therapists to prescribe roles (that is, set and well-defined roles) applicable to every stepfamily that comes into treatment. Theoretically, that is quite different from the approach applied to traditional families in therapy.

The dilemma for Mills, as for most other stepfamily therapists, is whether stepparents should assume a parental role. Mills suggests that they should not, because stepfamilies function effectively when stepparents accept the differences between their own roles and parental roles. We take a different perspective and attempt to separate familial adult roles from parental roles. If a stepparent chooses to move into a more parental position, that is acceptable to us, depending on the nature and willingness of the stepfamily. We also want the stepparent to be aware of the risks, however.

We feel the same about the adult position. Adults in families may behave like parents in some ways, but their cognitive framework is different. They act from the framework of a responsible adult, rather than assuming a parental status in the stepfamily.

For example, a fifteen-year-old girl comes home drunk after saying that she was going to spend the evening with a girlfriend. Her stepfather is the only adult home when she arrives, because her mother is working late. The stepfather is upset when he realizes that the girl is drunk. He sends her to her room, where she falls asleep. Before going to her room, the girl asks her stepfather not to tell her mother what has occurred. When he refuses, she verbally abuses him by yelling and using inappropriate language. When his wife returns, the stepfather has several options. His choice will reflect the length of time the family has been together and the developmental stage of relationships. If he chooses the parental role, the couple will discuss the incident and determine punishment and discipline together. The spouses will present their decision to the daughter and will both take responsibility for discipline. If the stepfather chooses the adult role instead, he will assume similar behavior initially in that he will talk with his spouse. His wife will see him as a consultant, however. She will determine and present the punishment and carry out the discipline. Her decision will be final; his role will be limited to input and support. Thus, in our view, the adult role is that of an involved consultant, and the parental role is more interactive. Each role has its positive elements and can work, depending on the nature of the family and the opinion of the therapist about which role will be most effective.

Stepfamilies often come to therapy with one of two parent-child problems with a stepparent. Either the mother is having difficulties with her biological children and wants the stepfather to be more involved in setting limits, or the father has his biological children in the stepfamily and wants to shift parental functions to the stepmother. In the first instance, if the stepfather does respond to his wife's urging, he will either find her criticizing his efforts or assuming a helpless role. Then, if the children actually improve, they are being disloyal to their mother. No one wins. In the second instance, if the stepmother attempts to move into the nurturing, organizing role, the children will get upset at what they perceive as her overinvolvement. Their reaction forces her to become even more involved, because at the same time her husband commands their obedience to her. The problem only gets worse. In both cases, families are stuck.

It becomes apparent that a stepparent-stepchild relationship can be troubled just because of the structure of the stepfamily. For example, a stepfamily may try initially to establish relationships. If the family contains adolescents, their needs and the family's needs will be directly opposed because the adolescents seek independence. It appears that young children are the only family members whose needs are consistent with the parent's. It can also be seen that the stepparent-stepchild relationship is nearly always secondary to the biological child-parent relationship. Stepparents have been with the biological portion of the family for a relatively short period. They have few legal rights and no place in society. Children can perceive a stepparent's status as a nonentity, and it is not reassuring. Children have already been through divorce, too. They may be afraid that the new relationship will not work, and so they seek to protect themselves.

When stepfamilies come to therapy, they tend to demonstrate typical adjustment problems. If a child is the "identified patient," then there are probably few clear household rules or expectations for different family members. The parents do not know whom their children are associating with or where they are spending their time, and they have only vague ideas about what the children are doing.

Once children get into trouble or are disobedient, their behavior is probably handled inconsistently. Parents in therapy tell us that our suggestions are foolish, or they say that they have already tried our approach and it did not work. With a few additional questions, we learn that trying and doing are different: that parents in a stepfamily do more talking than act-ing, and that they give up rather quickly. We tell parents that they need to make a commitment to discipline, and that if a certain kind of behavior has existed for some time, it will take repeated and consistent effort before the discipline will take hold and be effective.

Another typical finding is that in conflicts there will either be withdrawal from communication or angry verbalization cou-pled with lack of discipline. As we have indicated throughout this book, we insist that children's behavior be closely observed. Parents must be firm with rules and boundaries. We teach com-munication skills that involve the negotiation of mutual con-tracts between children and family members. These contracts discuss consequences for disobedience, positive reinforcement, responsibility within the family, and sometimes privileges. The marital couple needs to be strong enough to assume executive responsibilities if the stepfamily is to function effectively.

We believe that the stepfamilies, as a unit, needs to de-cide how it wants to be. There must be some sense of deter-mining what the family members perceive is wrong with the family, and then a switch to focusing more on positive elements. Therapists need to help families realize what types of relation-ships they are now capable of, and where they would like to go through the therapeutic encounter.

Bonding between the stepparent and stepchildren may take time. We believe that healthy bonding can take place in a short time, but it depends on the initiative and commitment of the stepparent and stepchildren. In traditional family units, parents have natural, biological time to bond with their chil-dren. That is a luxury that stepparents do not have. They are often obliged to set and enforce rules during the initial stages of the stepfamily's formation. It makes sense, from a theoreti-cal perspective, to involve the stepparent in nurturing, caring, and fun time with the children at first, saving rule setting and enforcing for later stages. In reality, however, when the family is chaotic or when the biological parents are disagreeing or when the noncustodial parent is actively sabotaging the new family in order to maintain contact with his or her ex-spouse, there is little choice but for the stepparent to be a stabilizing force. We have discovered that it is most helpful to have the stepparent help determine and establish structure for the family initially and then move on to a caring, loving relationship.

We take the opposite view, however, if the children are behaving appropriately. Then we lean toward giving the biological parent the majority of the say with the children, because this person has been successful as a parent, and the stepfamily should recognize excellence. In these family units, the stepparent can move into an adult role and can therefore also move into the scenario of the loving stepparent. We rarely see such families in a clinical setting, however, and usually do so only when the marital relationship is in trouble. In such cases, the children misbehave as a way of calling attention to the difficulties in the couple.

As the spouses define traditions and establish rules, they must also set boundaries for the other parents (that is, the ex-spouses who are no longer family members). In therapy, we work to reduce competition between ex-spouses. Realistically, cooperation between former mates may be unattainable; open communication and understanding are possible, however. Each family must recognize the other's right to a different set of rules and traditions, provided that each is a positive framework for the children. Often a stepfamily stagnates as it focuses on an ex-spouse's parenting. Unless the parenting is destructive and harmful to the children, we promote tolerance of different approaches, and we nurture the family to move past this point.

10

Fostering
Healthy Stepfamilies

We have said that thorough and accurate assessment of a stepfamily is critical to the success of intervention and to the overall achievement of therapeutic goals. Throughout this book, numerous suggestions concerning assessment have been presented.
Our underlying assumption has been that there exists a standard or norm to use in examining a stepfamily's functionality.
That standard encompasses the characteristics of a healthy stepfamily.

The Marital Unit

An inherent characteristic of healthy stepfamilies is a marital
couple functioning as the stable and bonding force behind all
familial relationships (Kosinski, 1983). Therapists observe whether
the spouses nurture, affirm, and support each other. Are the
individual marital partners happy with their relationship? Are
they intimate and overtly caring for each other? Although all
couples experience conflict, healthy couples know how to recognize and resolve dilemmas before and as they occur. The partners are sources of support for each other. The spouses need
to agree on principles of parenting. They must develop guidelines geared to meeting the needs of their children and enrich-
ing their development. Transactions between the spouses and
in parent-child relationships will influence how the children develop. If the family is healthy, the children will be able to become independent and function autonomously outside the family
(Rosemond, 1989).

Remarried couples are delighted with another chance to succeed. In some ways, remarriage is similar to an economic transaction with great potential for gain. Couples enter remarriage with high and positive expectations. Yet there are often issues that inhibit remarried couples from becoming viable and do not allow them to effectively recognize parenting and family needs. For instance, many couples believe the common myths about stepfamilies. One myth is that everyone in the new family will love everyone else instantly. This myth grows out of the natural desire to have a happy family and, in this age of instant gratification, to have it at once. Instead of fostering comfort and a climate for love to grow among stepfamily members, this myth leads to guilt feelings: "Why don't I love these people?" It also produces resentment of other members for not being overtly happy and leads to members' blaming one another for these perceived failures. Another myth inhibiting the development of the marital couple is that the mistakes of the past will not recur in the present, and family life will be better than it was before. Growing out of the hope to make a fresh start and build a future that makes up for the difficulties of the past, this myth leads to disappointment and frustration when the new family faces conflict. Instead of looking forward to the blending of lives enriched by past experiences, this myth encourages family members to separate themselves from the past.

In a remarriage, at least one partner has been divorced, and both usually have experienced that transition. Besides financial and other external interferences, there is a sense of mourning for a past spouse and children, particularly if they have emotionally suffered. Divorce is a serious life loss. While the children attempt to continue ties with a noncustodial parent, there may be a connection between the ex-spouses through the raising of the children. Messinger (1984) believes that it is important for remarried couples to reestablish roles and traditions as stabilizers. For example, there should be an understanding of who visits and who resides on a more permanent basis in the family, when children visit, what holiday schedules are, how all the parents will interact with the children around schoolwork and school visits, and other pertinent issues regarding living arrangements for the remarried couple and the children.

The promise of a loving and caring relationship is a prime motivator for people to remarry (Rubenstein, 1983). Most people want to live with someone and not be alone. Marriage seems to be one of the few acceptable options. It has always been considered a haven in our society. Secrets are shared and kept, and someone can provide support in a world that sometimes seems quite unforgiving. Most people also desire to begin a family. For many, having children adds a sense of completeness to adulthood. Remarried spouses may experience lack of family togetherness because they may see children only on a part-time basis and miss the feeling of having a more typical family, with two adults and children. This grieving may be alleviated by the hope that, through remarriage, a family will be born, and a sense of completeness will be achieved.

Others seek a new partner because, during the aftermath of divorce, economic or emotional circumstances have pushed them to return home with their parents. This journey to the past is difficult at best. Ready to leave the parents' home, people may be seeking help with family burdens, whether financial or emotional. This motivator is compounded by the fact that most single mothers are below the poverty level and are seeking greater economic resources. In addition to economic considerations, loneliness and the isolation of parenting children by oneself are often reasons for seeking a new marital partner. These feelings can be important motivators for remarriage, although the new union may not solve this dilemma. Burns (1985) has found one in four Americans suffering from loneliness; nearly 15 percent of married people say that they are lonely.

Like first-time married people, many remarried couples may get married for the wrong reasons. However, the effects of a bad decision are greater when the remarriage is a last-ditch effort to make things right. No one likes to get hurt in a relationship, and most people in remarriages have experienced divorce and have been emotionally scarred. Humans inherently protect themselves in relationships. This defensive behavior, along with the failure to understand the need for a strong remarital relationship in the stepfamily, may lead to difficult situations. If the prognosis for the marital relationship is poor, then the family unit will probably be disruptive. Spouses who do not cooperate and who are in conflict are the most blatant example of dysfunction in the parental unit.

It is important for therapists to realize that many remarrying individuals have not been emotionally divorced; they have not resolved their feelings about the past relationship, and they are emotionally stuck. Kübler-Ross (1969) in her pioneering research on grief, helps us examine the five stages that grieving individuals need to process: denial, depression, anger, bargaining, and acceptance. Ideally, this resolution will be achieved before remarriage, because otherwise any remaining stages will surface in stepfamily living and present unnecessary difficulties. Two emotions — anger and guilt — are typically seen in therapeutic cases. Carrying unresolved anger takes energy and preoccupies members of new stepfamilies when they should be concentrating on building new relationships. Even though the anger may remain unspoken, its presence will be sensed by others as an undefined tension in the new stepfamily. The new spouse may feel inexplicably insecure and jealous, while the children will experience heightened loyalty conflicts with their other biological parent.

Concerning guilt, Sager and others (1983) believe that most individuals feel remorseful about divorce and conclude, at some cognitive and/or emotional level that they were at fault or to blame. This perception damages one's self-concept and self-esteem. Again, it is difficult for adults to put full energy into new marital and familial relationships while battling emotions linked to the past. For instance, adults may feel guilty for leaving their children behind, and those feelings will influence budding relationships with stepchildren. As we have been saying, the future of the stepfamily is severely jeopardized by an incomplete divorce. Often the motivators for remarriage are linked to an unresolved divorce and produce haste to remarry. The belief is that somehow the new marriage will lessen the pain, solve the problems, take away the loneliness, and in all ways make life better. In fact, however, remarrying too quickly is a primary factor in the high divorce rates among remarried couples.

Without understanding and acceptance of themselves, many people marry mates who exhibit the same characteristics as previous spouses (Bowen, 1981; Satir & Baldwin, 1983; Minuchin & Fishman, 1981). Even when people remarry because they want to overcome horrible relationships from the past, these remarriages seem clouded by utopian dreams that will never be fulfilled. Seeking an unrealistic future can be a serious mishap, one with dire consequences for a remarriage. Therapists, because of their experiences with many types of married and remarried couples, can present the marital dyad with a more realistic picture of the general benefits and limitations of marriage.

It is also important for therapists to find out why, from their perspectives and observations, remarried couples decided to marry. When, where, and how did the partners meet? How were the children involved in the courtship, and was the stepparent considered to be a friend to the children before the remarriage? What did the former spouse think about the ex-spouse's remarriage? In remarriage, there are often changes in residence and financial status. What was each individual's life-style before the couple became married? How did the children behave in the single-parent family? What roles did relatives play in the divorce adjustment, and what relationships existed with both the ex-spouse and the ex-spouse's relatives? The therapist will examine the previous nuclear family of each individual and note how the previous relationship began. How did the marriage develop and change? How was the final decision made to dissolve the marriage? Each of the adults in the remarriage needs to have an understanding of past marriages and what those relationships meant.

Finally, the partners must be helped to examine their childhoods and the families in which they were raised. This understanding of the past helps clarify present dilemmas. It also adds vital information for the therapist in such areas as how each partner sees male-female roles and how children should be raised. What was each person's perception of his or her parents' marriage? Many of our values, ideas, and concepts about family life come from our families of origin. People react positively or negatively to what they experienced as children. Since the strength of the relationship for a married couple is significantly related to the strength of the family unit, understanding both the past and the present helps the couple determine covert and overt alliances, power struggles within the relationship, outsiders' influence regarding the depth of affection and intimacy, methods of bonding, and how people move in and out of the family system. This information may shed light on the couple's problems and provide the therapist with key ideas and a direction for therapy. The therapist hopes to see mature individuals who have learned from the past and who do not wish to repeat old problems. If the remarried couple is to be happy, the choice of a mate needs to be appropriate and to reflect personal growth.

Understanding Family Functioning

Brock and Barnard (1988) have arrived at six general areas of functionality, which they use as a standard of measurement for successful and caring families.

Roles

Brock and Barnard define this term as "repetitive patterns of individual behavior . . . [which] serve functional purposes in day-to-day family life. Roles delineate the family's structure and maintain the family's interactional processes" (1988, p. 23). In a functional stepfamily, the roles are clearly differentiated and boundaries are appropriately drawn. Yet there is flexibility and, as Brock and Barnard point out, roles can be shared or reversed, new roles can be tried out, and old ones can be modified. Members' roles complement one another, and all adults are involved in caring for the children.

Emotional Expression

Dysfunctional stepfamilies experience high levels of conflict, anger, and tension, even when these families are rigidly conflict-avoidant. Functional stepfamilies experience a normal range of emotions, but the primary emphasis is on positive feelings. Family members are comfortable sharing all their emotions openly and directly while observing family guidelines and understandings about such exchanges. There is obvious concern and affection for other members.

Interdependence and Individuation

While functioning interdependently, with consideration and respect for each individual's contribution to the whole, functional stepfamilies also promote individual development. Family members are encouraged to participate in activities separately from the rest of the family. Relationships with others are also encouraged as long as the family's routine and boundaries are not disturbed. Cooperation is a hallmark, and certain significant values are held in common about sexuality, money, religion, work ethics, and family loyalty (Brock & Barnard, 1988, p. 23). At the same time, differences of opinion are tolerated and discussed. Individuals take responsibility for their feelings and actions.

Power

As we said earlier, acquiring power or control over others is an important objective for individuals in dysfunctional stepfamilies. In functional stepfamilies, by contrast, power is shared and appropriately distributed. The marital couple is in the chief position. In different situations and settings, however, leadership will pass from member to member, according to each person's strengths. Coalitions, which can be very damaging to unhealthy stepfamilies, are generally not needed and so form only rarely, and for relatively short periods. When power is temporarily vested in one individual for a certain purpose, other family members willingly follow. Members of healthy stepfamilies make decisions jointly, and enforcement is through persuasion, not intimidation or coercion. Because the emphasis is on open, honest communication, conflicts tend to be short-lived.

Communication

Functional stepfamilies practice open, direct communication patterns. Verbal and nonverbal exchanges are congruent. The family environment encourages the discussion of differing opinions and the resolution of conflicts. In any family, some communications involve anger or misunderstandings, but in healthy families the majority of communications have a positive tone. Information and ideas are shared, and members express interest in one another's feelings, activities, and concerns. Parents have good problem-solving skills and teach these to children.

Subsystems

These groupings within the family (parent, spouse, and sibling groups) work to maintain the family system. Each has a function and, in healthy families, performs it adequately. Boundaries between subsystems are clear, and coalitions do not form between groups for the purpose of acquiring power. The parental subsystem is the primary one and holds the majority of the power. Members of subsystems share strong emotional bonds with one another and a strong family identity. They often participate in joint activities (Brock & Barnard, 1988, p. 25).

Dynamics of the Healthy Stepfamily

Messinger (1984) writes that remarried couples have little knowledge of what makes for a healthy stepfamily. There may be conflict between the children and their biological parent's new spouse, as well as confusion due to a new life-style, a new family group, different expectations for household management, new kin, and possibly a new ordinal position in the family. Stepfamilies need to redefine divisions of labor. There will probably be differences from past family situations, whether in a traditional nuclear families or single-parent units. All family members have to learn how to live in the new household according to the marital couple's expectations.

New partners need to experience disciplining the children, and the children need to learn how to treat the parent's new partner. Instant love is not possible, but respect is a reasonable expectation. The spouses must share their views about child rearing and discuss what their guidelines will be. They also need to discuss what constitutes satisfactory family life and how they view this marriage as compared to previous ones. Their thoughts about income are vital. If this is a dual-career marriage, they must determine how resources will be allocated, especially when money is shared between family units. Another area to examine is the thoughts and feelings of each family member about relationships between ex-spouses and kin and those between children and ex-spouses or absent parents. Thoughts and feelings about ex-partners are also important, as are ideas about children visiting regularly or sporadically or living regularly with an ex-spouse. A discussion of the difficulties in maintaining a new family and arranging private time for the couple should also take place.

Curran (1985) describes several characteristics of healthy couples, whether in stepfamilies or traditional family units. Let us examine these characteristics and relate them to the dilemmas of remarried spouses.

1. Stress is viewed as a normal part of family life. Couples who have healthy marriages are able to anticipate stressors from a whole spectrum of issues, ranging from child rearing to money. The coping skills required of remarried couples are greater than those required of traditional couples because of the complexities involved. Therapists can help couples explore the myths of marriage and methods of adapting effective framing to dilemmas and disagreements. Too often, many of the stressors associated with remarriage are avoided during courtship and must be faced after matrimony. The family budget, work, child rearing, and household chores are only a few of the items that must be addressed. Healthy couples expect both change and mistakes and understand that these are part of life and of the family's development.

2. Feelings, thoughts, and behaviors are shared. Communication is difficult for most couples; many people complain that their spouses are inattentive and rarely talk. Because of difficulties in past relationships, remarried spouses often see conflict as a call to arms. They blame each other and do not look at themselves or their individual responsibility for the conflict. Finding fault and blaming the other person is easier,

as is demanding that a spouse "change" while the other person does nothing or observes. Lerner (1985) discusses conflict and anger and how they are intertwined. She believes anger is a key to telling oneself that something is wrong: one is hurting inside. Sharing that hurt in an angry way will prove useless, yet this is the easiest and most predictable path for couples. Learning to share anger in a direct and productive fashion takes hard work and practice.

Reframing negative conflicts into more positive struggles helps couples accept conflict as a chance to renegotiate — a place where mistakes are understood as a way of life. Curran says that healthy couples learn to communicate feelings and develop nonthreatening techniques for achieving intimacy. They learn to stop "mind reading" when they need something and instead to ask for it. The feelings they share may not be acceptable, but belittlement is not the response. Healthy couples do have conflict, but they are willing to risk confrontation because they know there is no intimacy without risk. They care about what is important to them individually and together and are willing to have conflict about it. Intimacy is the most precious gift humans have to give one another, and achieving it is well worth the struggle.

In good relationships, couples see themselves as friends with the ability to talk about most issues. The basic characteristic of this friendship is that the partners have a right to their feelings; these are respected and not discounted.

3. Learning to resolve conflict is vital, as is being able to cope creatively. Healthy couples are both creative and persevering. If a remarriage is to last, the couple needs to make the commitment to solve problems and make decisions mutually and beneficially. Such issues as child rearing and money problems cannot be left to fester. Among the types of behavior that couples use to enable the habitual repetition of conflict patterns are avoidance, postponing, sidestepping, competing, accommodating, and compromising. When people believe that they are giving up or losing something in a conflict, then they will never collaborate on a final decision or resolution. Power

struggles are inherent in conflictual couples. Sometimes such couples exhibit a one-up/one-down pattern: the partners are constantly competing and will act without each other's knowledge to gain the winning advantage. In other instances, a partner may be too accommodating and will sacrifice on important issues to please the other person. Accommodators often tend to be passive-aggressive and may show their true feelings in indirect ways.

Obviously, couples who can collaborate have healthier relationships. Spouses who can tell each other what they want and openly share their feelings and thoughts about the real issues facing them as a couple, whether the issues are obvious or hidden, are more likely to be intimate. Healthy couples are adaptable. They learn how to negotiate differences and do not take life too seriously. The spouses learn how to respect each other's needs, rather than attempting to change each other. Couples who adapt to life's struggles remain optimistic and have a positive feeling about living. They learn to be flexible in the family and consistently work at communication. They know how to change and are willing to admit that they make mistakes. For most people, this is very hard to do.

4. Developing a supportive group of people and networking with others is vital. Remarried couples often feel alone in their frustrations and believe that no one else quite understands what they are experiencing. Because of the stigma attached to stepfamilies, they may want to avoid this label and not even tell people in the community their true history. In addition, as a result of increased mobility, families often do not have relatives or grandparents to help them cope with everyday functioning. That missing assistance may be of even greater importance to the stepfamily than to a traditional family. Sometimes substitute support groups can be structured; generally, however, they are groups of friends who get involved only when problems become severe. Without an extended family's support or an accessible substitute, family members come to believe that they cannot trust others and must handle all their problems alone. This increased stress can contribute to the difficulties.

Development of the Stepfamily Unit

While stepfamilies are different from traditional nuclear families, we believe that all healthy families are similar and that a healthy stepfamily displays specific characteristics. Although stepfamilies' structure may exaggerate typical developmental issues, they experience many of the issues and crises that other families face. Bowen (1981) says that healthy families are really not qualitatively different from dysfunctional families. There are core interactive processes in all families, but the disturbed or dysfunctional family displays more maladaptive behaviors. These are usually generated in the family of origin and transferred to the first family and then to the stepfamily.

Bowen also says that triangulation, which involves a dyad plus a less comfortable third person as an outsider, is very typical in families and a normal event. The goal of triangulation is to preserve a dyadic relationship by guarding against the discomfort that arises within it as the third party presents a more relaxing, comfortable alternative. Bowen believes that it is not the actual process of triangulation that causes problems but rather how the triangulation occurs, or the extent to which the triangulation promotes instability. One of the difficulties we have observed in stepfamilies is that these triangles are very secretive and prevent development of relationships. Unfortunately, stepfamilies use this method as a problem-solving process. In a healthy family, triangulation is not seen as a major method of solving problems; the family is able to talk about alliances and work free of them.

A typical triangulation involves a parent and a child united against another parent, as occurs quite often in stepfamilies. Haley (1984) and Minuchin and Fishman (1981) say that healthy families are characterized by clearly defined roles and a hierarchy, in which power is shared by the marital pair. The roles and operations of the family are known to all family members. The spouses discern their own measure of influence within the family, and the needs and demands of other family members are understood. There is a sense of protection within the marital dyad. The couple is able to be intimate as a marital pair and yet discharge parental functions. Curran (1985) and Walsh (1982) state that healthy families can be distinguished from more dysfunctional ones in four ways.

Identity Processes

Individuation among family members is evident, and people are able to stay connected to one another yet not feel suffocated or enmeshed. This is very difficult in any family and even more difficult for stepfamily members who exhibit a variety of loyalty conflicts. There is a sense of mutuality in healthy families. Each member helps the others, and they all participate in a variety of tasks, functions, and support systems rather than creating a sense of isolation.

Change Processes

Healthy families are open to new ideas and they are more flexible than rigid. Too often, stepfamilies are afraid of outsiders. They may begin to resemble chemically dependent families, where people are set in rigid roles and the family's direction is unclear. Functional families are unstable, although they may appear confused at times. Dysfunctional families exhibit a consistent pattern: family members do not know what the next day will bring, and routine tasks are not completed. A general state of confusion or chaos exists in dysfunctional families.

Information Processing

Healthy families eliminate distorted perceptions about each other. They try to share openly when there is ambiguity and to present clear messages, so that people will know what they think. Family roles are understood, and the expectations surrounding roles are clear, so that people are not always fighting about responsibilities and boundaries.

Role Structuring

There is a sense of reciprocity and mutual support regarding tasks and other functions in the healthy family. All members can help one another, and all are involved in diffuse areas of responsibility. Refusal to participate in the family is not an option.

Curran (1985) describes some parameters of family functioning that are also important. Reflecting on this notion, she sees developing family leadership as the first task of any family unit. This leadership is exhibited by the meshing of the parents' personalities, so that they complement each other and use their influence to help individuals rather than inhibit them. Second, Curran notices that family boundaries are clear. People understand the boundaries between parents and children, between children and ex-spouses and other family members, between relatives and other generations, and between the family and the community. Third, people in the family are intimate, and they are committed to sharing their feelings. Fourth, communications are consistent, and family members learn how to clarify and say what they are thinking. People understand both abstract and concrete messages. Finally, the family has a united sense of goals, exhibited in work and leisure activities. How the family copes with crises and how members of the family disengage from the family of origin will be proactive. Family members are able to individuate and yet remain close.

Becvar and Becvar (1988) believe that remarried individuals are confused about their roles in the stepfamily, feel unsure about themselves, and experience anxiety over belonging. They say that family members need to become aware of how to encourage feelings of self-worth and belonging in the stepfamily. Included in this unity is developing an awareness of new family values. Dysfunctional behavior may be exhibited because family values are not clearly understood and shared. These may include such values as the importance of education, hard work, manners, and cleanliness. Families need to explore the origins, the necessity, and the purpose of these value systems and discuss active and reactive behavior with respect to roles and expectations.

Another area of concern is establishing healthy attitudes in the children toward the parents. For example, in a single-parent family, the remaining parent may have experienced strong feelings about being a victim, and these feelings may have been modeled for the children. In the remarriage, these children may protect the biological parent from the stepparent. Sometimes a child's misbehavior is also related to family expectations. When a new adult enters the family, the child may feel that his or her role is being taken over by the stepparent. Without certain responsibilities in the family, the child may feel out of place. Too often, a child in a single-parent family may have taken the place of a spouse and formed a friendship with the parent. This confusion of rules can cause difficulties in the stepfamily. Becvar and Becvar (1988) indicate that cooperation, not competition or delegation, is vital in the stepfamily. Children need age-appropriate roles and responsibilities. When biological parents or stepparents disagree about the roles of children, the family will become dysfunctional.

Children have birth-order positions or ordinal roles in any family. This can create quite a sense of confusion. In one family, a child may be the youngest; in another, the second oldest or middle or oldest. This will increase conflict or confusion regarding significance, recognition, and a sense of belonging. Adults must be cognizant of how children withdraw from cooperative behavior and avoid responsibilities. Some such behavior may be due to sibling rivalry. Quiet withdrawal or lack of interest in family activities may be a sign of difficulties in the family, or the child may believe that he or she is being treated unfairly. Perceptions or misperceptions regarding these issues must be clarified, or else the child will continue to withdraw.

A child may naturally reenact a maladaptive role that he or she had in the original family and display it in the stepfamily. Parents may want a child to fill this role in an effort to hide their own issues or dysfunction. If the remarriage repeats the conflicts of the past marriages, the new spouse may help the child become a family scapegoat.

One can quickly realize that if each spouse has children from a previous marriage and new children are added, the combinations of interactions between family members become murky and overwhelming. Besides these structural difficulties, the step-family has a variety of issues related to individual and family identity, split loyalties, lack of emotional bonding between family members, and mourning for past family life.

Bonding issues are powerful influences inside and outside the family. These can produce crises, confusion, and jealousy. Problems with ex-spouses and relatives can accelerate very piv-otal issues around intimacy, power, exclusion, inclusion of others, and failure to negotiate or resolve past marital contracts. If ex-spouses are still bonded, whether in affection or in hostil-ity, any intrusion by them into the marital relationship will prob-ably weaken the remarital bond and affect the care of children.

Becvar and Becvar (1988) indicate that children express their hurt or anger in many ways but often do so to ensure their significance or sense of security. Change can promote confu-sion and misperceptions on the part of children. It can also en-hance the development of the family structure if dealt with effec-tively. Carter and McGoldrick (1980) say that it is difficult to define what a normal family is, whereas optimal family func-tioning is an easier concept to understand. Families vary greatly in their composition, but optimal family functioning ensures fairly predictable stages as the family progresses over develop-mental hurdles and is able to surmount issues in a supportive and helpful manner. The emotional and psychological needs of all family members are recognized, and parents prepare their children to be successful in a difficult world.

Concluding Thoughts for Therapists

Kottler (1986) discusses a variety of dilemmas that therapists need to address when working with clients. He warns that therapists can become involved with clients and lose objectivity. When work-ing with stepfamilies, therapists are subjected to continuous rein-tegration of their own emotional and psychological value systems. Conflict in stepfamilies focuses on male-female intimacy, parent-ing values, and issues surrounding divorce. Stepfamilies push the boundaries of loyalty and bonding to the therapeutic limit.

Some therapists grew up in families that are very different

from stepfamilies. They may have values and ideas that make it difficult for them to accept people who have divorced. They see ending a marriage as a selfish act, with children hurt in the process. Family members may touch on issues that the therapist has not resolved or may unknowingly point out difficulties in a therapist's own marriage. Working with this type of family, one will inherently question a great many values and philosophies that exist in a traditionally sexist culture. The stepfamily helps one question how couples function who are in one-up/one-down relationships, the economic situation in our culture, how males and females are treated differently in society, and what this treatment means for the family.

Stepfamilies exhibit many of the dysfunctions that exist in all family structures. A stepfamily is a cauldron of jealousy and anger. Adults may act like adolescents, and children may be messengers running through a war zone. The stepfamily may present people at their worst because they are in great pain and conflict. They do have the potential for a better life, however, if the therapist can be helpful in relieving the pain. This chaos, despair, hopelessness, and feeling of loss can affect the therapist's own life. Sager and others (1983) describe how a therapeutic team that they helped develop found itself putting its own relationships on hold or refusing to make commitments: the despair and depression of the stepfamilies that the team members counseled affected their own feelings and lives.

It takes insight and work for the therapist to encourage hope while understanding and recognizing the limits in a relationship. Therapists working with stepfamilies must ask, "What can this particular family accomplish? How close can the members be? What is a realistic expectation of the types of behavior that they are capable of exhibiting?" In our own practice and supervision, we find therapists who either limit stepfamilies too greatly or expect too much of them. Making a realistic assessment is difficult.

When spouses continually deny the destructive patterns between them, it is helpful to focus on past issues. Examine family-of-origin dilemmas. Be careful not to align with the children. This can be difficult, especially if a child's behavior is hurtful. Too often, parents tell the children that the remarriage is for their benefit, and this becomes a burden for the children. Therapists may not be clear about a child's needs, and this could affect therapy. If needs in a stepfamily are not clearly delineated, there will be problems. Thus, the therapist has to deal with his or her own feelings, being open and vulnerable with family members and at the same time being supportive of this process.

There are fears in stepfamilies, particularly about loss and abandonment. Therapists themselves often have the same fears. We have found that young therapists who have not been married and do not have children typically side with children and do not understand the parents' view. The opposite can occur when therapists have their own parenting issues and therefore side with unhealthy parents.

Generally, therapists are trained to protect children from pain; therefore, it is not unusual to side with a child in a stepfamily. We would suggest that therapists learn how to understand the pain of all family members. Stepfamily members have to learn how to support and care for one another, rather than staying isolated and alone (a typical stance in stepfamilies). One must remember that people tend to stand outside the stepfamily. To be of assistance, the therapist must be comfortable sharing emotions and helping family members become practiced in this type of behavior. This is a requirement, one that many therapists do not fulfill with their own families or do not learn in their families of origin (Sager and others, 1983).

Counseling stepfamilies is difficult, particularly because these families tend to be chaotic. Many therapists try to overcontrol or force these families to take action. Sometimes they rush or push too hard before the family is ready to have some sense of order. The family will pull away in response. When working with a chaotic family, therapists may get upset if the family does not seem to right itself immediately. We are not making excuses for therapists to accept failure with these families, but we realize that the boundaries and rules around these families present even more extenuating circumstances than with more typical chaotic families. If there is a very dysfunctional member in a stepfamily, it is even harder to help the members adjust because the family itself may continue to generate many dilemmas. Lack of family structure can inhibit change and will demand a great deal of patience and skill.

It is also important for the therapist to have a positive attitude about stepfamily life. It will probably be helpful if this individual knows a stepfamily that does exhibit positive characteristics and if he or she has a marital relationship that has functioned effectively. This may not be the case, however. Even if the therapist has a happy traditional marriage, stepfamilies bring up a host of dilemmas that traditional marriages do not encounter. They will force a therapist to question issues in his or her own marriage. If the therapist has a stepfamily relationship, he or she may experience the same sort of confused state that other families are facing. We have supervised therapists who are stuck in their own divorce issues and have not resolved personal intimacy issues with their families of origin or with past spouses. They cannot help stepfamilies. Other therapists may espouse feminist thinking yet not practice these "behaviors" in their relationships (Kottler & Blau, 1989).

It has been our experience in supervision that therapists living in traditional marital relationships encounter difficulties working with stepfamilies. Further, therapists who are willing to stay in unhappy relationships, where they feel unfulfilled, may experience consistent failure in working with stepfamilies. Because the stepfamily is chaotic and dysfunctional, it may solidify the unhealthy position of this type of therapist. In the therapist's viewpoint, this family is "worse." When this is true, the therapist will help the family stay stuck. If the family became more functional, it would push the therapist to examine his or her own family. If the therapist is fearful of change, is not very creative, and has difficulty with anger and tension, then the stepfamily is not one to counsel. Stepfamily members' lives are usually quite emotional and often on the edge.

Working with stepfamilies can be extremely rewarding, however. They are a therapeutic challenge, drawing on the therapists's acumen and understanding of the change process. We believe that a unique bonding occurs between competent stepfamily therapists and the families they counsel. It is a privilege and an honor to be allowed to "step" into the private world of these families. It is also immensely satisfying to make a contribution to the positive growth of these families as they journey along the path to healthy living.

References

Adler, A. (1964). *Problems of neurosis*. New York: HarperCollins.

Ahron, C. (1980). Joint custody arrangements in the post-divorce family. *Journal of Divorce, 3,* 189–205.

Ahron, C. (1981). Continuing co-parental relationship between divorced spouses. *American Journal of Orthopsychiatry, 6,* 86–90.

Ahron, C. (1983). Predictors of paternal involvement post-divorce: Mother's and father's perceptions. *Journal of Divorce, 6,* 55–69.

Anderson, J., & White, G. (1986). An empirical investigation of interaction and relationship patterns in functional and dysfunctional nuclear families and stepfamilies. *Family Process, 25,* 407–422.

Baptiste, D. (1983). Family therapy with reconstituted families: A crisis-induction approach. *American Journal of Family Therapy, 11,* 5–15.

Becvar, D., & Becvar, R. (1988). *Family therapy: A systemic integration*. Needham Heights, MA: Allyn & Bacon.

Bennett, P. (1981). Stepfamily survey: The final report. *Stepparent News, 2*(10), 3.

Berg-Cross, L. (1988). *Basic concepts in family therapy*. Binghamton, NY: Haworth Press.

Berman, W. (1988). The relationship of ex-spouse attachment to adjustment following divorce. *Journal of Family Psychology, 1,* 312–328.

Boss, P., & Greenburg, J. (1984). Family boundary ambiguity: A new variable in family stress theory. *Family Process, 23,* 535–546.

Bowen, M. (1981). The use of family theory in clinical practice. In J. Haley (Ed.), *Changing families*. Philadelphia: Grune & Stratton.

Bowman, M., & Ahron, C. (1985). Impact of legal custody status on father's parenting post-divorce. *Journal of Marriage and the Family*. 49, 483–488.

Brand, E., & Clingempeel, W. (1987). Interdependencies of marital and stepparent/stepchild relationships and children's psychological adjustment: Research findings and clinical implications. *Family Relations, 36,* 140–146.

Bray, J. (1988). Children's development during early remarriage. In E. M. Hetherington & J. Arastek (Eds.), *The Impact of Divorce, Single-Parenting & Stepparenting on Children* (pp. 279–298). Hillsdale, NJ: Lawrence Erlbaum.

Bray, J., & Berger, S. (1990). The developing stepfamily. *The Family Psychologist, 6,* 31–32.

Brock, G., & Barnard, C. (1988). *Procedures in family therapy.* Needham Heights, MA: Allyn & Bacon.

Bryan, H., Ganong, L., Coleman, M., & Bryan, L. (1985). Counselors' perceptions of stepparents and stepchildren. *Journal of Counseling Psychology, 32*(2), 279–282.

Burns, D. (1985). *Intimate connections.* New York: Morrow.

Buwick, A., Martin, D., & Martin, M. (1990). Issues in child custody determination in Illinois. *IACD Quarterly, 116,* 11.

Carter, E., & McGoldrick, M. (Eds.). (1980). *The family life cycle: A framework for family therapy.* New York: Gardner Press.

Carter, V., & Leavenworth, J. (1985). *Caught in the middle: Children of divorce.* Valley Forge, PA: Judson Press.

Cherlin, A. (1981). *Marriage, divorce, remarriage.* Cambridge, MA: Harvard University Press.

Clingempeel, W. (1981). Quasi-kin relationships and marital quality in stepfather families. *Journal of Personality and Social Psychology, 41,* 890–891.

Clingempeel, W., Brand, E., & Ievoli, R. (1984). Stepparent-stepchild relationships in stepmother and stepfather families: A multimethod study. *Family Relations, 33,* 465–473.

Clingempeel, W., & Segal, S. (1986). Stepparent-stepchild relationships and the psychological adjustment of children in stepmother and stepfather families. *Child Development, 57,* 474–484.

Coleman, M., & Ganong, L. (1985). Remarriage myths. *Journal of Counseling and Development, 64,* 116–120.

Coleman, M., & Ganong, L. (1987). The cultural stereotyping of stepfamilies. In K. Pasley & M. Ihinger-Tallman (Eds.), *Remarriage and stepparenting: Current research and theory* (pp. 19–41). New York: Guilford Press.

Crosbie-Burnett, M. (1984). The centrality of the steprelationship: A challenge to family theory and practice. *Family Relations, 33,* 459–463.

Curran, D. (1985). *Stress and the healthy family.* New York: HarperCollins.

Emery, R. (1982). Interparental conflict and the children of discord and divorce. *Psychological Bulletin, 92,* 310–330.

Emery, R., Hetherington, E., & DiLalla, L. (1984). Divorce, children and social policy. In H. W. Stevenson & A. E. Siegel (Eds.), *Child Development, Research, and Social Policy* (pp. 851–858). Chicago: University of Chicago Press.

Epstein, N., Bishop, D., & Baldwin, L. (1982). McMaster model of family functioning: A view of the normal family. In F. Walsh (Ed.), *Normal family processes* (pp. 115–141). New York: Guilford Press.

Furstenberg, F. (1987). The new extended family: The experience of parents and children after remarriage. In K. Pasley & M. Ihinger-Tallman (Eds.), *Remarriage and stepparenting today: Current research and theory* (pp. 42–64). New York: Guilford Press.

Furstenberg, F., & Allison, P. (1985). How divorce affects children: Variations by age and sex. Paper presented at the Society for Research in Child Development, Toronto.

Furstenberg, F., & Nord, C. (1985). Parenting apart: Patterns of childrearing after marital disruption. *Journal of Marriage and the Family, 47*(4), 893–904.

Furstenberg, F., Nord, C., Peterson, J., & Zill, N. (1983). The life course of children of divorce: Marital disruption & parental conflict. *American Sociological Review, 48,* 656–668.

Furstenberg, F., & Spanier, G. B. (1984). *Recycling the family: Remarriage after divorce.* Newbury Park, CA: Sage.

Ganong, L., & Coleman, M. (1983). Stepparent: A pejorative term? *Psychological Reports, 52,* 919–922.

Gardner, R. (1984). Counseling children in stepfamilies. *Elementary School Guidance and Counseling, 19,* 40–49.

Getzoff, A., & McClenahan, C. (1984). *Step kids: A survival guide for teenagers in stepfamilies.* New York: Walker and Company.

Giles-Sims, J. (1984). The stepparent role. *Journal of Family Issues, 5,* 116–130.

Glick, P. C. (1984). Marriage, divorce, and living arrangements: Prospective changes. *Journal of Family Issues, 5,* 7–26.

Glick, P., & Lin, S. (1986). Recent changes in divorce and remarriage. *Journal of Marriage and the Family, 48,* 737–747.

Goldner, V. (1982). Remarriage family: Structure, system, future. In J. C. Hansen & L. Messinger (Eds.), *Therapy with remarriage families* (pp. 198–211). Rockville, MD: Aspen Publications.

Goldsmith, J. (1980). The relationship between former spouses: Descriptive findings. *Journal of Divorce, 4,* 1–20.

Goldsmith, J. (1981). The divorced family: Whom to include in therapy. In A. Gurman (Ed.), *Practical problems in family therapy* (pp. 191–211). New York: Brunner/Mazel.

Goldsmith, J. (1982). The postdivorce family system. In F. Walsh (Ed.), *Normal family processes* (pp. 297–330). New York: Guilford Press.

Grunwald, B., & McAbee, H. (1985). *Guiding the family: Practical counseling techniques.* Muncie, IN: Accelerated Development.

Guidubaldi, J., & Perry, J. (1985). Divorce and mental health sequelar for children: A two-year follow-up of a nationwide sample. *Journal of the American Academy of Child Psychiatry, 24,* 531–537.

Gumaer, J. (1984). *Counseling and therapy for children.* New York: Free Press.

Haley, J. (1984). *Changing families.* Philadelphia: Grune & Stratton.

Hampson, R., Beavers, W., & Hulgus, Y. (1989). Insiders' and Outsiders' views of family: The assessment of family competence and style. *Journal of Family Psychology, 3,* 118–137.

Henggeler, S., & Borduin, C. (1990). *Family therapy and beyond.* Pacific Grove, CA: Brooks/Cole.

Hess, R., & Camaara, K. (1979). Post-divorce family relationships as mediating factors in the consequences of divorce for children. *Journal of Social Issues, 35,* 79–96.

Hetherington, E. M. (1981). Children and divorce. In R. Henderson (Ed.), *Parent-child interaction: Theory, research, and prospects.* New York: Academic.

Hetherington, E. M. (1987). Family relations six years after divorce. In K. Pasley & M. Ihinger-Tallman (Eds.), *Remarriage and Stepparenting today: Current research and theory* (pp. 185–205). New York: Guilford Press.

Hetherington, E., Cox, M., & Cox, R. (1978). The aftermath of divorce. In J. H. Stevens, Jr., & M. Mathews (Eds.), *Mother/child, father/child relationships* (pp. 149–176). Washington, DC: National Association for the Education of Young Children.

Hetherington, E., Cox, M., & Cox, R. (1979). Stress and coping in divorce: A focus on women. In J. Gullahorn (Ed.), *Psychology of women in transition* (pp. 95–128). Washington, DC: B.H. Winston & Sons.

Hetherington, E., Cox, M., & Cox, R. (1982). Effects of divorce on parents and children. In M. Lamb (Ed.), *Non-traditional families* (pp. 284–314). Hillsdale, NJ: Erlbaum.

Hetherington, E., Cox, M., & Cox, R. (1985). Long-term effects of divorce and remarriage on the adjustment of children. *Journal of the American Academy of Child Psychiatry, 24,* 518–530.

Hill, R. (1986). Life cycle stages for types of single parent families: Of family development theory. *Family Relations, 35,* 19–29.

Huey, G., Martin, D., & Martin, M. (1987). Remarriage: Understanding spousal dynamics and implications for counseling. *Illinois Journal of Counseling, 5,* 2–9.

Imber-Black, E. (1989). Women's relationships with larger systems. In M. McGoldrick, C. Anderson, & F. Walsh (Eds.), *Women in families: A framework for family therapy* (pp. 335–353). New York: W.W. Norton.

Irwin, H., Benjamin, M., & Tracme, N. (1984). Shared parenting: An empirical analysis utilizing a larger Canadian data base. *Family Process, 23,* 561–569.

Jacobs, J. (1983). Treatment of divorcing fathers: Social & psychotherapeutic considerations. *Journal of Psychiatry, 140,* 1294–1299.

Jacobs, J. (1986). Divorce & child custody regulations: Conflicting legal and psychological paradigms. *American Journal of Psychiatry, 143,* 192–197.

Jolin, P. (1981). *How to succeed as a stepparent.* New York: Signet.

Kalter, N. (1990). *Growing up with divorce.* New York: Free Press.

Kaslow, F. (1982). History of family therapy in the United States: A kaleidoscopic overview. In F. W. Kaslow (Ed.), *The international book of family therapy* (pp. 9–25). New York: Brunner/Mazel.

Kaslow, F. (1990). *Voices in family psychology* (Vols. 1–2). Newbury Park, CA: Sage.

Katz, L., & Stein, S. (1983). Treating stepfamilies. In B. B. Wolman & F. Stricker (Eds.), *Handbook of family and marital therapy* (pp. 387–420). New York: Plenum.

Kelly, J. (1988). Longer-term adjustment in children of divorce: Converging findings and implications for practice. *Journal of Family Psychology, 2,* 135–142.

Keshet, J. (1980). From separation to stepfamily. *Journal of Family Issues, 1,* 517–531.

Kim, A., Martin, D., & Martin, M. (1989). Identification of source traits and their role in marital stability. *Family Therapy Journal, 26,* 14–18.

Kosinski, F. (1983). Improving relationships in stepfamilies. *Elementary School Guidance and Counseling, 5,* 200–207.

Kottler, J. (1986). *On being a therapist.* San Francisco: Jossey-Bass.

Kottler, J., & Blau, D. (1989). *The imperfect therapist: Learning from failure in therapeutic practice.* San Francisco: Jossey-Bass.

Kübler-Ross, E. (1969). *On death and dying.* New York: Macmillan.

Kurdek, L. A., & Berg, B. (1983). Correlates of children's adjustment to their parents' divorces. In L. Kurdek (Ed.), *Children and divorce.* New Directions for Child Development, no. 19. San Francisco: Jossey-Bass.

Kurdek, L., & Siesky, A. (1980). Children's perceptions of their parents' divorce. *Journal of Divorce, 3,* 339–378.

Lerner, H. (1985). *The dance of anger.* New York: HarperCollins.

Leupnitz, D. (1982). *Child custody: A study of families after divorce.* Lexington, MA: Lexington Books.

Lutz, P. (1983). The stepfamily: An adolescent perspective. *Family Relations, 32,* 367-375.

McGoldrick, M., Anderson, C., & Walsh, F. (1989). *Women in families: A framework for family therapy.* New York: W.W. Norton.

Madanes, C. (1984). *Behind the one-way mirror: Advances in the practice of strategic therapy.* San Francisco: Jossey-Bass.

Martin, D., & Martin, M. (1985). *Families in transition: Divorce, remarriage, and the stepfamily.* Salem, MI: Sheffield.

Martin, D., & Martin, M. (1987). Blended legacies. *Focus, 10*(4), 10-20.

Martin, D., & Martin, M. (1992). *Step by step: A guide to helping stepfamilies.* Minneapolis, MN: Educational Media.

Martin, D., Martin, M., & Medler, B. (1983). *The marriage and family interview technique.* Dallas, TX: Wilmington Press.

Martin, M., & Martin, D. (1983). Children of divorce: Emphasizing the positive aspects. *Journal of Individual Psychology, 39*(2), 180-188.

Martin, M., Martin, D., & Porter, J. (1983). Bibliotherapy: Children of divorce. *The School Counselor, 30*(4), 312-214.

Messinger, L. (1984). *Remarriage: A family affair.* New York: Plenum.

Messinger, L., & Walker, K. (1981). Marriage breakdown to remarriage: Parental tasks and therapeutic guidelines. *American Journal of Orthopsychiatry, 51,* 429-438.

Mills, D. (1984). A model for stepfamily development. *Family Relations, 33,* 365-372.

Minuchin, S. (1974). *Families & family therapy.* Cambridge, MA: Harvard University Press.

Minuchin, S., & Fishman, H. (1981). *Family therapy techniques.* Cambridge, MA: Harvard University Press.

Nastasi, B. (1988). Family and child stressors: Research findings from a national sample. Paper presented at the annual meeting of the American Orthopsychiatry Association, San Francisco.

Papernow, P. (1984). The stepfamily cycle: An experiential model of stepfamily development. *Family Relations, 33,* 355-363.

Papp, P. (1980). The Greek chorus and other techniques of family therapy. *Family Process, 199*(1), 45–57.

Papp, P. (1984). The creative leap: The links between clinical and artistic creativity. *Family Therapy Networker, 8*(5), 20–29.

Pasley, K. (1988). Contributing to a field of investigation. *Journal of Family Psychology, 1,* 452–456.

Pasley, K., & Ihinger-Tallman, M. (1982). Stress in remarried families. *Family Perspective, 16*(4), 181–190.

Pasley, K., & Ihinger-Tallman, M. (1987). *Remarriage and stepparenting today: Current research and theory.* New York: Guilford Press.

Pasley, K., Ihinger-Tallman, M., & Coleman, C. (1984). Consensus styles among happy and unhappy married couples. *Family Relations, 33,* 451–458.

Peterson, J., & Zill, N. (1986). Marital disruption, parent-child relationships, and behavior problems in children. *Journal of Marriage and the Family, 48,* 245–307.

Poppen, W., & White, P. (1984). Transition to the blended family. *Elementary School Guidance of Counselors, 19,* 50–51.

Prosen, S., & Farmer, J. (1982). Understanding stepfamilies: Issues and implications for counselors. *Personnel & Guidance Journal, 60,* 393–397.

Resnikoff, R. (1981). Teaching family therapy: Ten key questions for understanding the family or patient. *Journal of Marital and Family Therapy, 12,* 135–142.

Rosemond, J. (1989). *Six-point plan for raising happy, healthy children.* New York: Andrews and McMeel.

Rubenstein, C. (1983). Forging the linked family. *Psychology Today, 13,* 59.

Sager, C., Walker, E., Brown, H., Crohn, H., & Rodstein, E. (1983). *Treating the remarried family.* New York: Brunner/Mazel.

Santrock, J., & Sitterle, K. A. (1985). The developmental world of children in divorced families: Research findings and clinical implications. In D. C. Goldbert (Ed.), *Contemporary marriage: Special issues in couples therapy* (pp. 142–161). Homewood, IL: Dorsey Press.

Santrock, J., & Warshak, R. (1986). Developmental relationships and legal clinical considerations in father-custody families.

In M. E. Lamb (Ed.), *The father's role: Applied perspectives* (pp. 135–163). New York: Wiley.

Santrock, J., Warshak, R., & Elliott, G. (1982). Social development and parent-child interaction in father custody and stepmother families. In M. E. Lamb (Ed.), *Nontraditional families: Parenting and child development* (pp. 289–314). Hillsdale, NJ: Erlbaum.

Satir, V., & Baldwin, M. (1983). *Satir step by step: A guide to creating change in families.* Mountain View, CA: Science and Behavior Books.

Sauer, L., & Fine, M. (1988). Parent-child relationships in stepparent families. *Journal of Family Psychology, 1,* 434–451.

Shapiro, J. (1984). A brief outline of a chronological divorce sequence. *Family Therapy, 11,* 269–278.

Skeen, P., Covi, R., & Robinson, B. (1985). Stepfamilies: A review of the literature with suggestions for practitioners. *Journal of Conseling and Development, 64,* 121–125.

Skeen, P., Robinson, B., & Flake-Hobson, C. (1984). Blended families: Overcoming the Cinderella myth. *Young Children, 39*(3), 64–74.

Stern, P. (1984). Stepfather family dynamics: An overview for therapists. *Mental Health Nursing, 6,* 89–103.

Touliatos, J., & Lindholm, B. (1980). Teachers' perceptions of behavior problems in children from intact, single-parent, and step-parent families. *Psychology in the Schools, 17,* 264–269.

Trotzer, J., & Trotzer, T. (1986). *Marriage and family: Better ready than not.* Muncie, IN: Accelerated Development.

Visher, E., & Visher, J. (1978). Common problems of stepparents and their spouses. *American Journal of Orthopsychiatry, 48,* 252–262.

Visher, E., & Visher, J. (1979). *Stepfamilies: A guide to working with stepparents and stepchildren.* New York: Brunner/Mazel.

Visher, E., & Visher, J. (1982). *How to win as a stepfamily.* Chicago: Contemporary Books.

Visher, E., & Visher, J. (1985). Stepfamilies are different. *Journal of Family Therapy, 7,* 9–18.

Visher, E., & Visher, J. (1988). *Old loyalties, new ties: Therapeutic strategies with stepfamilies.* New York: Brunner/Mazel.

Visher, E., & Visher, J. (1989). Parenting coalitions after remarriage: Dynamics and therapeutic guidelines. *Family Relations, 38,* 65–70.

Wald, E. (1981). *The remarried family: Challenge and promise.* New York: Family Services Association of America.

Waldron, J., Ching, J., & Fair, P. (1986). A children's divorce clinic: Analysis of 200 cases in Hawaii. *Journal of Divorce, 9*(3), 111–121.

Walker, K., & Messinger, L. (1979). Remarriage after divorce: Dissolution and the reconstruction of family boundaries. *Family Process, 18,* 185–192.

Wallerstein, J. (1985). Children of divorce: Preliminary report of a ten-year follow up of older children and adolescents. *Journal of the American Academy of Child Psychiatry, 24,* 545–553.

Wallerstein, J. (1990). *Second chance.* Boston: Houghton Mifflin.

Wallerstein, J., & Kelly, J. (1980). *Surviving the breakup: How children actually cope with divorce.* New York: Basic Books.

Walsh, F. (1982). *Normal family processes.* New York: Guilford Press.

Walsh, F. (1989). Reconsidering gender in the marital quid pro quo. In M. McGoldrick, C. Anderson, & F. Walsh (Eds.), *Women in families: A framework of family therapy.* New York: W. W. Norton.

Warshak, R., & Santrock, J. (1983). Impact of divorce, father-custody, and mother-custody homes: The child's perspective. In L. A. Kurdek (Ed.), *Children and divorce.* New Directions for Child Development, no. 19. San Francisco: Jossey-Bass.

Weed, J. A. (1980). National estimates of marriage dissolution and survivorship: United States. *Vital and Health Statistics: Series 3, Analytic Statistics: No. 19* (DHHS Publication No. PHS 81-1403). Hyattsville, MD: National Center for Health Statistics.

Weingarten, H. (1980). Remarriage and well-being: National survey evidence of social and psychological effects. *Journal of Family Issues, 4,* 533–339.

White, L., & Booth, A. (1985). The quality and stability of remarriages: The role of stepchildren. *American Sociological Review, 50,* 689–698.

Wynne, L., Jones, J., & Al-Khayyal, M. (1982). Healthy family communication patterns: Observations in families "at-risk" for psychopathology. In. F. Walsh (Ed.), *Normal family processes* (pp. 142–166). New York: Guilford Press.

Index

Index